STUDIES IN DIPLOMACY

General Editor: G. R. Berridge, Director, Centre for the Study of Diplomacy, University of Leicester

The series was launched in 1994. Its chief purpose is to encourage original scholarship on the theory and practice of international diplomacy, including its legal regulation. The interests of the series thus embrace such diplomatic functions as signalling, negotiation and consular work, and methods such as summitry and the multilateral conference. Whilst it has sharp focus on diplomacy at the expense of foreign policy, therefore, the series has no prejudice as to historical period or approach. It also aims to include manuals on protocol and other aspects of diplomatic practice which will be of immediate, day-to-day relevance to professional diplomats. A final ambition is to reprint inaccessible classic works on diplomacy.

Titles include:

Andrew F. Cooper (*editor*)
NICHE DIPLOMACY
Middle Powers after the Cold War

David H. Dunn (*editor*)
DIPLOMACY AT THE HIGHEST LEVEL
The Evolution of International Summitry

Brian Hocking (*editor*)
FOREIGN MINISTRIES
Change and Adaptation

Donna Lee
MIDDLE POWERS AND COMMERCIAL DIPLOMACY
British Influence at the Kennedy Trade Round

Jan Melissen (*editor*)
INNOVATION IN DIPLOMATIC PRACTICE

M. J. Peterson
RECOGNITION OF GOVERNMENTS
Legal Doctrine and State Practice, 1815–1995

Gary D. Rawnsley
RADIO DIPLOMACY AND PROPAGANDA
The BBC and VOA in International Politics, 1956–64

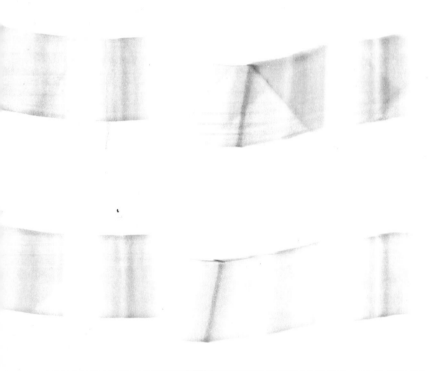

Studies in Diplomacy
Series Standing Order ISBN 0–333–71495–4
(*outside North America only*)

You can receive future titles in this series as they are published by placing a standing order.
Please contact your bookseller or, in case of difficulty, write to us at the address below with
your name and address, the title of the series and the ISBN quoted above.

Customer Services Department, Macmillan Distribution Ltd
Houndmills, Basingstoke, Hampshire RG21 6XS, England

Foreign Ministries

Change and Adaptation

Edited by

Brian Hocking
Professor of International Relations
Coventry University

Foreword by
Jacques Bilodeau
Deputy High Commissioner for Canada

First published in Great Britain 1999 by
MACMILLAN PRESS LTD
Houndmills, Basingstoke, Hampshire RG21 6XS and London
Companies and representatives throughout the world

A catalogue record for this book is available from the British Library.

ISBN 978-0-333-69242-4 hardcover
ISBN 978-0-333-69243-1 paperback

First published in the United States of America 1999 by
ST. MARTIN'S PRESS, INC.,
Scholarly and Reference Division,
175 Fifth Avenue, New York, N.Y. 10010

ISBN 0–312–21868–0

Library of Congress Cataloging-in-Publication Data
Foreign ministries : change and adaptation / edited by Brian Hocking ;
foreword by Jacques Bilodeau.
p.   cm. — (Studies in diplomacy)
Includes bibliographical references and index.
ISBN 0–312–21868–0 (cloth)
1. Diplomatic and consular service.   2. International relations.
I. Hocking, Brian.   II. Series.
JZ1419.F67   1999
327—dc21
                                                98–40522
                                                CIP

This book is printed on paper suitable for recycling and made from fully
managed and sustained forest sources. Logging, pulping and manufacturing
processes are expected to conform to the environmental regulations of the
country of origin.

Printed and bound in Great Britain by

CPI Antony Rowe, Chippenham and Eastbourne

Contents

List of Tables and Figures

Foreword

It gives me great satisfaction that the Canadian High Commission has been able to play a role in the development of this book by offering a venue for the symposium on which it is based. I am particularly grateful to the organizers for providing me with the opportunity to open the symposium and to offer the thoughts which are included in this foreword. The issues discussed on that occasion and within this volume are of particular interest to me mainly because, after 30 years in the diplomatic service, I have witnessed a considerable number of changes in the conduct of foreign policy. Certainly, Canada's Department of Foreign Affairs and International Trade in 1998 is in many ways a very different organization compared with the Department of External Affairs in 1968.

I agree with the assessment made in the introduction to the book that the conduct of foreign policy has become increasingly fragmented and diffused. I would add two additional points. First, it is also a fact that the number of external factors influencing that conduct has increased significantly over the last three decades. The globalization of the world – McCluhan's 'global village' – has made foreign affairs more closely linked to national affairs. The second change is that decisions by one government's bureaucrats have more and more influence on – and sometimes come close to interference *in* – other countries' national policies. One consequence of this is that officials of 'domestic' departments often want to play a more important role in the conduct of national foreign policy. Obviously this has implications for foreign ministries.

The growing 'bilateral' interaction between domestic ministries in different countries – for instance, between the UK's departments of Health and Social Security and Canada's Human Resources Development Department – has been pointed to by some scholars as evidence that foreign ministries are in 'decline'. As a representative of the profession, I claim the right to object to this proposition. Rather than in decline, I think foreign ministries are in a substantial period of mutation. This book addresses this precise issue in a very serious and substantial manner. Perhaps I could take advantage of this foreword to offer a few of my own thoughts based on our own experience in the Canadian Foreign Affairs Department.

Before arriving in London, I was briefly involved, as Head of Policy Planning, in a major review of our roles and functions in relation to the changing world environment and the approaching threshold of the third millennium. Clearly, the main challenge to any organization today – whether in the public or private sectors – is to remain relevant and perform a role that its managers consider important and useful. The Canadian Department of Foreign Affairs and International Trade is also facing similar pressures coming from a changing environment.

In Canada, our Department attempted to respond to this substantial challenge with a thorough review of its role and objectives and by reorganizing its own mode of operation. Four years ago, the Government of Canada set a task for all its departments. That task was to respond to its decision to set strict new deficit reduction targets and introduce more managerial realism. Our Department as a consequence made the necessary painful cuts in operations but at the same time started an in-depth analysis of how we do business. The overall objective being greater efficiency, delivering a high quality product with fewer resources.

In addition to fiscal pressures, the new international context forced us to re-examine our traditional way of doing business both in the international context and in helping the government set its domestic agenda. With the help of working groups, managers confirmed that foreign affairs should retain its basic roles which were clarified as being: the development and coordination of Canada's international policy; the promotion of our interests and values overseas; the provision of service to Canadians; and support for other government Departments abroad. Translating these expectations into a more streamlined and efficient structure required a major reorganization of the Department including changes to our day-to-day procedures. In doing this, we had two broad guidelines in terms of representation abroad, namely that we should remain visible and present in as many foreign sites as possible and that we should focus our activities in different countries by merging certain functions and examining the possible closure of certain offices. We had also to look at seemingly mundane topics such as:

- how policies are formulated and decisions made;
- how information is aggregated, especially when other government departments, provincial governments, corporations, non-governmental organizations and ethnic groups inside Canada are stakeholders in a particular issue-area;
- how ministers are advised and the process for taking recommendations forward;
- and finally, how policies are implemented.

In short, the fiscal situation in Canada coupled with a changing international environment made us become, I hope, more relevant for the government, the other stakeholders and the people. For instance, here in London our operations have been streamlined to the extent that we have cut our personnel by close to one-third since 1994. Yet it is arguable that we have now become more efficient, cover a wider territory and are more 'plugged-into' policy-making in Ottawa than before.

In terms of actual output, the level of political and economic co-operation between the two countries, channelled in some part through the High Commission, is greater than it has been for years. Certainly, two-way trade is surging. Obviously, none of these developments are due exclusively, or even primarily, to the results of the re-thinking, reorganization and re-energizing that has taken place at the Foreign Affairs Department. I leave it to others to judge the latter's contribution, but it seems likely that, at least, we are doing something right!

My final point is that this exercise demonstrated one thing clearly to all of us involved. We have entered a new world in which change is permanent – in fact the only permanent thing in the new global reality. The reorganization we have just gone through is not an end in itself. Rather, it is a beginning. As the process of globalization continues to unfold into the new millennium, foreign ministries everywhere will need to make constant change a permanent part of our activity. How we face this challenge will, to a significant extent, determine how successful we are in fulfilling our mandate and remaining relevant. This book makes a valuable contribution to a better understanding of the way ahead.

Jacques Bilodeau
Deputy High Commissioner for Canada
Canadian High Commission, London

Acknowledgements

The origins of this book are to be found in the first annual meeting of the Diplomatic Studies Programme (DSP) convened during the European Consortium of Political Research International Relations Standing Group's second pan-European conference held in Paris in September 1995. An outcome of this meeting was the formation of several Multinational Project Groups (MPGs) intended to facilitate cross-national, thematic research projects. One of these, of which I agreed to be convenor, is concerned with the administration of international policy in an era in which traditional distinctions between foreign and domestic policy arenas are becoming less tenable, and institutions – such as the foreign ministry – are subject to increasing pressures from both within and outside their national settings. The title of the MPG – 'Change and the Foreign Policy Community' – reflects one dimension of these developments, namely that a growing range of bureaucratic actors have become involved in the administration of international policy. This has helped to produce a widely-shared assumption that foreign ministries, seen as the traditional 'gatekeepers' between the domestic and international policy, are in some sense under threat. This 'declinist' scenario is bound up with the broader but obviously intimately related debate about the health of diplomacy itself.

Therefore, it seemed appropriate that the first enterprise of the MPG should be a comparative evaluation of foreign ministries themselves, setting as its goal the testing of the argument that foreign ministries are in some sense an endangered species. A group of academics and diplomats able and willing to provide studies of foreign ministries in a variety of settings around the world was assembled. As the introduction to the book explains, they were asked to consider the current role and status of the foreign ministry, and the ways in which it has responded to change. The first drafts of most of the papers were discussed at a two-day symposium held at the Canadian High Commission in London in February 1997. This was attended by academics and by diplomats from some 40 countries. The discussion that ensued was invaluable and provided an opportunity for the contributors to this book to revise their papers in its light.

In the period since the symposium the papers have been redrafted, some several times. Contributors have been patient during this process and my first thanks are directed to them. Although each of them assisted in different ways, I am grateful to Iver Neumann and Andrew Cooper for their general advice, ideas and encouragement as the project developed. Additionally, I would like to thank the professional diplomats who spared time from their busy schedules not only to prepare their chapters but also to offer support. Of these, especial thanks are extended to Andrés Rozental, then Mexican Ambassador in London and Kyoji Komachi, then Minister at the Japanese Embassy in London.

Without the framework provided by the Diplomatic Studies Programme at the University of Leicester, launching the project would have been immeasurably more difficult. The valuable assistance provided by Geoff Berridge (Director of the DSP and general editor of the series in which this book appears) is gratefully acknowledged as is that of Jan Melissen, Executive Director of the DSP. Tim Farmiloe and Sunder Katwala of Macmillan provided encouragement and advice.

The symposium on which the book is based was organized by the Centre for International and European Studies at Coventry University and supported by a conference grant from the British Academy. A particular debt is owed to the Canadian High Commission who generously hosted the meeting and to Vivien Hughes and her colleagues in the Academic Relations Unit for their invaluable assistance. As indicated in his foreword, Jacques Bilodeau, Deputy High Commissioner for Canada, kindly agreed to open the symposium and graciously offered hospitality to those attending it.

Finally, the work of preparing the manuscript for publication was ably assisted by Dominic Kelly, Research Fellow at Coventry University. But had it not been for the dedicated efforts of Kath Wright in assisting with the seemingly endless task of editing the chapters as they went through the various stages of revision, it is doubtful whether the book would have appeared.

Brian Hocking

Notes on the Contributors

Zakaria Haji Ahmad is Professor and Head of the Strategic and Security Studies Unit at the Universiti Kebangsaan Malaysia.

David Allen is Senior Lecturer in European Studies at Loughborough University, UK.

Jacques Bilodeau is the Deputy High Commissioner for Canada in London.

Andrew F. Cooper is Professor of Political Science at the University of Waterloo, Canada.

C. Edward Dillery is a former ambassador in the US Foreign Service.

Maurice A. East is Professor of International Affairs and Political Science at the Elliott School of International Affairs, George Washington University, Washington, DC, USA.

Paulette Enjalran is the former Head Archivist of the Archives Diplomatique, Paris.

Stuart Harris is Professor of International Relations at the Australian National University and former Permanent Secretary in the Department of Foreign Affairs and Trade, Canberra.

Brian Hocking is Professor of International Relations at Coventry University, UK.

Philippe Husson is a former ambassador in the French Foreign Service and Director of the Archives Diplomatiques, Paris.

Aharon Klieman is Professor of Political Science at the University of Tel Aviv, Israel.

Kyoji Komachi was Minister and Consul-General at the Japanese Embassy, London and is currently the Managing Director, General Affairs Department of the Japan International Cooperation Agency, Tokyo.

Richard Langhorne is the Director of the Center for Global Change and Governance at Rutgers, State University of New Jersey, USA.

Marie Muller is Professor of Political Sciences at the University of Pretoria, South Africa.

Iver B. Neumann is an adviser to the Norwegian Ministry of Foreign Affairs and former Head of Centre for Russian Studies at the Norwegian Institute of International Affairs, Oslo, Norway.

Andrés Rozental was formerly Mexican Deputy Foreign Minister and Ambassador in London. He is currently a private consultant in Mexico City.

David Spence is Head of Training and Information in DG1A European Commission, Brussels, Belgium.

Ivan Tiouline is Professor of Political Science and First Vice-Rector at the Moscow State Institute of International Relations, Russia.

William Wallace (Lord Wallace of Saltaire) is a Reader in International Relations at the London School of Economics and Political Science and is Liberal Democrat foreign policy spokesman in the House of Lords (the upper house of the British Parliament).

Introduction
Foreign Ministries: Redefining the Gatekeeper Role
Brian Hocking

Given the fact that the foreign ministry has come to be viewed from several perspectives as being in a state of relative decline, a book devoted to it might be regarded as a strange enterprise. There are, however, several reasons why this is not so. Firstly, despite arguments which suggest that fundamental changes in the nature of the international and domestic environments within which governments conduct their foreign policies have undermined the rationale of a department devoted to 'international' issues, foreign ministries are still a significant part of the bureaucratic landscape. Certainly, they confront increasing pressures, not least those imposed by resource constraints, but many of these are shared by most agencies of government and should not, of themselves, be regarded as an indicator of decline. The fact that foreign ministries continue to exist, then, in what is often assumed to be a hostile environment, of itself invites an examination of their responses to change and the roles that they are performing

A second and closely-related reason is to be found in the nature and impact of globalization and regionalization on the machinery of government. Enough has now been written on these contested concepts to challenge the more exaggerated claims which envision the state as an ever-weakening actor enmeshed by the globalizing forces of international capital and information technology.[1] Indeed, it is argued that the development of effective global governance in many areas demands enhanced state capacity.[2] In this context, the nature of the governmental machinery on which such a capacity to a large degree rests is of significance. And in a more general sense, it may be instructive to examine institutions which represent those aspects and activities of the state in their traditional guise rather than those which one might expect to be most obviously associated with these globalizing trends. What better example than that agency symbolizing the 'hard-shell' of the nation-state?

Third, the character and status of institutions are entwined with policy choices and this is no less so in the case of international than domestic policy.

1

There is a continuing dialogue between the choices governments make (or fail to make) in fashioning international policy and the machinery through which those choices are identified and articulated. Of course, this does not of itself imply that foreign ministries are significant actors, but their continuing presence within bureaucratic structures demands that their role be examined and their contribution evaluated.

Against this background, the contributors to this book were asked to examine the current position of foreign ministries (FMs) in a group of countries possessing widely differing characteristics with the aim of moving beyond simplistic images of the 'decline' of the foreign ministry. Thus they were invited to consider the broad operational environment of the ministry, its place within the structures of foreign policy management and the parameters of debates on reform. More specifically, authors were asked to examine the strategies and responses adopted by foreign ministries in a climate of change. Here, the assumption is that, like most bureaucratic actors, FMs adapt to perceived challenges to their role and status. It was not the goal of the project to erect some grand theory seeking to explain the place of FMs within the foreign policy processes but, far more modestly, to see whether there are broad trends that can be identified and whether these do indeed accord with the conventional wisdom of decline.

THE FOREIGN MINISTRY AS 'GATEKEEPER'

As Langhorne and Wallance indicate (see Chapter 1) in their overview of the changing diplomatic environment, the conduct of external relations has become increasingly fragmented and diffused for reasons which have received considerable attention. The impact of enhanced economic interdependence and state–societal interactions together with the erosion of the boundaries delimiting policy issues and arenas have been viewed as 'internationalizing' the domestic bureaucracy whilst challenging the role of the foreign ministry as the primary point of interface between the domestic and international environments. At the same time, the growth of transnational relationships provides an opportunity for a variety of non-governmental actors to impact on the conduct of foreign relations. One consequence of this, it is often argued, has been to diffuse the management of foreign policy and to produce a 'foreign policy community' embracing actors outside the confines of the FM. This, of itself, is taken as indicative of the relative decline of the FM from what might be regarded as a golden age, where it held sway in guarding the boundaries separating the state from its international setting.

However, there appears to be a considerable element of myth-making underpinning this 'gatekeeper' image which is only tenuously related to the development and role of foreign ministries. This is of some significance to an appreciation of the current position of FMs since the elevation of the gate-keeper image as the standard against which their contemporary significance should be judged has tended to distort the lenses through which the whole issue is viewed. Taken literally, the term implies exclusive control over the domestic–international interface, a claim which in the context of growing interdependence amongst economies and societies appears ridiculous. But there is considerable evidence that FMs rarely accorded to the role of gatekeeper defined in this way. Rather, they have been more usually engaged in bureaucratic bargaining processes with other government agencies intent on carving out for themselves a role in various areas of international policymaking.

It is not commonly noted in the contemporary international relations literature that the FM is a relatively recent phenomenon in the forms in which we know it, that its origins lie in a gradual dismantling of a unified administrative structure which did not distinguish (certainly in policy management terms) between domestic and foreign policy, and that conflict between foreign ministries and a variety of rival agencies with external concerns has been a continuing feature of their environment, certainly from the late nineteenth century onwards. Prior to the emergence of the earliest foreign ministries in the seventeenth and eighteenth centuries, the norm was to combine the management of domestic and foreign policy within a single department: 'The habit of combining both domestic and foreign policy administration in the same department was common throughout the greater states until the early eighteenth century.'[3] In short, the gradual evolution of the foreign ministry accompanied the development of the state system, reflecting the process by which the medieval world with its uncertain and overlapping jurisdictions came to be replaced by an order embracing territorially-based sovereignty and, indeed, the idea of 'foreignness' itself.[4]

It was the recognition by Richelieu of the need for continuity and coordination in the management of French foreign relations in the increasingly complex system of states that led to the emergence of a separate foreign ministry. In the case of Great Britain, up to 1782 the Northern and Southern Departments dealt with both domestic and foreign policy. From that date, the growing needs of dealing with the international environment and the inefficiencies and frictions that two often competing Secretaries could create were recognized in the form of two departments, one for home affairs and the other for foreign affairs.[5]

But the British Foreign Office (FO) conceived as gatekeeper in the sense of a department offering policy advice to the Secretary of State did not emerge until the reforms of 1906. Until then, its role was largely clerical whilst foreign secretaries conducted policy. This did not mean that the FO became the uncontested guardian of Britain's foreign relations. Far from it. The demands of World War I enhanced the status of bureaucratic rivals and tensions between the FO and other departments, particularly the Treasury and Prime Minister's Office and these were to grow in the inter-war years.[6] Against this background, the position of the Foreign and Commonwealth Office (FCO) today, as described by Allen in Chapter 12, can be regarded as a manifestation of successful adaptation in the context of a dramatically changed policy environment.

A number of the chapters in this volume make the point that the FM has not traditionally been the sole or even the main interlocutor with the international system. In the case of Israel, for example, Klieman points to the dominance of other departments, particularly Defence, in the shaping and implementation of foreign policy, with the events of the mid-1990s offering the foreign ministry a rare window of opportunity to influence the conduct of Israeli foreign policy. Australia, as Harris suggests, provides another case in which the foreign ministry has confronted powerful rivals in the shape of the Trade and Defence departments. In the face of this evidence, it seems surprising that the notion of the gatekeeper appears to have such considerable life in it. That it does reflects, in part, debates on the nature of international relations within the academic community.

Those approaching international relations from a pluralistic, world society perspective are likely to regard attention paid to the FM as a misguided preoccupation, privileging a representative of one element – the state – within a complex set of global structures and processes. Consequently, the field is left open to state-centric/realist approaches where the notion of the gatekeeper fits comfortably with core assumptions about the nature of international relations. This draws attention to one feature of the FM, its symbolic qualities as representative of the state and guardian of that key institution of the state system, the diplomatic network. Even though realists might be critical of the foreign ministry and its diplomats in their operations, that it is something special in the bureaucratic arena is readily accepted.

Moving to the 'real world' of the policymaker, arguments for the continued need for gatekeepers in a fragmenting policy environment are, of course, linked to the demands for coordination. This, as we shall see below, is a real issue but it is also used as a gambit in intra-bureaucratic struggles to gain advantage in diffused policy processes. In other words, arguments concerning gatekeeping become associated with a particular strategy for achieving coordination, namely the dominance of one department whose character, it is argued, equips it to perform this role. In the case of the foreign ministry, this rests on the assumed significance of the boundary between the domestic and international environments and the unique skills necessary for the management of that boundary.

In short, the gatekeeper image is both of questionable historical accuracy and has done a disservice to the very institution that it is intended to defend, in that it has established an inappropriate standard for evaluating the activities and worth of foreign ministries, and one that, paradoxically, is likely to result in the acceptance of the 'declinist' scenario. At the minimum, the concept of gatekeeping needs disaggregating and demystifying. To a considerable degree, the contributors to this book help to do this. As we shall see, the functions, roles and behaviour of FMs are far more complex than single, simplistic images suggest. Their capacity to respond to new challenges confronting governments is one reason for their continued survival in environments which, for differing reasons have not always been sympathetic to them. Underlying this reality is the fact that FMs have had some success in overcoming the preoccupation with 'exclusivities' to use the term employed below by Langhorne and Wallace, carving out for themselves roles in policy settings marked by dramatic domestic and international change.

FOREIGN MINISTRIES: CHALLENGES

The country studies in this book illustrate the difficulties confronting the foreign policy machinery as it responds to rapidly changing environments. Of course, the nuances are different given the varying circumstances of the countries concerned, but patterns show through. In some instances change has been dramatic as Tiouline describes in the case of Russia, but even in less turbulent environments, daunting problems confront the FM. One might characterize these at the broadest level in terms of diffusion and centralization. Diffusion reflects not simply the growing involvement of other government departments in the management of international policy but, additionally, the growing role of non-governmental organizations (NGOs) and a range of subnational actors. A globalizing economy changes the relations between government and business, and demands that FMs and their diplomatic networks respond to the need to enhance their country's competitive advantage and share of the global marketplace.[7] NGOs, particularly in the environmental and human rights areas, claim a voice in international policy and are increasingly part of the fabric through which official policy is developed and implemented. Moreover, the domestication of foreign policy arouses the interest of other arms of government – Congress in the USA is an obvious example – and subnational governments which, as Muller notes in the case of South Africa in Chapter 11, are increasingly aware of the impact that the international environment has on their interests.[8]

Centralization can assume several dimensions. Within the state there is a notable tendency to focus the management of international policy within special units often associated with head of government offices. Whereas the danger that this presents to FMs can be overstated – foreign ministry officials are not infrequently seconded to such offices and the relationships are usually very close – it presents another facet of an increasingly complex domestic environment. Outside the boundaries of the state, centralization of policymaking in regional organizations, notably the EU, provides another dimension to change which needs to be managed. Again, this is not to assume that such changes are detrimental to the FM, a point to which we shall return when discussing the coordination issue below.

RESOURCES AND THE RESTRUCTURING OF GOVERNMENT

Although not specific to foreign ministries, the emphasis during the 1980s and early 1990s on restructuring and downsizing government has presented particular problems to FMs and their diplomatic networks. Just as many governments were intent on reducing the size and costs of their diplomatic networks, so the end of the Cold War and the collapse of the USSR presented them with the need to cope with a growing number of newly-independent states. East and Dillery report that the State Department created (or upgraded) 20 new posts between 1991–6 but without additional funding. Indeed, there has been an 11 per cent reduction in funding since 1990. Some countries, of course, have confronted situations where changing circumstances have required them to greatly expand the size of their foreign ministries and diplomatic networks. This is particularly so in the cases of Japan and South Africa. In the former, Komachi portrays the foreign ministry as a bureaucratic 'growth industry' whilst in the South African context Muller describes what she terms 'phenomenal expansion' as the government has responded to the changed political situation and sought to prioritize foreign policy goals.

But elsewhere the picture is one of seeking to do more with fewer resources as economies are sought both at home and abroad. In part, this has been achieved by internal restructuring as Allen notes in the case of the FCO. However, cost-cutting and internal reorganization brings with it human costs and one of the themes running through several of the chapters is that of a decline in morale. Perhaps the most obvious instance, and one fortunately not replicated elsewhere, is that of Russia where Tiouline portrays a situation in which the diplomatic career has lost the prestige it once held as well as providing diminishing financial rewards. More generally, however, foreign services around the world have found it increasingly hard to attract and retain the calibre of staff which they need. Despite the popular view that a diplomatic career is glamorous, serving overseas presents very real problems in an era when both spouses have careers and the demands of family life are increasingly hard to accommodate. Moreover, cost-cutting and restructuring often has an impact on career structures by reducing the chances of promotion, particularly where reform manifests itself in recruiting to the foreign service in mid-career and offering head of mission posts to recruits from outside the service, by enlisting businesspersons, for example.

CONTEXTS AND SETTINGS

In analyzing the responses of the FM to these challenges, a clear relationship emerges between the status and role of the foreign ministry and the foreign policy preoccupations of a particular state, reflecting the relationship between policy and policy machinery noted earlier. In some contexts (Australia and Canada, for example) this has an evolutionary tone to it. Cooper's image of the Canadian Department of Foreign Affairs and International Trade in its various guises 'trying to get it right' as Canadian foreign policy moved from the internationalism of the Pearson era into the more testing foreign and domestic waters of the Trudeau era and beyond, conveys a sense of a laboratory for evolving foreign policy management. Other FMs have had to respond to more turbulent settings. In the case of Israel, Klieman's description of the rapidity of events surrounding the management of Israeli foreign policy in the mid 1990s illustrates how the Ministry of Foreign Affairs was presented with a window of opportunity in the context of the peace process which quickly closed in the face of international events and responses from intra-bureaucratic rivalries and political challenges. In very different contexts, the South African and the Russian foreign ministries have needed to respond to sudden changes which have altered both their objectives and their structures.

In the case of South Africa, Muller describes how, during the Apartheid era, the foreign ministry's main task was to defend domestic racial policies and how South African isolation reinforced the geographical rather than the functional organizational principle within the ministry. In the post-Apartheid era, the FM confronts a far more complex environment in which the need to select priorities has been accompanied by a shift towards multilateral diplomacy. Japan, as Komachi's study clearly explains, is another example where dramatic change of circumstance over the last 50 years has impacted greatly on the foreign ministry. Here, rather than decline, the position and the role of the FM has been reinvigorated by the lessons drawn from the Gulf War experience in 1991. Negative overseas responses to the Japanese stance at this time and the decision to seek to balance Japan's role as an economic superpower with a more overtly 'political' international role, has given the foreign ministry a platform on which to enhance both its role and resources.

Alongside the imperatives of the international environment, the status of the foreign ministry has been affected by characteristics of national political systems and their political cultures. The ambiguities that these factors present is conveyed by East and Dillery in their study of the US State Department. As they point out, in historical and constitutional terms, the State Department is a premier department within the federal government. And yet it has not enjoyed the prestige that such a position might be expected to confer upon it. In part, as they point out, this is because it is confronted by powerful rivals in the shape of Congress, the Defense Department and the National Security Council. But there are more deeply-seated reasons at work. Whilst charges of elitism are probably familiar to the majority of, if not all, foreign ministries and their diplomatic services, this is particularly true of the US with its pluralist and populist culture.

In the case of Norway, Neumann demonstrates how the foreign ministry has responded to an environment wherein its very legitimacy has been contested. In part this can be regarded as a functional issue in the sense that Norway's perceived requirements for international representation have been viewed in strongly commercial terms. Significantly, the business community has been positive towards the consular service but less so towards the foreign ministry. But this is related to a more fundamental problem, namely a lack of understanding within Norwegian society of the need for diplomacy as manifested in the fact that 'diplomat' is not a common usage. In such an environment, it is hardly surprising that identity has been a central issue in the operation of the ministry. Although the Mexican ministry appears, according to Rozental's analysis, to have had its ups and downs, particularly during the Echeverria presidency, a very different set of historical circumstances from those of Norway have endowed it with a degree of prestige both within Mexico and the diplomatic community.

Moving to the subnational level, the contributors to this volume clearly illustrate the significance of political and bureaucratic relationships to the position of the FM. As has been suggested above, this reflects the fact that the management of international policy has accorded more to a pattern of intra-bureaucratic tensions than it has to the sole dominance of any one agency. This is to be expected and it is only the assumption that foreign policy is something inherently different from other spheres of policy that produces the belief that this should not be so. Nevertheless, political leaders have a tendency to perceive foreign policy as something special if only because it provides them with an opportunity to carve a role on a more expansive political stage than that on which they are normally constrained to operate.

There is, of course, a long history of prime ministers and presidents acting, either formally or in effect, as their own foreign minister. Certainly this has been true of Australia in the past and is well-illustrated in the Malaysian case as Ahmad's paper demonstrates. Here, the Malaysian Prime Minister, Dr Mahathir, has developed a highly proactive foreign policy stance as spokesperson for the South. Not surprisingly, this has resulted in prime ministerial dominance of the foreign policy scene. To a not inconsiderable degree, however, personalities are a key factor as Klieman argues in the case of Israel. Indeed, he suggests that the foreign minister's character, political relationships, style of leadership and worldview are central to the Israeli foreign ministry's place in the policymaking process. Thus the period 1990–2 when David Levy was foreign minister and the two periods during which Shimon Peres discharged this role are regarded as periods of relative ascendancy for the ministry. The danger of strong ministers, however, as Klieman suggests in the case of Peres, is that they tend to run their own foreign policy outside the formal diplomatic network.

THE FUNCTIONS OF FOREIGN MINISTRIES

The fact that, as noted earlier, foreign ministries do not simply survive but appear to be engaged in activities of which the image of gatekeeping provides only an imprecise and misleading impression, invites the question as to what functions they are performing. This brings us up against debates concerning the requirements of contemporary government and the need for the traditional functions discharged by diplomacy. One of the central issues which the foreign ministry has to confront is that of whether the communication function of which it is part is any longer necessary. The 'CNN factor' highlights the challenges of virtually instantaneous news reporting provided by a global media. But several of the chapters draw a distinction between the reporting of events – on which the electronic media have an obvious advantage – and the analysis of those events tailored to the needs of a particular government. Harris makes this point forcefully in the case of Australia, arguing that the latter's geographical proximity to Asia demands an effective and independent capacity to analyze the societies of its neighbouring states. Reliance on outside information from whatever source is seen as having a negative impact on Australian foreign policy, a fact of particular concern given the apparent deterioration in the capacity of the Department of Foreign Affairs and Trade to provide this.

In a very different context, Klieman points to the advantages accruing to the policy debate from the additional source of analysis provided by the Ministry of Foreign Affairs after 1993. It may not always be the case, however, that the culture of the FM is supportive of a policy analysis role. In describing the elaborate processes employed by the State Department in terms of planning, both at headquarters and mission levels, East and Dillery note that there is an inherent scepticism within the department as to the possibility and worth of policy planning.

It is, however, the coordination function that comes through most clearly as the key activity performed by the majority of foreign ministries analyzed in this book. This reflects the changing nature of the policy environment within which governments are constrained to operate, one feature of which is the erosion of boundaries between issues and arenas.[9] This is not to suggest that coordination is a new preoccupation, but that it has become a much more central concern of policymakers as they need to operate in multiple arenas (often simultaneously), engage with a more diverse range of governmental and non-governmental actors, and to ensure that they maintain a coherent position on issues that are at once closely linked and embrace domestic and international constituencies. As Rozental points out in chapter 8, the lack of a unified voice on policy issues can offer an advantage to those who are skilled in playing off government departments in the course of complex negotiations. At its worst, one finds the situation described by Komachi in pre-war Japan where a 'dual diplomacy' developed as the military side-tracked the foreign ministry with ultimately devastating results. The need to avoid such a situation has made Japanese policymakers sensitive to the problem in its more modern manifestation where foreign economic policy has involved powerful actors outside the foreign ministry such as the Ministry for International Trade and Industry (MITI). And yet it is important to note the form and style of coordination. As Spence points out in Chapter 14, coordination may be achieved through various means, only one of which involves the dominance of one department.

In the context of the management of international policy, this returns us to the notion of the gatekeeper and the argument that FMs do and/or should perform such a role. But the evidence offered here makes it clear that coordination is a far more complex and subtle activity, albeit one where foreign ministries are providing a significant input. Certainly, in the case of the European Union (EU), national foreign ministries are portrayed as performing critical coordinating roles, but do so alongside other government departments. In the United Kingdom, Allen differentiates between internal coordination which the FCO has sought to improve both at home and over-seas and coordination with other government departments, particularly within the framework of EU policy processes. It is his conclusion that not only has the FCO met these challenges successfully but that its significance within the structure of government has been enhanced as a result.

RESPONSES AND STRATEGIES

Against the background of a changing and challenging environment, foreign ministries appear to have engaged in adaptive strategies at two levels: firstly, internally and within the broader governmental structures; second, outside the governmental setting by developing links with domestic interests, parti-cularly NGOs and business.

As we have seen in the context of the discussion on coordination, relation-ships with other agencies of government have been central to the evolution of the FM's role in the management of international policy. As coordination has become more critical to success in policy management, so FMs have needed to respond to a more complex milieu by sharing the coordination function with other departments whose functional responsibilities take them increasingly into the international arena. This is obviously true of the EU, but glimpses are offered in several of the papers of the processes through which the management of effective policy demands that working arrangements between departments, including the foreign ministry, be put in place. Hence Harris's reference to the agreement between the Australian Department of Primary Industry and the FM regarding the conduct of international negotiations in this policy area. Consequently, the FM appears to have become in many, if not all, of the cases examined in this book, a significant element in the management of growing interdependence. Thus the image of conflictual, zero-sum relations between an embattled foreign ministry and bureaucratic competitors – an essential element in the 'declinist' scenario – appears to be something of a caricature. This is not to deny that there are problems but these may have more to do with tensions between cost-conscious finance ministries and the foreign ministry than bureaucratic politics impinging on the conduct of external policy.

Interestingly, Komachi argues that the traditional picture of conflict between the Japanese Ministry of Foreign Affairs and MITI has become less significant due to the impact of globalization which has brought the approach of both departments towards foreign economic policy more closely into line. The experience of EU member states is also instructive in this respect given the growing involvement of domestic departments in the day-to-day interaction between member state governments and Brussels. The view from the 'centre' (Spence) and two member states – UK (Allen) and France (Enjalran and Husson) – all appear to suggest that foreign ministries continue to perform critical (but not exclusive) roles in this increasingly densely-textured policy environment, establishing their position rather than succumbing to the challenges of other actors.

What emerges clearly are the differing responses of governments to their own unique problems in managing fluid policy environments. One possible option is to alter fundamentally the structures of government concerned with the management of international policy. This route has been followed by both Canada and Australia in merging the international trade function with the foreign ministry. Given the long-running tensions between Foreign Affairs and Trade departments in the Australian case, this has been a significant development and one that has strengthened the role of the Department of Foreign Affairs and Trade (as it now is). But it is notable that in none of the national studies contained in this book does there appear to be a serious demand for the merging of the foreign ministry with the 'domestic' arm of government – as was suggested in the 1977 Central Policy Review Staff report on the UK FCO. Rather, pragmatic responses have been adopted, tailored to particular needs. One manifestation of this is the internal restructuring of FMs by fine-tuning the emphasis on the geographical versus the functional principle – an issue as old as foreign ministries themselves. Given the growing involvement of domestic departments in the management of international policy, this issue carries an added significance for the position of the FM within the overall governmental structures and policy processes.

Spence's Chapter 14 describes developments in the EU context, which may lead eventually to something approaching a European foreign service. Although there is a considerable distance to be travelled before that milestone is reached, there is significant interchange and cooperation between FMs within the EU that strengthens their role as agents of coordination both between Brussels and national capitals and between member state governments. The role of FMs is also strengthened by secondments within the machinery of national government, particularly to key policy units such as the Cabinet Office in the UK and the *Secrétariat Général du Comité Interministériel pour les Questions de Coopération Economique Européenne* (SGCI) in France.

Although the focus of the book is specifically on the foreign ministry rather than the diplomatic service which it administers, the two are obviously so closely intertwined that such a distinction is impossible to make in terms of analyzing the FM's role and distorts its significance as a policy actor. As noted above, one dimension of the FM's response to the resource pressures bearing down on it has been to experiment with new forms of diplomatic representation or to elaborate on existing patterns. This has been reinforced by another factor in the equation addressed by many of the papers, namely the impact of the revolution in information technology. In one sense, of course this can be viewed as a challenge. Indeed, the impact of enhanced communications and their impact on diplomacy is a theme that goes back at least to the mid-nineteenth century as observers grappled with the significance of the arrival of the railways and the electric telegraph.

At the same time, it can be argued that the IT revolution is providing an opportunity for foreign ministries to reconsider their role and activities, how core functions are discharged and the ways in which delivery of services can be improved. Recent reviews of the FCO in the UK, for example, have made the point, *inter alia*, that developments in this area have eroded the assumption that London makes policy whilst missions implement it; that overseas posts are increasingly involved in policymaking (depending on the size and location of posts) and that major missions – particularly delegations to international organizations – are key elements in the policy processes.[10] This casts a somewhat different light on the debates concerning the machinery through which diplomacy is conducted and the relative significance of bilateral versus multilateral diplomacy. Easier communications combined with the need to expand representation with fewer resources demands the adoption of a greater variety of modes of representation. Some of these are touched on in the following chapters. The Nordic countries, for example have for some years experimented with various forms of joint representation and Canada and Australia, amongst other countries, are currently exploring the possibilities of further cooperation in this area. Elsewhere, consideration is being given to employing home-based ambassadors covering countries or regions from the foreign ministry and the use of mini-missions with a skeleton staff whose primary role is often in the commercial sphere. As noted above, the example of innovation with the greatest long term potential lies in the development of EU representation.

The emphasis on the need to develop strategies outside the context of governmental structures is a consistent theme throughout many of the following chapters, reflecting the impact of the growing interaction between state and society on the operations of foreign ministries and their diplomatic services. In part this is connected to a long-standing problem confronting FMs, namely that, unlike functional government departments, they lack a domestic constituency whose support can be drawn upon. To a degree, the changing nature of much diplomatic activity with its growing emphasis on commercial work has helped to rectify this problem. But the expanding human rights and environmental agendas, for example, are requiring foreign ministries to develop their relationships with NGOs, not least because governments are increasingly reliant on the expertise and services that these can provide. Both Cooper (Canada) and Rozental (Mexico) see this as a major development. Even in the Japanese case, where as Komachi notes, the idea of civil society is not as well-rooted as in other societies, there is some evidence that the foreign ministry is becoming conscious of its potential significance. As the Mexican and Canadian examples point out, involving NGOs in the shaping of policy and as members of delegations to international conferences is not without its dangers since they may undermine national negotiating positions either at home or in the conference room. It goes without saying that foreign ministries are conscious of the increasing importance of the media, particularly the electronic media, to the management of international policy and place considerable emphasis on the management of media relations.

CONCLUSION

Two broad and perhaps obvious conclusions emerge from the studies which follow. The first is the diversity of factors that determine the role and status of the foreign ministry. These, it has been suggested, operate at three interactive levels: (a) the international context within which national governments and societies are located; (b) the nature of national socio-political settings and, in particular, patterns of bureaucratic relations; and (c) the impact of individual policymakers on the management of international policy. Thus countries confronting dramatic change in their international environment, such as South Africa, have needed to expand their foreign policy capabilities and that means strengthening the foreign ministry and diplomatic network. That dramatic change does not, however, necessarily confer beneficial results on the foreign ministry is confirmed by the example of Russia.

The national level focuses attention on the historical position of the FM in its political and bureaucratic setting and cultural attitudes towards it and the practice of diplomacy. In very different contexts, the studies of Norway and the USA illustrate the ways in which political culture and social norms have conditioned the operation of their foreign ministries. In terms of the impact of personalities, so clearly of major significance in the case of Israel and also of Malaysia, it is obviously the case that *who* is foreign minister at a given period can be critical to the influence that the FM is able to exercise. Given the potential complexities that the interrelationship between each of these factors can create, generalizations about foreign ministries, their role and significance are fraught with danger.

The second broad conclusion follows from the first and suggests that the image of foreign ministries suffering from a state of perhaps terminal decline is a distortion of reality. It has been suggested above that this is due in part to a misreading of the nature and historical evolution of foreign ministries and their relations with other government agencies in the management of international policy. To some extent, this is because diplomats have been their own worst enemies, arguing that their pre-ordained role, underscored by history, is to act as the gatekeeper between the domestic and international policy environments. Not surprisingly, as a rapidly changing policy milieu made such a claim look distinctly tenuous, so some, taking the pretension at face value, have been tempted to conclude that the days of foreign ministries are indeed numbered. The following studies demonstrate that this is not the case. But they also suggest that the core functions that FMs can provide, often relating to complex coordination processes, are much more nuanced and relate to their role as a key part of the processes through which national governments are required to operate in increasingly fragmented policy environments.

As suggested earlier in this chapter, foreign ministries have and are responding to the demands of managing access rather than focusing on the imperatives of control which is implicit in the notion of gatekeeping in its crudest forms. Rather, 'gatekeeping' continues to be what it has frequently been, namely a shared activity, on occasions involving conflict with other key government departments. This form of activity – perhaps more appropriately designated as 'transboundary facilitation' – is, somewhat paradoxically, likely to be both more valued yet increasingly challenged by other government agencies engaged in similar processes within specific policy areas. However, this is not to be equated, as the following chapters suggest, with some generalized pattern of decline. Rather, if an overarching lesson can be drawn from the diverse examples presented in this book, it is that foreign ministries appear to be highly flexible organizations; that, indeed, they exhibit many of the characteristics which students of organizational change term the 'virtual' organization where this is understood as 'the name given to any organization which is continually evolving, redefining and reinventing itself . . . .'[11] Perhaps the key test now lies in adapting to a situation in which the post-modern state exists in an environment wherein the separation of the foreign and the domestic, through which the contemporary foreign ministry was born, is gradually reversed.

NOTES

1   See, for example, P. Hirst and G. Thompson, *Globalization in question: the international economy and the possibilities of governance* (Cambridge: Polity Press, 1996).

2   This point is developed in E. B. Kapstein, *Governing the global economy: international finance and the state* (Cambridge, Mass: Harvard University Press, 1994).

3   K. Hamilton and R. Langhorne, *The practice of diplomacy: its evolution, theory and administration* (London: Routledge, 1995), p. 73.

4   See G. Mattingly, *Renaissance Diplomacy*, (Harmondsworth: Penguin University Books, 1973), especially ch. 23. For an overview of the differences between the medieval and the modern conceptions of space and territoriality, see S. J. Kobrin, 'Back to the future: neomedievalism and the postmodern digital world economy', *Journal of International Affairs*, 51(2), Spring 1998, pp. 362–86.

5   Sir John Tilley and S. Gaselee, *The Foreign Office* (London: Putnam's, 1933), pp. 26–49; N. Hart, *The foreign secretary* (Lavenham: Dalton, 1987), pp. 9–27; V. Cromwell, 'The Foreign and Commonwealth Office', in Z. Steiner (ed.), *The Times survey of foreign ministries of the world* (London: Times Books, 1982), pp. 542–51.

6   E. Maisel, *The Foreign Office and foreign policy, 1919–1926* (Brighton: Sussex Academic Press, 1994), p. 63.

7   See S. Strange, 'States, firms and diplomacy', *International Affairs*, 68(1), January 1992.

8   B. Hocking, *Localizing foreign policy: non-central governments and multilayered diplomacy* (London: Macmillan, 1993).

9   On the changing nature of the foreign policy environment see B. Hocking and M. Smith, *Beyond foreign economic policy: the United States, the Single European Market and the changing world economy* (London: Pinter, 1997). ch. 1.

10   S. Eldon, *From quill pen to satellite: foreign ministries in the information age* (London: Royal Institute of International Affairs), 1994, p. 22.

11   R. Hale and P. Whitlam, *Towards the virtual organization*, (Maidenhead, McGraw-Hill, 1997) p. 3.

1 Diplomacy towards the Twenty-first Century

Richard Langhorne and William Wallace

The general context in which diplomacy and the functioning of foreign ministries occurs has always been subject to very particular events and circumstances. That is not just to say that their environment has undergone constant modification, though plainly it has, but also to note that the pace and style of change have had no cyclical form. Over time, modifications have been both gradual and sudden, shallow and profound, occurring in response to highly irregular sea changes in the organization and expectations of human societies. We can recognize, however, that, if not uniquely, the contemporary international environment is inducing strikingly rapid changes in the objectives of foreign relations by both states and non-state entities, in the institutions involved and among the personnel employed to pursue these objectives. How might we create a taxonomy of at least the most compelling of contemporary pressures?

First, we would want to look at the underlying structure of international relations. Here, first and foremost we would note the consequences of the globalization of the world's communications systems. At one level, this has produced a revolution in global social interaction which flows from cheap and rapid travel and from globally available television, video and film. Tourism has now become one of the world's largest and most profitable industries. There is an increasing tendency in richer societies for people to own second homes in other countries. Global flows of foreign students continue to rise, and both short- and long-term migrations are being simultaneously induced in poorer areas and resisted by destination states.

Even more significant, however, is that the technology involved has reached the point where the global economy has been stitched into a single garment. It is not yet a seamless robe, but it has advanced far enough to have created important new layers of globally arranged human activity which behave horizontally and cut across the traditionally vertical divisions inherent in a system composed of sovereign states, relating to each other as distinct geographical and administrative entities. The effect has been to shift the boundary between domestic and international politics producing a consequent movement in economic regulation and efforts at multilateral consultation on economic policies. The result is an inevitable and uncomfortable mixture of old and new. States have not been swept away by the globalized economy, but they have been in some ways emasculated by it.

They have also been affected by it very differently depending upon their level of development. The new areas and levels of activity have not in some cases yet developed any form of governance and are thus unable to represent themselves, or do so defectively. For the continuing state, and for associations of states or any other organization that has some governance, this presents one of the most serious difficulties of the contemporary international system. For the foreign services and ministries of states, it is the basis, sometimes more emotional than seriously quantified, of the sense that they had become an expensive irrelevance, and thus an easy target for cost cutting in a generally post-collectivist political atmosphere.

The unfolding and unwelcome stresses of the post-Cold War world may have begun to turn this particular tide a little. Both the departing and incoming US Secretaries of State remarked in January 1997 on the need for Congress at least to maintain the present levels of funding for the State Department and ideally increase it; and this seems to have become an acceptable idea. Even this change of mood, however, if it were to be paralleled in other countries, would still leave foreign services struggling with the task of coping with an ever growing agenda on reduced resources. Nor will the basic changes induced by enhanced communications be reversed. The widespread and immediate availability of electronically produced information about national and international developments coupled with the ease of international travel has permanently altered the balance of power between foreign services and their political masters. Direct negotiation between senior members of governments may not be the best practice – it has been specifically warned against by diplomatic theorists from the earliest times – but it has become irresistibly attractive in contemporary circumstances. Heads of government devote a large proportion of their time to international activity, as do most other senior ministers and officials. Personal likes and dislikes, understandings and misunderstandings have thus intruded into diplomacy. The ready availability of real time global information not only feeds this development, it also produces a difficult paradox. What CNN tells the world about wars, refugees and atrocities induces a public demand that something must be done; but the same public also thinks that governments – rightly sensing that they are genuinely less effective than hitherto – should do less and that taxation should consequentially fall. This produces inevitable but contradictory surges of popular concern, relapsing into criticism of over-engagement when governments respond.

This growing work load is a consequence of other characteristics of the contemporary system. States may have suffered a decline of authority, but they have markedly increased in numbers, a development sharply increased in recent years by the collapse of the Soviet Union and Yugoslavia, which has added 21 new states to the system. By 1986, the UN had acquired 158 members, two-thirds of whom spoke for less than 10 per cent of the world's population: by 1997, the figure was 185. It has further flowed from this that the range of physical size, economic power, demographic weight and military power to be observed among states has to be represented on a vastly extended scale of difference. So great are these differences that it stretches credulity that the single word 'state' can still be used to describe them all, and it is a tribute to the overwhelming significance of the state since the early seventeenth century in Europe that the notion continues to have such power.

Nor has it only been states that have increased in number. The ever growing environmental and economic complications of the world have led to a corresponding increase in the number of international organizations of every kind at every level. Here, too, the scale of difference has sharply increased; government and non-government, global and regional, ethnic and economic, military and commercial, large and small, significant and insignificant, long-lived and brief, all and more can be found. Organizations that are associations of states have inevitably shared in the fate of their members; organizations that are not derived from states have increased in numbers and importance and have acquired significant diplomatic functions. Several recent episodes of humanitarian interventions have shown how important this shift has become and how difficult it is for the parties to manage their relationships in such situations.

The result is a thickening texture of exchanges both horizontally and vertically with accompanying uncertainties and confusions. This has led to a proliferation of non-governmental actors – media conglomerates, television networks, banks, companies, expert 'policy-communities' and transnational campaigning groups. Policymakers can no longer rely on tailoring the messages they present to different domestic and foreign audiences; the feedback between the two is close, with domestic interests also engaged in lobbying other governments and sitting-in on multilateral negotiations. The range and expertise of the personnel involved has gone beyond and threatens to dwarf the numbers engaged in more traditional diplomatic activities. The old rules continue to provide some framework, but they have to be bent and recreated: nobody can yet tell what the new rule book will contain, nor who its publishers will be.

A further major influencing factor in diplomatic development has been the steadily rising number of matters which both states and non-state entities must discuss: some obvious examples are environmental and climatic issues, the position of women, working conditions and civil rights. These kinds of issues, together with the ever increasing significance of various forms of economic, financial and trading practice negotiation tend to shift the boundary between what is considered political and non-political. Some of these issues require the active participation of a wide range of scientific experts and can only be effectively dealt with on a global scale. Some elements of both have been observable in recent times, particularly with reference to arms control, but they go against the grain of the evolved diplomatic structure and, despite some important developments underpinning, for example, the series of Habitat conferences, they have been difficult to achieve and coordinate.

For the future, the progress of the major non-governmental organizations in more rapidly developing their diplomatic activity, as the Red Cross has always quietly done, is going to be highly significant for the functioning of the global system. Acceptance of a diplomatic role leads to the need for training and deciding, as states have had to do, what kind of balance between specialist and generalist skills their personnel should deploy. More difficult still, perhaps, is the hurdle that has to be crossed by both governments and non-governmental organizations if they wish to cooperate and take part in joint representations. A traditionally adversarial relationship has to change: the NGO may lose the cutting edge of its protest role, a government may have to take risks with information and confidentiality. But as it becomes widely accepted that environmental crises have to be dealt with both in the form of contemporary disasters on the ground and by minimizing their long-term causes as rapidly and completely as possible, there is an increasing convergence in the positions of governments and NGOs. Certainly the mutual benefits from cooperation are self evidently immense, and it seems likely that this trend will eventually solidify into fairly routine practice. In addition, a new diplomatic need is developing, as yet largely unmet from within the system, for a means of organizing the preparatory work for major conferences on issues comparatively new to the global agenda. The combinations to be brought together may include professional organizations, local government, national government, regional interests, commercial interests and expert advisers. The likely assembly tends to be unwieldy and becomes impossibly so if there has not been adequate preparation beforehand, followed by highly skilled management of the proceedings. Either diplomacy will do this, or those who do so will become diplomats.

Among the other developments in the fundamental structure of the global system which affect the objectives of international actors has been a notable change in the nature of war, both in the expectation of its likelihood and in the manner of its conduct. It is no longer major, overwhelming, possibly terminal, inter-state or inter-alliance conflict that is feared, so much as the effects of low level domestic turbulence on regional security, or the possibility of its spreading to other states. The pursuit of cultural or religious agendas by fomenting low level conflict has also, together with improving opportunities for terrorism, been a beneficiary of the heady mixture of types and centres of power that characterize the post Cold War and post Internet global system.

Naturally, the onset of serious change in the global international structure is producing changes in the nature of its business, its machinery and its personnel. It might be said that the chief objective of governments is now to put themselves into the best position to benefit from the existence and opportunities of the global economy. This may mean adopting particular and uncomfortable domestic economic policies, with a consequential decline in domestic political legitimacy. At another level, it may mean participating in the global market rather than relying on economic autarchy, justified by ideological rejection of capitalism, or even still the legacy of colonialism. It may also mean raising the significance of belonging to and being important within international economic organizations both regional and global. Within Europe, it means even more; it means facing and adapting to the institutional consequences, whether a member or not, of the existence of the EU, whose purposes transcend the purely economic. In Europe particularly, direct and continuing contacts among officials and ministers make for cross-cutting coalitions; defence ministries support each other against finance ministries within NATO; central banks form an effective transnational 'club'.

This particular feature has meant that within states the conduct of foreign affairs has long since fractured into very different elements spread across most of the functions of government. In their different fields, each deals with the equivalent part of other state administrations, or the relevant sections of international entities. Within the global system, the elements have also fractured, so that some remain with and between states, however variously they may be managed by individual states, but others have fallen into the hands of a very varied assemblage of organizations, both governmental and non-governmental. Some crucial activities, particularly global financial operations, have so far not evoked any system of governance and thus create major areas of economic uncertainty. One result of this particular aspect is that a crisis is developing about how to handle the control and prosecution of global economic crime. It is a good example of how economic globalization has de-territorialized a definable and growing activity. It plainly requires international negotiation and cooperation at a highly specialized level and it would normally have been the task of diplomacy to enable this to happen. But there are no obvious principles, no clear basis of legal authority and no effective punishments available. The issue is too serious and too damaging to the essential good order of the global financial system: without such order, it cannot function, and some kind of mechanism will undoubtedly emerge. Whatever it turns out to be, it will require personnel with very particular skills, and they will have to engage with other sources of authority and power: diplomacy will begin again in yet another new context.

It is popular on the part of cost-cutters, but wrong, to assume that these changes can be regarded in a mercantilist way: that what is no longer within the control of states has simply passed somewhere else and thus reduced the responsibilities of states and the flow of their business. On the contrary, states do not have less to do, they have more, merely at different points of contact within the system. The same is true for organizations. They, too, have to deal with a far more thickly textured world, and to find the funds with which to do it. One of the ways in which the force of these developments can be seen is in the rapid growth of multilateral diplomacy, whether involving combinations of states or combinations of states with non-state or inter-governmental entities. This shift has led to changing requirements from bilateral embassies, giving them a new role as an additional dimension to multilateral negotiations, providing briefings on the domestic constraints under which other governments operate and laying the groundwork for bilateral deals. In the case of the EU, there has been a noteworthy expansion of its multilateral diplomatic structure with the opening of representation across Central and Eastern Europe and within the CIS.

The overall costs of the current global international system are bound to be greater than they have ever been. If the business of the world is thought of in terms of the number of items on its agenda – particularly increased by the emergence of the great environmental issues – and by the extraordinary range of the people involved in conducting it, neither its significance nor its scale can be ignored.

With such a variety of issues and actors, requiring many different levels of expertise, and interacting both internally and externally with so many different elements in human societies, the outstanding function of diplomacy and foreign ministries at this stage of development is coordination. There has to be coordination between the parts of individual governments, between governments themselves, between governments and international bodies of every kind and between officials and unofficial, or only temporarily official, representatives, particularly academic and commercial experts. Freed from the responsibilities of being the sole managers of foreign policy, and from the exclusivities and occasional paranoia that went with it, foreign ministries, who are already playing such a role to some degree, will need to make it their principal purpose; and governments will need both to support such a purpose and pay for it. Moreover, in a world where the ease of communication has made a very public management of external affairs available to political leaders, and thus equally available to service their domestic agendas, coordination of this kind is at a premium. It is not easy to see how to turn this role into a politically desirable goal, but at least politicians need to be brought to see that success, whatever that might be deemed to be and to the extent that states can individually expect it in today's global environment, will not be achieved by short term domestic gestures. It can only accrue from a steady, persistent, support for routine, but vital, coordinative management. Zbigniew Brzezinski once said that if foreign ministries and embassies 'did not already exist, they surely would not have to be invented'. Of course, we do not need either as they were in 1914, but we need both in expanded ways more than we have ever needed them before. Nor will they be alone – the activity of diplomacy has spread to many other entities and across many categories of people; and there is no zero sum game in contemporary diplomacy. What states have lost, they have regained with interest in different types of activity; what the state system has lost, the global system has more than replaced with the largest agenda of communication, negotiation and coordination on crucial issues of every kind that has ever faced human societies.

2 Australia
Change and Adaptation in the Department of Foreign Affairs and Trade

Stuart Harris[1]

Although the erstwhile colonies in Australia came together in 1901 to create the Federation that it is today, '(a)t the time of Munich Australia . . . had *no* diplomatic missions in any *foreign* country', unlike other comparable dominions, Canada and South Africa.[2] There had been an external affairs division of the prime minister's department from 1921 but, except in a limited form from 1901 to 1916,[3] a stand alone foreign ministry was not established until 1935 and the first diplomatic mission in a foreign country was that of Australian Minister to Washington in 1940. Essentially, until World War II – and in many respects for a period after then – Australia was content to let Britain speak for what was then the British Empire. Dependence on Britain was only partially diminished during World War II and the early postwar years, with the wartime reliance on the USA and the increased importance of that relationship, and the recognition of the growth in the economic and ultimately strategic significance of Asia.

Dominant historically in Australia's international context is the sense of dependence, first on Britain and then on the USA, that came from being a small/medium sized country which has had through much of its history, and to some extent still has, 'a sense of being a small and vulnerable society potentially under threat from more populous societies'.[4] Added to the wide appreciation of the US role in Australia's emergence from the dangers of World War II there is a continuing general acceptance that Australia's security still depends ultimately on the USA. Indeed, Coral Bell describes Australia as 'still a province of the English-speaking world, whose capital was once in Britain but is now in the USA'.[5] While, in recent decades, Australia's geographic and social characteristics have continued as major influences on the form in which Australia's foreign policy is developed and managed, the foreign ministry has also had to respond to the substantial geopolitical changes in the international system, as well as to domestic institutional and bureaucratic pressures.

Although a high level of bipartisanship has existed, and still does, in the political support for Australia's foreign policy, with notable past exceptions, such as the recognition of China and military involvement in Vietnam, more subtle differences exist. Over the postwar years the underlying philosophy of the two major parties differed in that the Labor party has been more internationalist in orientation, and particularly supportive of the United Nations,[6] while the conservative parties have been more specifically alliance oriented, with the USA becoming the centrepiece of a globally oriented security policy.

This mainly concerned security issues, although during the Cold War actions on economic issues were to a large degree predicated upon their security implications. Australia, in moving from economic dependence upon Britain, and in engaging economically with Asia, embraced economic multi-lateralism to gain the protection sought by less powerful countries from rules based international systems.[7] Post Cold War US trade unilateralism, and the US's lack of comfort with the ideas of the open regionalism, diffuse recipro-city and rapid trade liberalism of the Asia–Pacific, have created tensions domestically as well as in the relationship.

Having been a loyal liegeman of first the British and then the USA in much of the early postwar period, a continuing challenge for Australia's foreign policy, and one not always fully met, has been to avoid being seen as a clone of the USA; how, that is, to express Australia's individual point of view on the many issues on which it differs from the USA and its policies, and specifically with respect to Asia, without substantially undermining the fundamental ties with that country still politically important domestically. Its overall success in this respect has led to Australia being termed 'odd man in' in Asia. Suggestions that the new Conservative government in Australia is seeking to return to closer links with the USA raise the question: will Australia still be odd man in, or become odd man out, in Asia?

Apart from its geographic location and its consequent policy assumptions, other factors important to the way Australia manages its foreign policy include its development as a multicultural society, with a large immigration programme. Consequently, it needs to maintain links with countries of original settlement. Given the wide spread of settler origins, this includes many countries with which Australia would otherwise have only limited contact.

In addition, Australia's ability to respond to the changing international environment is conditioned by its federal system. The closer integration of domestic and international policy and the expansion of the foreign policy agenda from the previous substantial dominance of security and alliance diplomacy has magnified this constraint. Although the central government has overriding constitutional power to pursue foreign policy, the increasing internationalization of economic interchange and the growing range of inter-national treaty commitments has been seen as threatening the sovereignty of individual states within the federation.[8]

ORGANIZATION AND AGENDAS

When established in 1935, the Department of Foreign Affairs (DFA)[9] was 'originally perceived as a small elitist institution, primarily focusing on overseas representation and negotiation...' and reflecting British norms and styles of diplomatic practice.[10] That it is now a major department of state with a wider perspective on its functions, reflects Australia's changing interaction with the world as well as a response to domestic pressures.

From the mid-1950s until 1987, there were three departments primarily concerned with international affairs: DFA, the Department of Trade (DT),[11] and the Department of Defence (DD). Given the importance of trade to Australia, its difficulties in its export marketing in the face of agricultural protectionism in Europe and the US, the shift in Australia's trade relations from largely bilateral links with Britain to Japan and the USA, and then more widely in Asia, and the increasing importance of multilateral trade discussions, DT became a major international player. DFA, however, 'was not highly ranked in the informal Canberra public service pecking order until the 1970s'.[12]

Differences in the cultures of the two departments – the elitist culture of the DFA contrasting with the 'can-do' pragmatism of DT – are often given as a major element in the conflicts of the two departments. More important, however, were other factors. These included the competition for priority in their agendas, and the shift in political power of the respective ministers. As well as the growing importance of economics, for many years DT had had powerful ministers from the Country (subsequently National) Party associated with rural – and therefore agricultural export – interests. Although the Country Party was part of the Liberal (conservative) coalition, strains were often evident within the coalition over the dominance of DT.

The alternative governing party, the Labor Party, developed a strong antipathy to DT, seeing it as too closely aligned politically to the Country Party. Efforts to weaken it by Labor ministers when in power in the early 1980s were successful but at the cost of an effective trade policy, since the DFA was in no position to fill the gap. Whereas in DFA the international development assistance function was made autonomous in 1986, working directly to the foreign minister[13] but with successful coordination arrangements, the dismantling of the trade portfolio by giving independence to the trade commissioner service responsible for trade promotion, seemed designed as much to weaken DT as to improve trade promotion efficiency. Coordination was less than fully effective for a number of years.

Links among various parts of the bureaucracy reflect at any time not just the formal organizational arrangements but also the influence of personal and political factors. The relationship between DFA and DT was influenced particularly by the fluctuating influence of prime ministers on foreign affairs, sometimes to the short term advantage of the department, as under Mr Whitlam in the early 1970s, but often to the longer term disadvantage of both the foreign minister and his department.

Australia's membership of the British Empire and then of the Commonwealth gave prominence to the role of the prime minister in foreign affairs,[14] as did World War II. In part because of the decline of these influences, and the greater complexity of international relations, the role of the foreign minister relative to the prime minister has tended to increase in importance. This does not mean that the prime minister's department will not try to provide alternative advice but that will be increasingly difficult to have this accepted except on very specific matters.

Two prime ministers, Menzies and Whitlam were, for periods, also their own foreign ministers, and other prime ministers, Fraser, Hawke and Keating, played important, more general, roles in foreign policy – the latter two in shifting Australia's focus most directly towards Asia. The increased complexity of the range of foreign policy issues is one reason for the inability of a prime minister to dominate foreign affairs except on one or a few issues. The shift to a wider agenda, and away from a largely security based agenda, is another. Hawke was unusual in having an interest in economic issues, both in themselves and as a component of an engagement process with newly emerging Asian countries, notably China – but he was also involved in Australia's international environmental approach, as the Australian policy on Antarctica illustrated. The Prime Minister's role remains important, nevertheless, given the personal participation in the Asia Pacific Economic Cooperation (APEC) forum, the Commonwealth and the Pacific Forum.

In the case of DFA and DD, defence and alliance diplomacy were for a long time the priorities, both because of the importance of the US alliance and the regional impacts of the Cold War, the two departments accepting, within a bipolar global system, the primacy of the USA with which DFA and DD felt very comfortable.[15] Consequently, although DD had acquired a strong, even dominant, position post-Federation because of its role in Empire security, and despite the overwhelming dominance of DD in the early post World War II period, coordination problems did not have the high profile that attached to the DFA/DT relationship. With the easing of the Cold War, and its eventual ending, differences could and often did emerge with DD over threat potentials of countries such as India, Japan and China, as did the two departments' more general perceptions of future security interests and concerns, particularly in the South Pacific. Nevertheless, lack of coordination on substantial policy, as distinct from administrative matters, was not a characteristic feature of the relationship.

Coordination problems with other departments were emerging, however, as the internationalization of domestic issues proceeded. Most departments now have international interests or responsibilities and are involved in actions with international implications. This has always been so with the treasury portfolio and with departments concerned with primary (rural and mining) industries and with immigration. It now extends into policies concerned with indigenous peoples, education, communications, science and industry, tourism, health (aids), social security (pensions and social security benefits for settlers), environment, law and order (drugs, international crime, extradition treaties).

The problem of coordination has changed in character overseas as well as domestically. Given the intensity of international exchanges, embassies often know less of an Australian presence in a country than once was the case. Multinational corporations now represent a major interface between countries, but many government business enterprises or semigovernment authorities also have or are developing overseas links that may impinge on government to government relations. Problems can emerge when there is ambiguity about the nature of such enterprises. Thus, some Asian governments find it difficult to accept that critical comments about them made by the Australian Broadcasting Corporation come from other than an Australian government source.

The assumption may be that, for the most part, decisions about foreign policy are made by foreign ministers and their advisers in the DFA but that is often somewhat distant from reality. The role of interest and pressure groups has grown substantially and they are now an important factor in the decisionmaking on foreign policy. Their influence can be strong whether on other Cabinet members, on backbench members or through the media and public opinion.

It is, of course, less easy to influence legislative programmes in Australia than, for example, in the US where legislation comes from the floor of the Congress rather than from the executive. In Australia the range of counter pressures is frequently enough to cancel out substantially the impact of individual lobby or interest groups but it is a growing influence nevertheless on policy decisions. In some cases, the path is direct to ministers or the prime minister. Ethnic lobbies, such as the Jewish lobby concerned about policies towards Israel and the Middle East, or the Greeks concerned with Macedonia, tend to follow this course, as does the mining industry. Others, such as the motor vehicle lobby, like to raise public concern by threatening unemployment, the nuclear lobby is concerned to raise the public consciousness of the dangers of nuclear power, and the environment lobby seeks to bargain over voter preferences in a preferential voting system, all working through the media and through that to public opinion. Some use direct action, as is often the case with trade unions, and at times, the environmental lobby.

That foreign ministries have always been distant from the general public appeared less apparent as a problem when issues of security and diplomacy were comfortably left in the hands of a small group of insiders and a small number of ministers. With the greater impact of international relations across the board, and the greater transparency of international affairs, the existence of a domestic constituency has become a major factor in the political bargaining that goes on in resource allocation for DFA against other governmental activities.

Parliament

Although foreign policy is seldom now a major electoral issue, DFA has had to respond to changes in political interest in foreign affairs. The interaction between parliament and foreign affairs remains limited in a direct sense although many individual parliamentarians take special interest in particular issues and often raise them in party meetings. There is, however, no formal constitutional requirement for parliamentary scrutiny of foreign policy decisions, including the accession to treaties, except where complementary Commonwealth and state legislation is required. While parliamentary statements on foreign policy are made from time to time, debates on the statements are less frequent.

The parliamentary committee process, however, has grown in importance. The public profile of administrative committees such as the public accounts or estimates committees varies, the latter in particular often being a partisan forum for political point scoring. The substantive committees, whether joint committees of both Houses, or the Senate foreign affairs and defence committee, have become more significant in their depth, quality and commonly non-partisan nature of their conclusions. They have also been more significant through the acceptance by the government that there will be a formal response tabled in parliament to the recommendations of a parliamentary committee. Moreover, they have provided a means for the foreign ministry to put its assessments of foreign policy issues more effectively into the public arena.

Given a series of legal decisions that have reinforced the view that international treaties dealing with issues in one context may flow over into domestic policies in another, political sensitivity by parliament to the impact of international treaty making has grown significantly. Thus, although treaty making is an executive function, pressure for increased parliamentary scrutiny has increased.

In addition to overcoming the 'democratic deficit' at the Commonwealth parliament level, even more concern has been expressed at the state level. The Commonwealth Senate, which was developed constitutionally as a states' house, supported Commonwealth parliamentary reform on treaties in part to pursue their role as protectors of state interests. Given that, in very broad terms, the Commonwealth, with constitutional responsibility for external relations, can adhere to treaties which may have a significant effect on the role and responsibilities of state parliaments, and ultimately override state laws, the strong pressure from the states for more effective consultation before treaties are signed is perhaps not surprising.

Proximity to Asia

A challenge to the management of foreign policy that is particular to Australia and few other countries comes from its proximity to an Asia that has shown more or less unprecedented growth and a consequent increase in political and strategic importance. Being in the Asia–Pacific region is more than just a geographic fact. It has had, and will have in the future, continuing importance for Australia's material welfare and for its security.

Its geographic location, however, means that Australia lives closely with neighbours that have traditions, languages and views of the world which are largely foreign to it. Yet over 60 per cent of Australia's exports go to the Asia–Pacific region, and two thirds or more of that go to Asia, much of its growing tourism intake comes from Asia, investment links both ways have grown significantly and an increasing, if still relatively small, proportion of migrants are from Asia. That Australia shares no tradition or history with the countries of its region to provide a common and widespread understanding of cultures, values and social systems,[16] has a number of implications. While Western countries may not need a deep understanding of these societies, Australia needs to be able to analyze in depth their processes of cultural and social change and of nation building. Moreover, as a developed country, Australia is almost unique in that, excepting New Zealand, its neighbours are developing countries.

The growing relationship with Asia continues to create domestic stresses. Some are unreal, such as the argument often put in terms of how far the links with Asia should be at the expense of traditional relationships with Europe and North America; the persistence of Western values does, however, impose genuine stresses, as in the case of issues such as human rights.

Media Coverage

Although media coverage of security issues is still limited by information gaps, media coverage of international events is now substantially greater, and of greater depth and substance than only two or three decades ago. It is now covering not only the new agenda items, such as the environment, human rights, refugees, drugs, energy and development issues, but broader foreign policy issues. In the post-Cold War period, as the coverage of regional issues has increased greatly, regional issues have to some extent increased as a particular focus of media and public interest: for example, Indonesian forces in action in East Timor have replaced the activities of East German border guards in public attention.[17]

A more general problem is that, despite a small number of experienced and able journalist commentators on foreign affairs, Australia's links with the USA have an influence, not only directly through the alliance relationship, but also on Australia's perceptions and attitudes. The Australian media is very dependent upon USA media material and has tended to be more interested in alarmist than in considered and analytical reporting. This has been important in influencing a public opinion that has tended to be more threat oriented than elite opinion, and the quality of public debate overall is consequently affected. This makes it difficult for Australia to pursue an independent foreign or security policy without facing significant public opinion problems if they differ from Western mainstream views, a factor that has been important in many issues concerning Asia.

This is reinforced in some respects by the fact that Australian foreign policy and security elites gain much of their intelligence and analysis, and their attitudinal stances, from US intelligence and policy sources. Despite the availability of alternative sources of opinion, the intelligence briefings have been important in moulding the views of the official defence and foreign policy community. These have at times been helpful, as over the China 'threat', but at times they have not.

STRATEGIES AND RESPONSE

The challenge to the management of Australia's foreign policy is being met in a number of different ways, which are discussed here in terms of a series of arguments which fit within the 'decline of the foreign ministry' thesis. The decline of the foreign ministry thesis can be predicated on a number of general propositions.

Organization and Style

The first is concerned with an organization and style of foreign ministry that reflected a diplomatic elite that is now insufficiently able to cope with more complex, more competitive and more transparent international relationships. The different cultures in DT and DFA were real, if less important than often stated. It was frequently argued, for example, that private school students had an advantage in recruitment to DFA than those from state schools: yet frequent surveys indicated otherwise, and that the majority of the diplomatic stream came from state schools. Nevertheless, that DFA, in its early years, recruited for the diplomatic stream at university graduate level at a time when the public service traditionally recruited from school leavers, helped create its exclusive reputation. Efforts have been made to break down the sense of an elitism based on anything other than merit. First, steps taken initially in the early 1980s to permit lateral recruitment were subsequently expanded and facilitated, and promotion procedures became more open and transparent.

Second, there was a basic division within DFA between consular and administrative (c&a) officers and the diplomatic stream with very little lateral movement. Arising from the amalgamation of DFA and DT (see below), this process was broken down so that there is now no barrier of a formal kind, and a much higher degree of interchange.

Third, a more demanding training programme was introduced for new entrants based on university courses[18] in part to ensure a spread of both political and economic skills in DFA staff. Access to the course was made available to those who had entered the department in the old c&a stream.

DFA still attracts some of the best graduates from universities and in general, recruitment problems are not major; problems of retaining skilled staff are. Salaries at senior levels have always been below comparable levels but this would be offset by job interest while postings were available and the pressures at head office were not too unreasonable. Both have changed under the budgetary restraints, the ideological pressures for smaller government and the preference given, in the international sphere, to defence. Some would argue that the emphasis on managerialism, rather than area or subject specialization, has also been a factor. For some more traditionally minded, the loss of the exclusivity of the diplomatic stream may have been a factor.[19] A more general problem is the declining attraction for families of overseas postings, compounded by the problems of two career-families and the inability, in most countries, for non-diplomatic partners to obtain professional appointments.

The response by DFA to the rise of lobby groups and of NGO interest has been to expand its processes of information provision, briefing and consultation with the growing range, effectiveness and professionalism of lobby and interest group representatives. Moreover, it often either includes representatives of NGOs in delegations to important international meetings such as the UN summits on the environment and development, on social issues or on women's issues, or helps with parallel meetings of NGOs or both. In Antarctic treaty meetings, both environmental and industry NGOs have been included in Australian delegations, as was the case with meetings of the Framework Convention on Climate Change (FCCC). That such inclusion is not always successful is indicated by the withdrawal from the FCCC delegation of environmental representatives who disagreed with the position being taken by the delegation.

In the case of greater public involvement in decisionmaking, and the need to develop a domestic constituency, the public affairs function has been expanded, although DFA had been to the forefront of departments in recognizing the need for an effective public face for the department. Moreover, while DD can put large sums into publicity campaigns, ostensibly as a recruiting requirement, DFA cannot do this. It therefore has to try to develop closer links with business, a process that has been facilitated since the DFA/DT amalgamation, and to explain itself more effectively to the media and to the public.

Its outreach to industry and business includes not only formal consultative processes with respect to particular aspects of policy, such as a trade policy advisory council. Efforts to achieve closer links with industry, through exchanges of staff with the private sector, and the use of state offices for closer contact with business, have also become an important element of its activities.

To meet the needs of increased parliamentary interest, among other things, the existing treaties unit in DFA has been enlarged to coordinate information, dissemination and consultation to ensure the fullest opportunity for consultation and to provide the secretariat for a Joint Standing Committee on Treaties.[20] In the first six months following the establishment of the standing committee it considered and reported on over 50 treaties.

In the face of increasing state hostility generated by the seeming use of international treaties to overcome state opposition to Commonwealth policies, notably in the environment field, and supported by legal decisions which seemed to enhance the power of the Commonwealth relative to the states because of the international treaties power, agreement was reached for a more cooperative and consultative process in treaty making between Commonwealth and state governments. This process, although already working reasonably well, has been reinforced by the government's decision to create a Treaties Council.[21]

Technology Changes

A second argument suggesting a declining role for foreign ministries is that global changes, notably in transport, communications and information technologies, have reduced the need for overseas representation and the specialist advice of a DFA. Direct communication, it is argued, is possible by telephone or through visits of political figures or experts from the specialist departments. At the same time the flow of information from non-diplomatic sources is much greater and often more rapid.

For a variety of reasons, this argument does not hold.[22] Certainly these developments have changed the role of the overseas mission. The foreign ministry has had to put greater emphasis on its domestic establishment and this has seen some apparent diminution in the relative importance of the diplomatic function overseas, given that the qualities required for diplomatic representation are not always those required for policy analysis. From 1988 to 1996, the proportion of DFA staff overseas declined from a little less than a third to a little more than a quarter of DFA's total staff. Yet, in many respects, the changes have increased rather than diminished the need for overseas on the spot representation. For example, that much more information is available to the public on international developments through the media in particular puts greater pressure on politicians and their advisors to be able to respond to the public reactions to that information. A response specific to Australia (and perhaps New Zealand), is that specialist knowledge and expertise about the Asian countries is in limited supply and that there are many fewer (reliable) alternative sources than the overseas missions than is the case in Europe and North America. Moreover, given the different, usually greater role of governments in Asia, commercial success for Australian enterprises often involves some acceptance of Australian government association with the enterprises in their contacts with the governments involved.

Expanded International Agenda

The third argument stems from the expanding international agenda and the difficulty for the traditional DFA to maintain a coordinating role as the new agenda extended into the bureaucratic responsibility of other departments. Three principal factors have countered this in the Australian case. The major one was the amalgamation of DFA and DT. In part in recognition of the problems of coordination in the management of foreign policy at a time when reforms were being attempted to resuscitate a domestic economy with major structural defects, in part as a reaction to recollections of past bureaucratic conflicts, and in part because of the increasing illogicality and impracticability of keeping economics and politics in separate boxes and the need to raise the priority of economic and trade issues, DFA and DT were amalgamated in 1987. The amalgamation has generally been accepted as successful.[23] Various factors contributed to this, including acceptance by a number of the senior staff of DFA that the Department was becoming increasingly marginalized in the management of Australia's international affairs.

The amalgamation was rapid and substantially integrated the functions of the two departments.[24] DFA was already organized on a largely area desk basis and this was continued in the new structure, as shown in figure 2.1, but with each desk handling both economic and political relations with their respective areas. Multilateral trade (essentially GATT/WTO) remained as a separate division largely, but increasingly not wholly, staffed by trade experts while in the case of international legal issues, the reverse was true. Although the foreign minister is normally the senior minister,[25] both that minister and the trade minister sit in cabinet but officials work to either depending on the

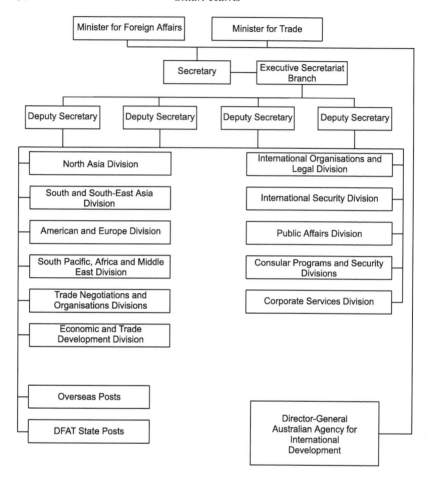

Figure 2.1 Organizational Structure as at 30 June 1996

matters at issue. Both also act for the other during their frequent absences overseas, a factor that facilitates internal coordination. Illustrations of the benefits from a coordination viewpoint of the amalgamation were quickly evident in the policies towards Taiwan and South Africa, compromises coming readily on issues that were previously major points of contention.

The second factor was the implementation of the recommendations of the review of the overseas service carried out in 1986 which made a series of proposals for changes in the management, administration and decisionmaking in DFA and for the coordination of overseas activities.[26]

Among other things, these changes improved staff use efficiency and flexibility, and offset to a significant extent the reduction in staff numbers at overseas posts.

The third was the prime minister's guidelines. The coordination problem between DFA and DT, although already minimized by agreement between the two heads of departments before 1987, had been helped further by the renegotiation and acceptance in 1985 of the prime minister's formal guidelines for overseas missions[27] which reinforced the coordinating role of the head of mission.

In practice, effective coordination of the international interests of other departments so that Australia could speak with one voice overseas was not guaranteed, especially where communications through faxes and the Internet made it easier for those who wanted to evade official coordination to do so. The impression seems to be, however, that such coordination is working, if not totally; the Treasury, largely following the path of the major financial players, is usually given as an example of independent uncoordinated activity although some improvements in that context seem apparent. The broad acceptance of the coordinating role of DFA may be the awareness of the damage from past lack of coordination, the greater public transparency of international affairs, and the resource scarcity that greatly diminishes the incentives to departments to establish or maintain their own officers in overseas posts.

A further help was the negotiation, at the time of the 1987 amalgamation, of an aide memoire between the primary industry department and DFA over the responsibility for international commodity discussions and negotiations. The agreement that intergovernmental negotiations were the responsibility of DFA but discussions and consultations other than such negotiations should be with the technical department, despite occasional disputes as to whether an international meeting was a negotiation or simply consultations about negotiations, seems to have reduced conflict – as has a broadly comparable understanding with the environment department.

As a result of these changes, and notably the amalgamation, DFA became an important department of state. It lost much of its exclusivity, and its own sense of being an elite department derived from its mission as a diplomatic service and the way it recruited its diplomatic staff. It has become like other departments within the public service. It has gained in professional credibility among other departments, however, and improved its effectiveness in interdepartmental discussions and negotiations, a critical gain as domestic aspects became more basic to a wider range of foreign policy issues. By an amalgamation that incorporated the trade function, DFA gained a function which already had a domestic constituency and this has contributed to overcoming a gap in its public image that was becoming increasingly a problem.

Response to the Rise of Asia

In the Australian case, the developments in Asia have posed particular challenges to the bureaucracies concerned with international relations. The rise of Asia in economic and increasingly in political and strategic terms has had major impacts on Australia's foreign ministry in two respects: Australia's geographic proximity; and the broader regional and global implications of the changes involved.

Australia's interaction with Asia at the official level has now been substantial for over 30 years with a consequent wide spread of experience among DFA staff. In particular, this has come from Australia's long and growing involvement in regional economic and security cooperation – an increasingly important part of Australia's foreign policy and a field where it has had a major initiating role. This has been a major process for networking and sharing of experience and, indeed, developing elements of a common historical tradition. A greater expertise in and understanding of the nature and cultures of these societies has in practice been accumulated by DFA staff.

Particular efforts have been made to enlarge regional language skills in DFA, through training of existing staff or giving a degree of preference in recruiting to those with Asian language skills, now much easier with the rapid expansion in the numbers of students of Asian languages in Australia. Nevertheless, the analysis function is still deficient. Dependence is therefore increasing on the supply of analytical information and assessments from other sources many of which start from different presumptions and interests than those appropriate for Australia. Inevitably, therefore, Australia's policy becomes more derivative and less independent while this situation continues.

A challenge to foreign ministries generally has been the pressure on resources due to tighter budgetary processes and a general unwillingness to meet the growing costs of public services, particularly the increased costs of overseas representation. Measures being taken in response to resource pressures have included closing of less essential posts, sharing of overseas representation costs with other like-minded countries such as Canada and New Zealand, greater use of locally engaged staff and cutting out functions. DFA's total overseas (Australia-based) staff declined from 1019 to 837 in 82 overseas diplomatic posts.[28] Staff in posts in Northeast and Southeast Asia, however, has increased slightly, from 255 to 259, now constituting about 30 per cent of total overseas staff, and a substantial increase in the proportion of DFA's total overseas staff.

One consequence of the downsizing of the DFA relative to its growing agenda is that the analysis function tends to be seen as discretionary rather than as essential, in competition with crisis issues or day to day but non-discretionary functions, and therefore to be the function that, while not dropped formally, tends not to be done. To counter this, to a degree at least, a special analysis unit has been established to study East Asia.[29] This can draw on outside expertise as well as its own assessment capacity and so far has been substantially protected from immersion in day to day problems. Nevertheless, overall analytical capacity has greatly declined.

CONCLUSION

Any traditional foreign ministry that has not, or cannot, adjust flexibly to the major changes in the international environment, to the greatly enlarged international agenda and the consequent domestic changes, or to the seemingly common, at least in the Western world, resource pressures reflecting demands for smaller government, is or will become increasingly marginalized in the policymaking and implementation process. If for no other reason, the traditional security and alliance diplomacy areas of international relations have greatly diminished in relative, if not always in absolute, importance, new agenda items, often linking economic and political/security issues and domestic issues, have a greater international impact, and decisionmaking transparency continues to grow. In that sense the 'decline of the foreign ministry' thesis is appropriate and applies in Australia.

In the Australian context, the impact of those changes was being felt in the foreign ministry and would have been much more evident had major changes, both as a result of the 1986 review and the 1987 amalgamation, not been put in place. There are reasons to be concerned about the adequacy with which the foreign ministry function is being performed in the light of the greater demands imposed on it alongside its diminishing real resources. Countries achieve their international objectives 'by threatening, by bribing (bargaining), or by persuading – whether through diplomatic skills, logic, cultural affinities or ideological drives'.[30] Australia has little capacity to bribe and less to threaten and has therefore to depend substantially on its capacity to persuade. Given its geopolitical situation, with few natural allies, it needs a wide ranging and highly knowledgeable overseas representation, proportionately more than large and powerful countries, to build coalitions and to magnify its bargaining strength on particular issues important to it. Its capacity to do this is diminishing, as is its own capacity for the analysis needed to support this approach. Without that, it is subject to greater influence from populist views normally coming originally from outside the region and reflecting different national interests. This could lead to Australia becoming 'odd man out' rather than 'odd man in' in Asia.

Organizationally and institutionally, however, much of the needed institutional change has been introduced that makes it possible at least to meet the new challenges without being unduly hindered by deficient organizational structures or inability to handle or coordinate efforts related to the new international agendas.

NOTES

1   Information from the Department of Foreign Affairs and Trade and comments on an earlier draft from Greg Austin are gratefully acknowledged.

2   Alan Watt, *The Evolution of Australian Foreign Policy 1938–1965* (Cambridge: Cambridge University Press, 1967), p. vii.

3   Russell Trood, 'Australian diplomatic practice: methods and theory', *Journal of Asian and African Studies*, 25: 1–2, 1990, p. 93.

4   Coral Bell, 'The international environment and Australia's foreign policy', in F. A. Mediansky and A. C. Palfreyman, eds, *In Pursuit of National Interests: Australia's Foreign Policy in the 1990s* (Sydney: Pergamon Press, 1988), p. 74.

5   Coral Bell, *Dependent Ally: A Study in Australian Foreign Policy* (Sydney: Allen and Unwin, 1993), p. 186.

6   For a substantial assertion of Australia's internationalist role, see Gareth Evans and Bruce Grant, *Australia's Foreign Relations In the World of the 1990s* (Melbourne: Melbourne University Press, 1991).

7   See Stuart Harris, 'Managing Australia's shift to multilateralism', in L. T. Evans and J. D. B. Miller, eds, *Policy and Practice: Essays in Honour of Sir John Crawford* (Sydney: Pergamon, 1987), pp. 51–65.

8   I considered the various issues involved in Stuart Harris, 'Federalism and Australian foreign policy', in Brian Hocking, ed., *Foreign Relations and Federal States* (Leicester and New York: Leicester University Press and St Martin's Press, 1993), pp. 90–104.

9   This form is used here to cover the various departmental titles that have evolved over time: External Affairs, Foreign Affairs, and Foreign Affairs and Trade.

10 Nancy Viviani, 'The bureaucratic context', in Fedor Mediansky, ed., *Australia in a Changing World: New Foreign Policy Direction* (Sydney: Maxwell Macmillan, 1992), p. 49.

11 Although established in 1956 from a reorganization of two departments (Commerce and Agriculture and Trade and Customs), the department had a number of name changes, usually according to whether industry responsibilities were also included: so that it was at times, with no particular logic except perhaps that of individual ministers (or their advising officials) wanting more power, Trade and Industry, Trade and Resources and then finally Overseas Trade.

12 Commonwealth of Australia, *Management and Operations of the Department of Foreign Affairs and Trade*, Report of the Senate Standing Committee on Finance and Public Administration, 1992, p. 8.

13 At times, subsequently, assistant ministers have been given responsibility for development assistance.

14 Peter Edwards, *Prime Ministers and Diplomats: The Making of Australian Foreign Policy 1901–1949* (Melbourne: Oxford University Press, 1983).

15 Hugh Collins, 'The impact of the international system in the shaping of postwar Australian foreign policy', paper to a workshop on the making of Australian foreign policy, Griffith University, November 1992.

16   Stuart Harris, *Review of Australia's Overseas Representation* (Canberra: Australian Government Publishing Service, 1986), pp. xvi, 18–19.

17   Roderick Alley, 'The politics of Australian and New Zealand foreign policy', *Working Paper No. 40*, Australian Defence Studies Centre, Canberra, August 1996, p. 16.

18   In the early years of the department such courses had been the practice but they gradually came to lack substance.

19   Russell Trood, 'The Foreign Service: diplomats as advisers', paper to a workshop on the making of Australian foreign policy, Griffith University, November 1992.

20   Bill Taylor (Chair, Parliamentary Joint Standing Committee on Treaties), 'Trick or treaty: an Australian perspective', paper to Institutionalising Communities Conference, University of Southern Queensland, November 1996.

21   *Parliamentary Debates* (The Senate), 2 May 1996, pp. 217–18.

22   This question has been dealt with at some length in Stuart Harris, *Review of Australia's Overseas Representation*, pp. 19–20.

23   This seems to be the general view of commentators: see, for example, Nancy Viviani, 'The official formulation of foreign policy or A student's guide to the bureaucratic galaxy', in Mediansky and Palfreyman, eds, *The Pursuit of National Interests*, pp. 45–65; Lara Bancroft, 'The Amalgamation of the Departments of Foreign Affairs and Trade, 1987', *Research Report*, Australian National Internship Program, Australian National University, May 1996; Richard Woolcott, 'Amalgamation of foreign affairs and trade', *Canberra Bulletin of Public Administration* 59, 1989, pp. 30–3; Report of the Senate Standing Committee, pp. 18–22.

24   See Stuart Harris, 'Amalgamation of foreign affairs and trade', *Australian Foreign Affairs Record* 59, 1988, pp. 71–4.

25   From 1996, with the change of government, the Minister for Trade was also the Deputy Prime Minister and therefore senior in Cabinet status.

26   Harris, *Review of Australia's Overseas Representation*; and Stuart Harris, *The 1986 Review of Australia's Overseas Representation Revisited* (Canberra: Department of Foreign Affairs and Trade, October 1988).

27   *Guidelines for Management of the Australian Government Presence Overseas*, October 1985, (reproduced as Attachment 19 in Stuart Harris, *Review of Australia's Overseas Representation*, pp. 262–8).

28   There are a further 22 posts, 19 concerned with trade, and three with immigration.

29   This was in response to one of a number of recommendations made by Ross Garnaut in his influential report *Australia and the Northeast Asia Ascendancy* (Canberra: Australia Government Publishing Service, 1989).

30   Harris, *Review of Australia's Overseas Representation*, p. 17.

3 Canada
Trying to Get it Right: the Foreign Ministry and Organizational Change
Andrew F. Cooper

The Canadian experience in terms of change and the foreign policy community presents a paradoxical case study. The stylized image of Canadian governance has been one of cautious and hesitant adaptation. Yet, over the last three decades, the Canadian foreign ministry (the Department of Foreign Affairs and International Trade and its predecessors, External Affairs and International Trade Canada and the Department of External Affairs) has gone through a series of reorganizations in a bid to reinvent itself. While clinging on to many of its older habits of behaviour with respect to international activity (most notably an acute concern with diplomatic skill and reputation),[1] the Canadian pattern of internal reform has been one which features a marked focus on re-thinking and re-jigging. Indeed, the concern with trying to get its organizational structure right serves as the dominant leitmotiv for the Canadian foreign ministry.

In trying to ascertain the reasons why the Canadian foreign ministry has featured such a strong dynamic of change, both an outside-in and inside-out mode of analysis needs to be incorporated. From an external perspective, the response must be located vis-à-vis the context of the multiple currents of global forces which made the management of foreign policy more complex through the entire span from the 1970s to the 1990s. In common with most other countries, Canada had to respond to the increased volatility introduced by the widened international sphere of discourse/action in which the traditionally paramount first (security) agenda was challenged by the ascendancy of the second (economic) and third (social) agendas. Concomitantly, 'cascading' pressures have been exerted via the accelerating mix of interdependence and globalization.[2] While increasingly assuming the appearance of the level of cliché, these pressures have to be taken seriously as factors influencing the nature of the adjustment process. This is particularly so given Canada's distinctive character, namely its combination of vulnerability to the international structure balanced by its willingness/ability to act as an agent of change on a differentiated basis. With its relatively open economy, bicultural/multicultural society/culture, and vast territorial distances, Canada remains highly exposed as a receptor of change. Given the high stakes involved, however, Canada also has some considerable incentive to move ahead of other countries in terms of global problem-solving via the building of international conventions and institutions.[3]

While the conditioning effect of external factors must be taken fully into account, domestic circumstances have played an important part as well in shaping Canada's adaptive process. The manner in which the issue of bureaucratic decline has been responded to is particularly salient here. Canada, through the so-called Pearson or 'golden era' of Canadian diplomacy in the immediate post-1945 period, served as the model of concentrated authority in the domain of foreign policy with the Department of External Affairs (DEA) enjoying what amounted to a near monopoly position. Few sources of competition existed on either a state/societal or an interdepartmental basis. Over recent years, by way of contrast, there has been a significant dispersal of influence. Not only has there been a marked expansion in the Canadian foreign policy community,[4] the overarching position of the foreign ministry has been contested in a comprehensive manner. If ultimately successful in hanging onto its privileged position as the core actor in foreign policymaking, the task of meeting these challenges has been a laborious and protracted one.

Three specific, albeit overlapping, stages may be captured through this pattern of organizational reform. The first stage, corresponding largely with the period of the Trudeau government (1968–79, 1980–4), centred on the process of horizontal adjustment. During this period, the institutional mode of operation practised by the DEA was soundly critiqued as being out of date and irrelevant. This sense of 'decline' was reinforced by the rise of a number of rivals within the governmental apparatus, both at the federal and provincial level. In response to this set of challenges, DEA attempted to reassert its position through task expansion. Not only did DEA try to extend and upgrade its own level of expertise, but it tried to broaden its responsibilities into new areas of activity through a push towards 'integration' and 'consolidation'. The second stage, which came to the fore when the Mulroney government was in office (1984–93), opened the way to vertical integration. Moving beyond state-centric concerns, the prime challenge to the Canadian foreign ministry during this period came via societal groups generally and non-governmental organizations more specifically. Accorded a greater credibility by the mix of a putative crisis of governance, together with a philosophical and instrumental concern with 'offloading' responsibilities away from the state, these societal actors offer a very different (and often formidable) source of competition to the traditional managers of foreign policy. At the same time, though, the Canadian foreign ministry moved out ahead of the bulk of its counterparts in other countries by its explicit attempt to forge

a more constructive relationship with societal actors. The third stage, paral-
lelling the time of the Chrétien government (1993–), has accorded greater
salience to the question of task definition. During this more recent period,
the primary challenge for the Canadian foreign ministry has been to demonstrate that it could modify many of its established organizational weaknesses.
One of these deficiencies relates to the set of internal differences (and even
competing cultures) found within the foreign ministry. Another relates to the
top heavy organizational structure. The reform drive, currently in train, has
been motivated by an on-going concern with administrative streamlining and
a more efficient delivery of services.

THE TRADITIONAL DEA MODEL UNDER SIEGE

A number of interlocking factors allowed the DEA to secure a tight grip over
foreign policy in the immediate post-World War II period. Held together by a
uniformity of background, and sense of purpose, the senior officials (or 'wise
men') from External Affairs formed a cohesive cohort eager to 'to lead
Canadian public opinion in the direction of new obligations' in terms of
international affairs.[5] The relative autonomy of this group of state officials
was strengthened by the sense of consensus which existed through the late
1940s and early 1950s about what policies promoted the Canadian national
interest. This consensus was linked, in turn, to the ingrained centrality of
geo-security issues. Issues of war and peace, which mattered most to the
DEA officials, were also most relevant to the Canadian public.[6]

This unique set of circumstances provided a long moment of opportunity
for the DEA. Between the time Mackenzie King left the political scene and
the time Pierre Trudeau appeared, the 'External Type' reigned supreme.
Among the large caste of 'Ottawa Men'[7] only the mandarins at the Department of Finance and the Bank of Canada could be said to be rivals as the
Canadian equivalent of the best and brightest in the Anglo-American world.[8]
While some vigorous differences of view did exist among this foreign
policy elite, their ability to work as an effective team was testimony to
their common pattern of intellectual/policy socialization and 'on the job'
experience.

The strength of this model lay in the ability of the DEA to react decisively
in times of international crises. The Suez crisis, in particular, stands out as the
defining episode of Canadian diplomacy during the immediate post-war
period. Canada revealed that on a major controversy, which had enormous
spillover implications on intra-bloc relations and institutions, it could have an
impact on the international system by utilizing its skills of communication and
negotiation. By exploiting these skills, Canada could also win recognition and
kudos, as exemplified by Pearson's winning of the Nobel Peace Prize in 1957.

The weaknesses of the model were equally obvious. To begin with, the model relied heavily on the skills of diplomatic improvization. The classic 'External' style was tactical not strategic, geared to operational agility rather than to working within definitive guidelines. The DEA had long prided itself on its ability to deal flexibly with external situations, due to the high quality and experience of its diplomatic personnel. As one key member of the 'Old External' cohort readily acknowledged, 'principle or theory' played little part in the success obtained by Canada as a mediator during the Pearson years. Pearson, himself, was said to have operated by getting 'into the middle of a mess or crisis and by some kind of intuition, [getting] himself out of it – and in the process, [helping] others out of the mess too.'[9]

A second problem related to DEA's narrow composition. A bastion of 'English' (or more precisely Anglo-Celt) unilingual elitism, the DEA had found room for only the most talented (and like-minded) individuals from other backgrounds. Not only did this narrow form of representation hit a sensitive political nerve as bilingualism and biculturalism became more salient on the political agenda, it made the DEA the target for on-going criticism concerning the need for sensitivity to other factors of recruitment – multiculturalism, gender representation and other forms of diversity.

A third problem related to the lack of appreciation by DEA of attitudinal change within Canadian society. Through the 1960s, accordingly, the department was held up as the quintessential anti-model of an organization disconnected from the heightened interest and politicization of Canadian society with respect to international affairs. A telling example of the foreign ministry's lack of appreciation for these attitudinal changes came in 1968 during the Biafra civil war ('our Bay of Pigs', as one DEA official put it) when the DEA stance of non-interference clashed with the desire of the increasingly attentive Canadian public to do something to mitigate the suffering inflicted by the war.[10]

A number of other factors increased the intensity of the criticism concerning the DEA's mode of operation. To begin with, this negative perspective was part of a wider intellectual backlash against the profession of diplomacy in the 1960s and 1970s. Largely because of its failure to resolve the Vietnam crisis, diplomacy was perceived by a wide variety of academics and media analysts as morally and practically bankrupt. Moreover, the established practices of diplomacy were viewed as being increasingly out of touch with the surge of technological/communications change. A prominent University of Toronto professor of international relations, James Eayrs led the critical charge. Indeed, Eayrs questioned the corpus of accepted wisdom about the function of diplomacy as an institution. Not content with charging diplomacy with 'moral turpitude', and 'inefficiency', Eayrs described the practice of diplomacy as being in 'deliquescence' ('melting into nothingness, fading away into limbo') in a rapidly evolving global environment.[11]

More decisively, this critical outlook was shared by Prime Minister Trudeau. As an advocate of rational management, of the extension of bilingualism and biculturalism, and (at least in a declaratory fashion) of participatory democracy, Trudeau had little sympathy with the old DEA model. On top of this, came a critical targeting of External's 'reactive rather than active concern with world events.'[12] To win back favour, the DEA had to demonstrate that it was not 'outmoded' in terms of its administrative skills and operational techniques.

A more tangible challenge to the familiar ways of doing things underscored the closer intermeshing of domestic politics with foreign policy. This challenge came in the form of the intrusion of a wide array of competing actors at the governmental level, the combined effect of which was to fragment the process of decisionmaking. The most dramatic – and pervasive – of these challenges was presented by the Canadian provinces. Propelled by the momentum of the Quiet Revolution and the outward-looking expression of Québecois nationalism, Ottawa and Québec became an intense site of struggle over legitimacy and power. Amid the wider dynamics of this struggle over legislative powers, 'domestic' issues spilled over the 'international' arena. Québec argued that in international relations, as in other areas of government, it should be able to proceed autonomously in matters falling within its own jurisdiction. Specifically, it claimed the power to negotiate and sign treaties within the limits of its constitutional rights.

Affixed to the Québec factor was a more generalized provincial challenge. Fundamental differences existed between the federal government and a number of other provinces (and especially, Alberta) over decisionmaking and the conduct of foreign economic policy. These differences led to a good deal of frustration and tension at the inter-governmental level. Prime Minister Trudeau, for example, could lecture the gathering at the February 1978 economic conference of first ministers on the constitutional limitations on provincial activity: 'We all surely agree that international trade is a federal responsibility.'[13] Notwithstanding the deepening sense of rivalry between Ottawa and these other provinces, though, this category of differences must be distinguished from the struggle which persisted between the federal government and Québec. Rather than being concerned with the symbols of statehood, this wider challenge was tied directly to the furtherance of material interests. The issues under debate on the broader inter-governmental plane did not concern 'the international independence', or even many of the nuances of the 'international personality' of these other provinces. They centred on practical questions concerning effectiveness and equity and the regional distribution of benefits.

Another main source of institutional crowding on the authority of the 'old' External Affairs came via the extension of bureaucratic politics. As an array of traditional 'domestic' departments moved into the international arena, turf battles over responsibility and influence predictably ensued. This type of behaviour was driven in a large part by ambitious ministers eager to embellish their personal and departmental standing and power base. This phenomenon was most evident in newly created departments with a mandate over environmental and energy issues.[14]

Under the cumulative weight of these various challenges, DEA was forced to go through an extensive period of renewal. Indeed, the foreign ministry has to be given credit for parlaying these challenges into opportunities to upgrade its skills and expand its interests in a horizontal direction. Jettisoning much of its familiar mode of operation, the Department through the 1970s and early 1980s bought into scientific management theory and the construct of a coherent context for Canadian foreign policy. While the DEA old guard could (with some solid justification) decry all of the paraphernalia or baggage that went along with the embrace of this technocratic model – with its expanded bureaucratic apparatus, its organizational charts, its mania for consultation, and concern for cost-benefits evaluation – this administrative transformation allowed DEA to go on the offensive in terms of winning back its lost status and authority. At the core of this strategy, as indicated by a senior official, was the extension of the DEA's 'coordinating and overview capacity' with respect to international trade.[15] That is to say, the aim was to re-define and re-exert DEA's traditional 'lead' position over foreign policy.

Tactically, the means chosen meant an on-going process of reorganization in the machinery of government. An impetus towards consolidation in the trade issue-area under the authority of the DEA built up in the Trudeau period, culminating in the January 1982 reorganization, which merged the Trade Commissioner Service and the trade promotion units of the Department of Industry, Trade and Commerce. This amalgamation, of the 'old' DEA into a revised structure was designed to place 'a greater priority on trade objectives in the conduct of our international relations, give greater emphasis to the international marketing of resources and services, and strengthen Canada's ability to adapt to changing world economic conditions' and to 'integrate the department more effectively into the broader economic process in Ottawa.'[16]

The DEA buttressed its revised claims for bureaucratic leadership through a concerted drive to raise its game in terms of economic expertise and capacity. As the role and visibility of the trade policy side of the 'new' DEA were elevated, so were the rewards provided to a core group of responsible officials. In some instances, this shift in emphasis was accomplished by an infusion of talent with specialist skills from other areas of government. The commonplace practice, however, was to tap into these sort of specialist skills within the ranks of the newly integrated DEA. Neither of these tendencies represented a substantial departure in itself. The Department of Industry, Trade and Commerce (together with other elements of the national bureaucracy) had long had a presence in overseas posts and in the exercise of power in decisionmaking. What was different was the degree of visibility accorded to the trade side of DEA, and extent of their influence. Through the integrated foreign service, an assertive cohort of state officials from this stream worked hard to make foreign policy and trade policy one and the same. The benefits of this activity were obvious, both in providing DEA with greater resources and muscle in inter-bureaucratic terms and in enhancing it with a greater sensitivity and capability for dealing with the issues which loomed so large on the international agenda. But so were the additional complexities placed on politics and policy. As they contributed to the DEA's organizational capacity, this ascendant wave of trade-oriented officials posed a very different set of challenges to the established ways of doing things. To some extent, the resultant tensions were based on status and turf. Trade specialists not only held more influence in Ottawa. They increasingly held high-profile ambassadorial posts abroad. But, as witnessed most notably on the issue of bilateral free trade with the USA, this tension also had an important policy dimension.[17]

In an analogous fashion, the pressures emanating from the Québec challenge contributed to a series of organizational responses. Structurally, the most important of these changes came with the formation of the Federal-Provincial Co-ordination Division as a means of coordinating the provincial dimension. As Hocking describes, this division (subsequently changed to the Federal-Provincial Relations and Francophone Affairs Bureau) acted as 'a channel of communication between Ottawa and the provinces, a transmitter of information from the DEA to provincial capitals, a monitor of provincial activities, and an advocate of regional interests within the political process.'[18] In terms of an organizational culture, the infusion of talented francophones into the DEA during the late 1960s and 1970s had a profound impact on the Canadian foreign service. Not only did this process go some considerable way towards improving the DEA's organizational image (thereby opening the doors for a more inclusive process of recruitment generally), it also facilitated the shift towards dealing with issue-specific change in the global agenda. Previously neglected issues, including cultural diplomacy, received a higher priority. Shaped by its instrumental motivation, the wider provincial challenge did much to reinforce the shift of the foreign ministry towards the trade promotion/sales function and a more client-oriented mode of operation.

THE OPENING UP OF THE FOREIGN POLICY PROCESS

All of these organizational adjustments improved the ability of the foreign ministry to compete with its challengers. In no way, though, did they translate into renewed dominance. Once opened up, the shift towards an extended degree of pluralism could not be closed. On the contrary, a number of other (both centrifugal and centripetal) tendencies contributed to an atmosphere of on-going competition and crowding. The first of these tendencies relates to what may be termed the challenge of politicization. The ability of the foreign service to rebound completely as the 'lead' department over international affairs was complicated by the presence of alternative – and well-connected – sources of foreign policy advice. These pressures were inextricably intertwined with the rise of a number of powerful central agencies, most notably the Prime Minister's Office (PMO) and the Privy Council Office (PCO).

Part and parcel of this design, key individuals assumed prominent roles in foreign policy decisionmaking. Under Trudeau, Ivan Head (a former law professor and DEA official) operated out of the PMO as the central conduit between DEA and the Prime Minister between 1970 to 1978. Likewise, Derek Burney stood out as the pivotal figure under Prime Minister Brian Mulroney. Following in the footsteps of Head, Burney established himself securely as Mulroney's chief foreign policy advisor. Formalizing his position of power after his success (when associate under-secretary at DEA) in orchestrating the 1985 Shamrock Summit between Mulroney and Reagan, and getting the US–Canada FTA negotiations off the ground, Burney became the Prime Minister's chief of staff in the spring of 1987. Throughout this time span, as Nossal notes, the channelling of politically sensitive questions through the PMO/PCO further 'contributed to the distancing of the Prime Minister from the external affairs portfolio.'[19]

The second of these tendencies came from the opposite direction through the opening-up of the pattern of foreign policy decisionmaking. In the economic agenda generally and the trade agenda more specifically, this development was to a large extent externally-driven. As Canada in the 1980s entered into a new and delicate phase of negotiations on both the multilateral and bilateral front, an infusion of legitimacy and credibility was required through new forms of vertical integration. A closer domestic state-societal relationship, in which business groups were allowed access to policymaking on an institutional basis, facilitated this approach. To bargain effectively in the international arena, as much agreement as possible on the substance of a domestic 'game plan' was necessary. The most important illustration of this integrative approach on the trade side came during the Canada-US free trade negotiations, as 15 Sectoral Advisory Groups on International Trade (SAGITs) were established.

The move towards a pattern of vertical integration was even more dramatic on the social agenda. The contrast between the closed-off system found in the Pearson years and the opening up of the decisionmaking process in more recent years is also evident in the area of the social agenda, encompassing the areas of human rights, social justice and the environment. To a large extent, this process has been limited to an agenda-setting role with the focus on information exchange and an alternative form of discourse.[20]

In some cases, it is important to note, Canadian NGOs have become integrated into the policy process itself. The episode which epitomizes this trend is the activity surrounding the 1992 Rio United Nations Conference on Environment and Development (UNCED). Furthermore, the integrative pattern achieved in the Rio conference was important not only in issue-specific terms but also as a model for on-going activities on a broader plane. From a functional viewpoint, there is abundant evidence of a spillover effect from Rio onto other UN conferences. One excellent example of the spillover of the Rio model could be witnessed in the process developed for the 1993 Vienna World Conference on Human Rights and another involved the 1994 International Conference on Population and Development held in Cairo.

Societal pressure played a part in pushing this integrative process. As one editorial from a Canadian newspaper stated, after the release in 1986 of the Mulroney government's Green Paper on Canada's International Relations: 'Canadians are knocking on the door of this country's foreign policy with more than messages to deliver: they want in.'[21] But, unlike the activity centred on agenda-setting, this type of pressure was not the major motivating force for opening-up the process of policymaking. The government, for its own part, tried to pull non-state actors into a closer sort of relationship. As on the trade agenda, this dynamic is wrapped up with both questions of legitimacy and technical skill.[22] For the Canadian government, like many other governments, recognized the need to negotiate and bargain with their publics (including the components of the so-called counter-consensus)[23] in a more direct and comprehensive fashion. On top of this, important technical and administrative reasons existed for trying to draw societal groups more deeply into the decisionmaking process. One common feature found among NGOs has been an expanded repertoire and focus on specialized skills. Some groups have worked to improve their monitoring, witnessing and interlocutory skills (for example, Amnesty International, Asia Watch and other organizations involved in the monitoring of human rights violations). Others have expanded the range and sophistication of their legal competence.

Giving considerable added impetus to these tendencies have been the philosophical and bureaucratic motivations for integrating societal groups more closely into the policymaking process. Transferring responsibilities from the state to societal actors meshed well with the push towards privatization and downsizing of governments. An expanded and strengthened client base also provided a useful tool in administrative 'turf' conflicts. As Stairs suggested in a seminal article on the domestication of Canadian foreign policy, competing bureaucratic actors 'exploit the opinions of their respective constituencies as a source of leverage in the policy process.'[24] This point has had even greater relevance in the 1990s given the context of the on-going, intense and multidimensional bureaucratic competition in which this adaptive approach took place.

It was one thing though to adopt an integrative approach towards societal participation on a segmented basis, it was quite another to implant a com-prehensive system based on the 'democratization' of Canadian foreign policy. Some considerable momentum was generated towards this alternative goal because of the promises made in the Liberal 'Red Book',[25] and the Liberal Foreign Policy Platform, both of which raised the 'democratizing' notion to the status of organizing principle. Once established in office, moreover, the Liberal government tried to show its continuing commitment to this ambi-tious objective through the establishment of two special joint parliamentary committees (with a wide-ranging mandate to hold public hearings) and the staging of a Foreign Policy 'National Forum' in March 1994.

The innovative design of these measures stand out. An extensive dialogue about Canadian foreign policy was conducted through the channel of the parliamentary hearings. The massed voices of Canadian NGOs were heard in all of their diversity. A significant piece of evidence concerning the will-ingness of the Chrétien government to listen to this activist (and often critical) component of civic society may be found via a comparison of the NGO presentations before the Standing Committee of External Affairs and National Defence, reviewing Canadian foreign policy in 1970–1 (29), and the numbers that appeared before the Special Joint Committee of the Senate and House of Commons in 1994 (277). Another sign of this same trend was the generous space given to NGO representatives at the 1994 National Forum.[26]

The long-term impact of these new features should, nevertheless, not be overestimated. In some ways, the Liberals were willing to take a very differ-ent path in pursuit of a new direction in foreign policymaking. In other ways, the Chrétien government moved to consolidate the machinery of foreign policymaking on the basis of its own evolving calculus of a hierarchy of interests and capabilities.

To some extent, this retreat came about by default. When put to the test, the intended goal of 'democratization' was simply too difficult to reach in practice. 'Democratization,' as it has been implemented through the hearings of the Special Joint Committee and the 1994 National Forum, certainly did not move ahead in a smooth, uni-directional fashion. Instead it was marked by volatility and unevenness. For one thing, the marked increase in parti-cipation from activist societal groups was offset by an apparent decline in the willingness of business groups to engage in public consultation (with all the attendant risks of exposing their views to criticism). Relatively few members of the business community either appeared before the Joint Committee or attended the first National Forum.[27] For another thing, the representative nature of the participating NGOs was increasingly called into question.[28] Finally, frustrations developed at the governmental level about the capacity of this 'open' system to deliver precise policy proposals.

Against this background, it is not surprising that there were several signs of a recalibration of this pattern of 'open' consultation. By the time the second National Forum was held, in September 1995, representation had been tilted away from the NGOs with a heavier emphasis on the inclusion of members of the business community, and foreign policy experts from academia and other professions.[29] Furthermore, the ambitious proposal of a new mechanism for 'foreign policy consultation, research and outreach that will bring together government practitioners, parliamentarians, experts and citizens' (as proposed in the government response to the Joint Committee's report, *Canada in The World*) was dropped. Instead a more concentrated 'advisory board' of foreign policy was created.

Design played a part as well. The basic dilemma for the Chrétien government has centred on the need to show that an effective foreign policy could be pursued during a time of budgetary pressures. In an attempt to recover the Canadian foreign ministry's traditional sense of organizational esprit, a number of gestures of confidence were bestowed on it. Many of these were symbolic in nature, intended to signal the return of foreign policy to the foreign ministry.[30] The name of the ministry was changed from External Affairs and International Trade Canada (EAITC) to the Department of Foreign Affairs and International Trade (DFAIT). The top bureaucratic position of deputy minister of foreign affairs was given to a veteran foreign service officer, Gordon Smith, whose institutional memory extended back to the early Trudeau period.[31] A number of other key senior officials (including the new assistant deputy ministers for Global Security Policy and Corporate Services) were brought back into the department's senior management after extensive stints in central agencies. Experienced professionals including Raymond Chrétien, in Washington were assigned key diplomatic posts.

Other gestures had a stronger instrumental dimension. DFAIT certainly has not been excluded from cuts imposed as part of the on-going attempt by the Liberal government led by Paul Martin and the Department of Finance to put Canada's fiscal 'house in order,'[32] but two crucial factors mitigated the impact of these cuts. First of all, the means by which they have been imposed featured an ongoing dialogue with the departmental personnel (through memos and internal electronic messages). This operational mode could be contrasted with the approach adopted by the EAITC senior management in its response to the budgetary cuts imposed by the Mulroney government in the February 1992 budget. These earlier cuts had been characterized by a closed rather than an open approach. Emphasizing the need 'to return to basics', a number of activities of the department had been summarily offloaded (including the transfer of the department's immigration role to the department of Employment and Immigration). Secondly, in relative terms, DFAIT appears to have survived the series of cuts quite well.[33] Many other government departments and agencies (including the Department of National Defence and the Canadian International Development Agency (CIDA)) have been cut more deeply. As Doern and Kirton detail: 'the first Chrétien budget, of February 1994, reduced defence spending by 10 per cent, reduced [Official Development Assistance] by 2 per cent, and increased DFAIT spending by $74.1 million, or 5 per cent, to $1.41 billion. In the budget of 27 February 1995, DND suffered further substantial reductions, CIDA was reduced by 15 per cent from $2.03 to $1.73 billion, and DFAIT was cut 7 per cent to $1.30 billion.'[34]

STREAMLINING THE FOREIGN MINISTRY STRUCTURE

To suggest that the diplomats staged 'a comeback',[35] is not to imply that the purpose to which the foreign ministry has been put has returned to the traditional DEA model. Under the influence of systemic change in the international arena (and the direction of a cohort of senior officials, who remained thoroughly imbued with the ethos of bureaucratic rationalization), foreign policy has become a key element in the Chrétien government's effort to demonstrate its ability to act as an effective manager of public policy. Rather than going back to the past in terms of organizational style (with an onus on 'flying by the seat of the pants'), the emphasis has been on coordination and value in terms of the specific Canadian interests.[36]

The criteria for success of such a strategy lies in the delivery function. Using results as the guide for action,[37] Canadian foreign policy has become increasingly mission-oriented. Although this theme extends well beyond the framework of this paper, this evolution has meant an enhanced focus on well-defined areas of Canadian comparative advantage (peacebuilding for example). It has also meant that the notion of Canada acting as a 'global boy scout' has been downplayed to accommodate an instrumental results-oriented concern with the national interest and the 'main game' of economic competitiveness and securing market access. This reshaping of Canadian foreign policy comes out most strikingly in the Chrétien government's various 'Team Canada' initiatives which explicitly privilege the aim of trade diversification over human rights.[38]

The high priority given to delivery has also influenced a number of changes with respect to the nature of Canadian diplomatic missions. With the proliferation of new states since the collapse of the Soviet Union and Yugoslavia, the number of missions has expanded (from 110 in 1981 to 121 missions in 107 countries in 1997).[39] Measures to increase efficiency (and cut costs) have been sought, therefore, in other ways. A number of creative approaches have been developed in regard to the sharing of resources, both with other countries (as illustrated by the Canada–Australia Consular Sharing Agreement) and on an inter-departmental (with an emphasis on the 'single window' or 'one stop shopping' service delivery model at Canadian missions) and inter-governmental basis (with a number of provinces entering into 'co-location' agreements with the federal government). There have been moves as well towards the establishment of 'micro' missions. The Canadian embassy in Zagreb, Croatia, for example, has been located in a hotel room. The mode of diplomatic operation is primarily through the use of a laptop computer.[40] Throughout all of Canada's diplomatic activity, there is a pronounced trend towards a greater use of locally-engaged as opposed to Canada-based staff.

This strong onus on results provided a renewed momentum towards the internal reorganization of the Canadian foreign ministry. The array of changes made over recent decades left the department with a number of contradictions in its administrative structure. One of these contradictions has been the push and pull between centralization and decentralization. In attempting to achieve coordination, the Canadian foreign ministry had moved towards a centralized model in the 1980s and early 1990s. The span of control allocated to the secretary of state for external affairs/deputy minister foreign affairs appears to have been much greater than in most other comparable countries. Not only did a large number of subordinates report directly to the deputy minister; the instruments for the delegation of work were far more restricted. As such, the foreign ministry's administrative structure gave the impression of being top-heavy.

To deal with this first problem there has been a move towards task differentiation. As seen in Figure 3.1, one of the most significant changes in the process of restructuring currently in train has been a reduction of the number of the deputy minister's immediate subordinates, from 12 to seven assistant deputy ministers (ADMs). Moreover, the remaining ADMs have become integrated as part of a corporate or collective executive within a new Executive Committee. In other words, the prime responsibility of these ADMs putatively will be to help provide the ministers of foreign affairs and international trade, the secretaries of state (Latin America, Africa, and Asia-Pacific) and the deputy ministers of foreign affairs and international trade with strategic direction. There has been a corresponding drive to move decisionmaking downwards. The Bureau (headed by a director-general, albeit with the ADMs having oversight responsibility) has become the most important component of the organizational structure in terms of programme management.

The other contradiction has been between the push and pull between issue-specific and geographic concerns. Despite the continued salience of 'functionalism' in Canadian foreign policy, another striking feature of the

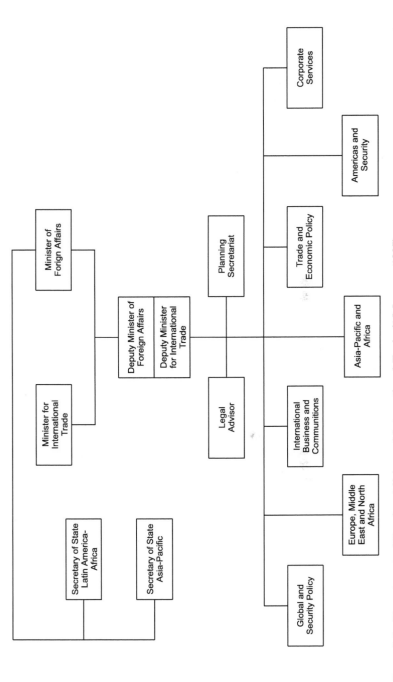

Figure 3.1 Department of Foreign Affairs and International Trade (15 January 1997)

foreign ministry's structure as it evolved in the 1980s and early 1990s was the comparatively large number of officials with bilateral/geographic responsibilities. This fissure, coming on top of the deeper split between the political and the trade side of the department, impeded a coherent mode of decision-making. At the very least, this high degree of fragmentation was a recipe for extensive consultation and 'micro-management'. More seriously, the compartmentalization resulted in complaints about exclusion, inflexibility and duplication.

To deal with this problem there has been a move towards consolidation. The current reorganization not only cuts down on the basic units (over 100 divisions existed in the department by the beginning of the 1990s), it streamlines them in a cross-cutting fashion. One illustration of this type of change has been the establishment of a Global and Human Issues Bureau, containing the Environment and Nuclear Division, the Human Rights Division, the Human Security Division, and the Peace Building and Human Development Division. Another illustration has been the establishment of an International Security Bureau, containing the North-American and Euro-Atlantic Security and Defence Relations Division, the Regional Security and Peacekeeping Division, and the Arms Control, Disarmament and Non-proliferation Division. The overall goal, as the deputy minister, stated was not only to change 'the [organizational] charts'; but to foster a 'new departmental culture' to set clearer priorities, provide clearer direction, and make better use of resources.[41]

By moving to re-invent itself, the foreign ministry has consolidated its ability to act as the 'lead' department over Canada's international relations. This does not mean that DFAIT has either the will or the capacity to act as though its former monopoly of influence had been restored. In some selected cases, it has moved to try to re-exert its authority. This assertive behaviour has been facilitated by DFAIT's capacity as coordinator and its leverage in terms of specific forms of oversight. For example, DFAIT's supervisory powers over CIDA were tightened after the election of the Chrétien government. All of CIDA's major policy and programme decisions (with their funding requirements) had to be approved by DFAIT, with overall responsibility for CIDA firmly positioned in the hands of the minister of foreign affairs.[42] This assertive behaviour is encouraged, it may be added, by the diminished resources among its bureaucratic rivals. Even the relatively well-placed Finance department has had to reduce its international profile (as witnessed, most notably, with the cut back in finance counsellors attached to Canadian G-7 embassies).[43]

More commonly, the foreign ministry has responded by working out a new set of relationships on an interdepartmental basis. One illustration of this type of relationship – based on a perceived coincidence of interest – has been the partnership forged between DFAIT and Industry Canada. Industry

Canada has access to a client/information base among Canadian firms that is hard to match. Equally, though, Industry Canada needs to tap into DFAIT's expertise in trade promotion. Because of its context and complexity, it may be argued, this relationship will never be completely trouble-free. A sense of competition still exists between the two departments. Viewing trade and industry policy as the dual components of a 'full tool kit',[44] Industry Canada has repeatedly tried to get back DFAIT's trade functions. DFAIT, for its part, has tried to reinforce it mandate over international business development by a greater emphasis on the integration of policy and the delivery of programmes.

CONCLUSION

Rather than confirming the image of decline, the Canadian case appears to highlight the capacity for adaptability among foreign ministries.[45] The role of the Canadian foreign ministry has gone through a series of changes brought about by a combination of international and domestic forces. No neat – and decisive – breakthrough has been made in the search to get its organization 'right'. Rather the process has been incremental and fluid, with a number of discrete and distinctive changes in the transition from the old External Affairs model and the on-going attempt to build an alternative model based on administrative rationality and efficient service. During this process, the foreign ministry has lost any claim it had to exclusive responsibility for Canada's international relations. Yet, the role of DFAIT remains central to any sustained analysis of Canadian foreign policy. Despite all the pressures towards fragmentation and specialization, the foreign ministry remains at the heart of the process of managing change. DFAIT remains the key source of articulation, aggregation and the determination of outcomes with respect to Canada's global activities. Moreover, DFAIT has been drawn in a more concerted and elaborate fashion to the internal policy agenda. From its insulated position established during the Pearson era, therefore, the Canadian foreign ministry has been transformed into the main vehicle by which the intricate and varied interactions between the domestic and the international domain are carried out. With their emphasis on bargaining, persuasion and delivery, these multiple 'two level games' are often extremely messy and frustrating.[46] At the same time, though, the method of evaluation by which its activities are judged have become increasingly focused. Although the tests to which the Canadian foreign ministry has been put have been fundamentally altered, and diversified, the judgment of performance is based much more on instrumental criteria linked to the retaining of confidence of its varied publics. If the application of international skills retain considerable import, domestic imperatives have come to the fore in shaping the direction of the Canadian foreign ministry's organizational response.

NOTES

The author would like to thank Brian Hocking and Evan Potter for their help with this chapter. He also wishes to acknowledge the support of the Social Sciences and Humanities Council of Canada.

1   Andrew F. Cooper, *Canadian Foreign Policy: Old Habits and New Directions* (Scarborough, Ontario: Prentice Hall, 1987).

2   James N. Rosenau, *Turbulence in World Politics: A Theory of Change and Continuity* (Hemel Hempstead: Harvester Wheatsheaf, 1990).

3   The recent government statement, *Canada in the World*, states that co-operation along these lines enhances the sovereignty 'for smaller and medium-sized countries since the growing number of international rules on security, trade and other matters better protects states from arbitrary and unilateral action by other international actors.' Canada, Department of Foreign Affairs and International Trade (Ottawa: DFAIT, 1995), p. 4.

4   On this theme, more generally, see Lauri Karvonen and Bengt Sundelius, *Internationalization and Foreign Policy Management* (Aldershot: Gower, 1987), p. 14.

5   John Holmes, *The Shaping of Peace: Canada and the Search for World Order*, vol. 2 (Toronto: University of Toronto Press, 1979), p. 110.

6   Peter Dobell, 'The management of a foreign policy for Canadians, *International Journal* 26, Winter 1970–1, pp. 218–19.

7   J. L. Granatstein, *The Ottawa Men: The Civil Service Mandarins, 1935–1967* (Toronto: Oxford University Press, 1982).

8   On the wider intellectual climate see G. John Ikenberry, 'A world economy restored: expert consensus and the Anglo-American postwar settlement', *International Organization* 46: 1, Winter 1992, pp. 290–6; 'Rethinking the Origins of American Hegemony,' *Political Science Quarterly* 104:3, 1989, pp. 375–400.

9   George Ignatieff, quoting Hume Wrong, in a review of *Conflict Among Nations: Bargaining, Decision Making, and System Structure in International Crises*, Glenn H. Snyder and Paul Diesing, *Queen's Quarterly* 85: 4, Winter 1978/9, pp. 714–15.

10   Bruce Thordarson, *Trudeau and Foreign Policy: A Study in Decision-Making* (Toronto: Oxford University Press, 1972), p. 150.

11   'Farewell to diplomacy', *Saturday Night*, December 1968, p. 21. See also his *Diplomacy and Its Discontents* (Toronto: University of Toronto, 1971).

12   Canada, Secretary of State for External Affairs, *Foreign Policy For Canadians* (Ottawa: Information Canada, 1970), p. 8.

13   Jeffrey Simpson, 'PM lectures provinces as meeting bogs down,' *Globe and Mail*, 15 February 1978, p. 1.

14   G. B. Doern and T. Conway, *The Greening of Canada: Federal Institutions and Decisions* (Toronto: University of Toronto Press, 1994); Glen Toner and G. Bruce Doern, *The Politics of Energy: The Development and Implementation off the National Energy Program* (Toronto, Methuen, 1985).

15   Robert Johnstone, testimony to the Standing Committee on External Affairs and National Defence, *Minutes of Proceedings and Evidence*, 30 January 1981, 30: 15.

16   Office of the Prime Minister, *Release*, 12 January 1982, quoted in Andrew F. Cooper, Richard Higgott, and Kim Richard Nossal, *Relocating Middle Powers* (Vancouver: University of British Columbia Press, 1993), p. 37.

17   On this policy conflict, see Michael Hart with Bill Dymond and Colin Robertson, *Decision At Midnight: Inside The Canada-US Free-Trade Negotiations* (Vancouver: University of British Columbia Press, 1994), pp. 89–91.

18 Brian Hocking, 'Regional governments and international affairs: foreign policy problem or deviant behaviour? *International Journal*, 45: 3, Summer 1986, p. 503.

19 Kim Richard Nossal, 'The PM and the SSEA in Canada's foreign policy: dividing the territory, 1968–1993,' *International Journal* 50: 1, Winter 1994–5, p. 203.

20 Leslie A. Pal, 'Competing paradigms in policy discourse: the case of international human rights,' *Policy Sciences* 28: 2 May 1995, pp. 185–207.

21 *Montreal Gazette*, 'Coming of age,' 10 December 1986.

22 Tom Keating, 'The state, the public, and the making of Canadian foreign policy' in Robert J. Jackson, Doreen Jackson, and Nicolas Baxter-Moore, *Contemporary Canadian Politics: Readings and Notes* (Scarborough: Prentice-Hall, 1987), pp. 363–4.

23 Cranford Pratt, 'Dominant Class Theory and Canadian Foreign Policy: The Case of the Counter-Consensus,' *International Journal* 31: 1, Winter 1983–4, pp. 93–125.

24 Denis Stairs, 'Public opinion and external affairs: reflections on the domestication of Canadian foreign policy,' *International Journal*, 33: 1, Winter 1977–8, pp. 144–5.

25 *Creating Opportunity: The Liberal Plan for Canada* (Ottawa: Liberal Party of Canada, 1993), p. 157.

26 Andrew F. Cooper and Leslie A. Pal, 'Human rights and security,' in G. B. Doern, Leslie A. Pal and Brian W. Tomlin, eds, *Border Crossings: The Internationalization of Canadian Public Policy* (Toronto: Oxford University Press, 1996), pp. 209–38.

27 Denis Stairs, 'The public politics of the Canadian defence and foreign policy reviews,' *Canadian Foreign Policy* III, 1 (Spring 1995), pp. 91–116.

28 Kim R. Nossal, 'The Democratization of Canadian Foreign Policy,' *Canadian Foreign Policy* 1, 3, Fall 1993, pp. 95–105.

29 Paul Knox, 'Canadians wrestle with global change', *Globe and Mail*, 12 September 1995.

30 Andrew Cohen, 'The diplomats make a comeback', *Globe and Mail*, 19 November 1994.

31 Jeff Sallott, 'Mr. Smith goes to Foreign Affairs', *Globe and Mail*, 5 August 1994.

32 Paul Koring, 'Deep cuts at Foreign Affairs target Ottawa bureaucracy,' *Globe and Mail*, 4 July 1996.

33 Evan Potter, 'A question of relevance: Canada's foreign policy and foreign service in the 1990s,' in Fen Osler Hampson and Christopher J. Maule, eds, *Canada Among Nations, 1993–94, Global Jeopardy* (Ottawa: Carleton University Press, 1993), pp. 48–51.

34 G. Bruce Doern and John Kirton, 'Foreign Policy,' in Doern, Pal and Tomlin, *Border Crossings*, p. 256.

35 Cohen, 'The diplomats make a comeback'.

36 See for example, *Canada in the World*.

37 Gilbert Winham, 'The Impact of System Change on International Diplomacy', Ottawa: Canadian Political Science Association, 1993.

38 See for example, 'So long Dudley do-right: Canadian foreign policy reflects self-interests of the '90s,' *Montreal Gazette*, 12 February 1995; Gordon Barthos, 'Radical foreign policy banks on trade liberals' pro-business agenda, stands tradition on its head,' *Toronto Star*, 8 February 1995.

39 Robert Wolfe, 'Still lying abroad? Why Canadian ambassadors proliferate in the era of globalization,' paper presented to the International Studies Association, Toronto, 19–22 March 1997, p. 1.

40   'Cyber-Diplomacy,' Speaking Notes for Mr. Gordon Smith, Deputy Minister,
      Foreign Affairs and International Trade, to the Technology in Government
      Forum, Ottawa, Ontario, 18 September 1996.
41   Koring, 'Deep cuts at Foreign Affairs.'
42   Cranford Pratt, 'Development assistance and Canadian foreign policy: where
      we are now,' *Canadian Foreign Policy* 2: 3, Winter 1994–5, pp. 77–85.
43   Doern and Kirton, 'Foreign Policy,' p. 250.
44   G. Bruce Doern and Brian W. Tomlin, 'Trade-Industry Policy,' in Doern, Pal
      and Tomlin, *Border Crossings*, p. 175. On the earlier tensions between the
      foreign ministry and the then Department of Trade and Industry, see Ernie
      Keenes, 'Rearranging the Deck Chairs: A Political Economy Approach to
      Foreign Management in Canada,' *Canadian Public Administration* 35: 3, 1992,
      pp. 381–401.
45   Brian Hocking, 'Beyond "Newness" and "Decline": The Development of Cat-
      alytic Diplomacy', *Discussion Paper in Diplomacy* No. 10, Centre for the Study
      of Diplomacy, University of Leicester, October 1995.
46   Peter B. Evans, Harold K. Jacobson and Robert D. Putnam, *International
      Bargaining and Domestic Politics* (Berkeley, California; University of California
      Press, 1993).

4 France
The Ministry of Foreign Affairs: 'something new, but which is the legitimate continuation of our past...' (Paul Claudel – *Le soulier de satin*)

Paulette Enjalran and Philippe Husson

In France, Foreign Affairs is one of the state's oldest departments. The first body to deal specifically with external relations emerged during the Renaissance. Heirs to the royal notaries of the Middle Ages, from 1557 Secretaries of State shared the responsibility of French diplomatic activity on a territorial basis. However, with a view to obtaining a coordinated and unified policy, King Henry III, as early as 1589, decided that only one Secretary of State should be in charge of Foreign Affairs. The latter presided over clerks who, over a period of time, were organized into bureaus and finally, during the seventeenth century, became a veritable ministry. Simultaneously, to fulfil the requirements of royal policy, a network of permanent diplomatic missions was developed. As early as the sixteenth century, envoys had been sent to the Pope, the Emperor, Venice and Great Britain and also to the Swiss Cantons and Turkey. Other missions of the same type developed later, in Madrid, Moscow and subsequently Philadelphia. At the close of the Ancien Régime, France had 11 embassies, 20 legations and four residencies, and also a large number of consulates throughout Europe and the Ottoman Empire.

In spite of an initial upheaval, the French Revolution brought but few durable changes to the structures of diplomacy. However, the French Constitution of 1791 set forth the principle of legislative participation in discussions concerning external policy. During 1793, consulates which had heretofore reported to the Navy were attached to Foreign Affairs. Finally, by the Order of Messidor 22, Year 7 (17 July 1797), the Ministry was renamed Department of External Relations and granted exclusive jurisdiction over relations with other countries. Under the Consulate and the Empire, Napoleon privileged this body and by a Decree of 25 December 1810, confirmed its structure and functions.

The alternating monarchic and republican regimes, characteristic of French political life in the nineteenth century, brought about various reforms but their scope was limited. In 1814–15 the Ministry of Foreign Affairs (MFA) resumed its original name. During 1825, a Commercial Department was created and in 1852, four geographical subdepartments shared political affairs. The map of diplomatic and consular posts was revised several times, especially in America and in Asia. But the constitutional principles of handling foreign policy and the organization of the Ministry were not modified. In particular, the progressive implementation of the parliamentary system and the existence of a Chairman of the Council of Ministers did not eradicate the Head of State's traditional role in diplomatic affairs.

On the other hand, since the beginning of the twentieth century, the MFA has developed significantly. After World War I, new sections were created such as those to monitor the affairs of the League of Nations and to administer French schools and institutes in other countries. From 1920 on, it was placed under the authority of a Secretary General whose mission was to supervize the Central Administration and to ensure the coordination of diplomatic action.

However, in 1945, the MFA found itself faced with new problems. The East–West rivalry and nuclear threat, the growth of international relations in practically every area, the increase in the number of states, the increasingly intricate web of national and international questions, the speed of communications and finally the influence of economic agents, NGOs and of the media, each imparted a more public and multilateral character to diplomatic action. Meetings and conferences multiplied at the same rate as the actors and very prominent political figures were frequent participants.[1]

Faced with the globalization of business, the MFA's near total monopoly in the management of external policy was questioned. However, the Ministry undertook various organizational changes, new desks were added, both functional and territorial, and its activity, far from being reduced, actually increased. Therefore, is it possible to speak of its decline, as do some observers? What lessons can be gleaned today from its organization and operation? In other words, what is its position in the state since the adoption of the current constitution of 1958?[2]

ORGANIZATION AND AGENDAS

Before attempting to answer these questions, the MFA's main responsibilities should be defined, as well as the means available for discharging them.

The Ministry's Tasks

During recent years the MFA (Quai d'Orsay) has been faced with a number of problems, some shared by its counterparts in other countries, but others the result of factors specific to it. Within the first category, as already mentioned, are those factors relating to the ever-growing complexity and technical nature of international relations. Be they political, economical, cultural or humanitarian, it was necessary to face new situations and new requirements. Because of the Cold War, it was increasingly important to strengthen the mechanisms of collective security and multilateral diplomacy. To do so, the Quai d'Orsay had to deal with the problems of coordination of French external action which had not assumed such significance heretofore.

Likewise, France's membership of the European Community[3] engendered in this country, as it did for its partners, the need to adapt the Ministry's structures and methods. As European cooperation developed, a larger number of departments were involved with many policy decisions being transferred to the Community. Thus there gradually emerged in French administration policy areas with fluctuating boundaries, touching simultaneously on internal and external issues, where the part played by the MFA appeared more as that of a leader, coordinating the action of the various parties involved. However, since the implementation of the Treaty of Maastricht in 1993, this role of coordinator has assumed greater importance. It has given the MFA a new basis to launch French action in all areas pertaining to the European Union, be they economic, financial, social, political or security oriented.

Aside from these problems, which are to be found in other countries, there are others resulting from specific national preoccupations. As a former colonial power, France devoted particular attention to relations with its former territories. Here, the MFA not only continued to pursue active diplomatic relations but also furnished significant technical support.[4] Mention must also be made of the assistance the Ministry brought to other Third World countries through bilateral aid within the context of UN programmes. Globally, France leads G-7 countries in terms of assistance expressed as a percentage of GNP.

Moreover, after the emancipation of the colonies, relations with French-speaking countries were developed. Canada, Belgium, Luxembourg and other countries joined France and the new states to create in 1970 an Agency for Cultural and Technical Co-operation.[5] Since 1973, French and African leaders meet each year and have periodically held 'summits' of French-speaking countries since 1986. These various events in French-speaking states are important, in particular to the MFA. In fact, the scope of cultural, scientific and technical exchange, humanitarian aid, or development assistance are one of the main characteristics of France's external policy. Also, actions conducted in this area are considered of prime importance by the Quai d'Orsay which devotes to them nearly a third of its resources. Another of the MFA's major objectives is to maintain contact with French expatriates and to ensure, where necessary, their protection. This goal has become increasingly difficult to achieve in view of the surge of terrorism and insecurity in certain parts of the world.

Finally, but by no means the least of the problems confronting the MFA, is that resulting from the policy of stringent financial austerity implemented for several years now by the government due to economic conditions. Although its resources are not increasing, the MFA is called upon to handle many more tasks, and this presents certain difficulties. These challenges resulting from the change in international relations, the goals set by France for its external action, and the financial situation are permanently on the Ministry's agenda. The means available to the Ministry for discharging its role must be analysed in this context.

THE MINISTRY'S STRUCTURE

The Ministry's structure is the result of several partial reforms implemented in 1958 together with subsequent reforms.[6] The present organization of the Central Administration was created by a Decree dated 4 November 1993,[7] completed by an MFA Order of the same date. The purpose of these texts is to eliminate certain overlapping responsibilities which existed and to strengthen coordination between departments. The organizational chart is essentially as follows:[8]

1) At the head, a Secretary General who supervises all departments under the direct authority of the Minister.
2) Two Assistant Secretaries General each responsible geographically and functionally for a department, that is:
   - The Department of Political Affairs and Security is in charge of United Nations and international organizations affairs, of strategic affairs and disarmament, of the Atlantic Alliance and finally, of European political co-operation. It is also in charge of matters concerning French-speaking countries, humanitarian affairs, terrorism and drug trafficking.
   - The Department of European and Economic Affairs is in charge of European economic co-operation, bilateral relations between France and other European countries and, more generally, economic and financial affairs.
3) Four territorial Departments:
   - Department of African and Malagasy Affairs

- Department of North Africa and the Middle East
- Department of the Americas
- Department of Asia and the South Sea Islands

The above departments are in charge of coordinating all matters concerning relations between France and each of these territories.

4) Operational Departments
   - The Department of Scientific, Technical and Cultural Relations. This section is in charge of the implementation of cultural policy and scientific and technical co-operation between France and other countries. It oversees all cultural and educational (schools and universities) institutions outside France. It organizes exchanges with universities and institutions in industrialized countries and, jointly with the Ministry of Co-operation, programmes for co-operation with developing countries. A current reform aims at a fuller integration of the above with the Ministry's other activities.[9]
   - The Department of French Citizens Abroad and Foreigners in France. As its name indicates, it takes care, on the one hand, of French citizens living abroad and negotiates agreements on their behalf and, on the other, applies regulations concerning immigration. For this reason, it is in charge of the supervision of OFPRA (Office Français de Protection des Refugiés et Apatrides). It also acts as secretary to the Council of French Citizens Abroad (Conseil Supérieur des Français de l'Etranger), a consultative body representing expatriates which is elected by universal suffrage and has no counterpart in other countries.
5) Supporting Departments
   - The Department of Administration handles the Ministry's personnel and is in charge of the Cipher Bureau, of equipment and communications as well as budgetary, administrative and financial affairs.
   - The Department of Legal Affairs is consulted by the Ministry and by the other departments regarding all questions of international law. It represents the state before international jurisdictional or arbitral authorities.
   - The Department of the Press, Information and Communication, headed by the Ministry's spokesman.
   - The Department of Archives and Documentation. A living memory of the Ministry since 1680, it conserves archives and collects documentation other than the press; it runs the library and the map office.[10]
   - Protocol. This department is at the disposal of the President of the Republic, the Prime Minister and the Minister of Foreign Affairs.
6) Tasks and sections directly attached to the Minister.

- Bureau of Analysis and Planning
- General Inspection of the Central Administration and External Posts
- Security Officer
- Historical Advisor
- Advisor for Religious Affairs

In addition, the Minister has a Cabinet, members of which he appoints to handle political affairs and to serve as an intermediary with the various internal departments, other ministries and the Parliament.

The structure of the Central Administration takes into account the diversity of external policy nowadays and clearly reflects the priorities of French diplomacy. Outside France, it supports a network of diplomatic and consular posts, which is among the densest in the world. In 1945 it included 50 diplomatic or similar representations, two general residences and 166 consulates general and consulates. In 1996, this figure had increased to 151 embassies (three posts are closed and three others are temporarily in the hands of chargés d'affaires), 17 permanent representations, four delegations to international organizations and 116 consular posts (88 consulates general, 23 consulates and five separate chanceries).

The growing number of embassies after the decolonization of the 1950s and 1960s, and the dislocation of the Soviet Union, Czechoslovakia and Yugoslavia in the 1990s, were compensated in part by the removal of consular posts judged less useful because of the decrease of certain communities or the improvement in communications. Other changes are contemplated to keep abreast of the evolution of the international situation.

The importance of this network which is permanently in contact with the Central Administration was stressed during the 1993 reforms. It is one of the typical traits of the French diplomatic apparatus and one of the main advantages the FMA possesses over other departments, which have nothing comparable. Information, instructions and reports can be transmitted almost instantaneously between posts throughout the world.[11]

Ministry Personnel

The Ministry's structures, however well they have adapted, would be of little use were it not for its qualified personnel.[12] Since 1946, employees of the MFA are subject to the General Status of Civil Servants, but with provisions that take into account the particular qualities of their profession.[13]

There are two methods for the recruitment of MFA officers (Class A), namely embassy secretaries and counsellors. Firstly via the 'Ecole Nationale d'Administration', as is also the case for the higher echelons of the other ministries. Second by a competitive exam, of a comparable level, known as

'Concours d'Orient' to choose experts of the languages and cultures of Eastern European countries, Asia and Africa. This is also applicable to other Class A officers, (deputy secretaries and administrative attachés) where there are also three specific competitive exams to select public servants with generalist skills and expertise in more difficult languages.

The intermediate staff of the Ministry (Class B) is selected through four competitive exams for recruiting personnel to work in France or abroad, in various specific areas such as programming, ciphering and transmitting messages, all tasks which have become increasingly complex. As regards operational officers (Class C), they are selected by four competitive exams, which have grown more difficult in view of the increasing numbers of candidates. They fill posts either in the central administration or abroad and they are entitled to assume supervisory responsibilities when they reach a certain rank. Finally, the promotion of 'insiders' enables officers to pass from one class to another if they fulfil certain conditions. This type of promotion is frequent, involving approximately one quarter of the total.

Members of the cultural staff of MFA had been recruited for the most part from teachers from the Ministry of Education working under contract. But following the reform of the Department of Cultural, Scientific and Technical Relations, implemented in 1994, it was decided to align, as closely as possible, their method of recruitment and career profile with those of other staff. This change is currently being implemented. The means of recruiting officers for Foreign Affairs is, therefore, based on diversity but also on strict requirements concerning initial qualifications. This makes it possible to select each year people whose background and profile are different but whose skills are useful in view of the ever-growing diversity of the ministry's tasks.[14]

STRATEGIES AND RESPONSES

The examination of the MFA's 1993 structures reveals a tightening of the hierarchical pyramid and a strengthening of the coordination between its sections, with a greater emphasis on the functional rather than territorial sections. It also appears that the diversity of the officers' origins, combined with strict recruitment standards, broadens the range of available or potential skills and thus benefits the Ministry. However, measures implemented three years ago were and remained internal; they have not modified the distribution of competence between other ministries called upon to engage in international policy. Under these conditions the capacity of the Ministry to lead and coordinate foreign policy is a question of strategy as much as organization. In fact, it depends on the procedures and means at the disposal of the Quai d'Orsay to ensure its influence not only at a political level but at an administrative level.

The MFA's Political Authority

The Constitution of 4 October 1958 confirmed the French tradition by recognizing the pre-eminence of the Head of State in defining foreign policy. However, it also confers on the Prime Minister, responsible before Parliament for the country's general policy, authority in these affairs. Along with them, the Minister of Foreign Affairs is the only legal authority for conducting external policy. Other ministers may only intervene if he sees fit or by special permission. But certain ministers, of Defence, of Economy and Finance and of the Interior, are influential in various aspects of foreign policy, because their respective departments are called upon to co-operate in the formulation of policy.

From a constitutional point of view, French diplomacy is in the hands of three people. There can be differences of opinion between the President of the Republic and the Prime Minister (and this has occurred).[15] In practice, this is rare. The Head of Government, although always informed, intervenes primarily when a foreign policy decision may have serious repercussions inside the country, particularly in the economic field. Generally speaking, the authority of the Head of State prevails as far as major diplomatic trends and problems are concerned. For this reason, there is a direct relationship between the Head of State and the Minister of Foreign Affairs which enhances coordinated action.[16] Such was the case with General de Gaulle and his successors.

Moreover, Ministers of Foreign Affairs have had ministers delegated to assist them in their various tasks for several years. Their number varies from one cabinet to another; they are in charge of areas of external action of specific interest to France including cultural and French-speaking community relations, humanitarian aid, co-operation with developing countries and European affairs. These 'assistant' ministers sometimes have the full title of minister, but more often that of Secretary of State or of 'delegated' minister and they are attached to the Head of Diplomacy.[17] Such delegations of power were unavoidable because of the development of diplomatic activity but in no way jeopardize the coherence of external policy. Public opinion and Parliament still consider the Minister of Foreign Affairs as being in charge of diplomacy as a whole and as the person responsible for the implementation of French international policies.

Procedures and Means of Conducting Foreign Policy

The terms of the Constitution as well as the government's organization confer a wide range of action on the Minister of Foreign Affairs. But in practice, to exercise it at an administrative level, the Quai d'Orsay must be equipped with adequate means to ensure the cohesion of its department, establish useful contacts outside and effectively coordinate intervention of the various actors on the foreign policy scene. Where do matters stand in this respect?

In order to fulfil its mission the Ministry devotes considerable effort to preparing and training personnel on the new aspects of diplomatic work. Today diplomats can no longer merely handle political and consular problems which, not so long ago, were their main concern. This was once again clearly emphasized in 1996 by the President of the Republic during the ambassadors' annual meeting. They must now keep watch over economic and commercial activities. They must continue to implement cultural, scientific and technical programmes. It is up to them to establish a confident relationship with the media and important associations in the countries where they are living. They may be called upon also to work in insecure parts of the world and must be prepared to do so. Finally, in the numerous posts where staff is limited, they must know how to use modern data processing and communication equipment without the help of qualified personnel.

Recently, training programmes and refresher courses in various areas have been made available to Quai d'Orsay staff. The aim is to avoid excessive specialization and to have officers move from one task to another, both in France and abroad, on a frequent basis. At the same time, diplomats were often encouraged, according to their aptitudes and tastes, to develop with the help of the Ministry particular knowledge of geographic or technical areas. Thus the Ministry has at its disposal an increasing number of officers who have attained a very high level of proficiency in certain areas. However, it does not oblige them to remain in one area of specialization throughout their career.

Training, together with a search for efficiency, are essential. As mentioned above, the tasks of the MFA have multiplied, but have not been matched by its human and material resources. Manpower has been fluctuating for over 15 years at around 10 000 officers (of which a third are employed by the Central Administration) whereas the personnel of some other ministries has increased by ten per cent over the same period.[18] Its budget has remained approximately stable for several years and represents barely one per cent of the general budget, that is, approximately 15 billion French Francs in 1996.[19] The Ministry has made efforts to improve its productivity. Tasks that were accomplished manually have been automated. Members of the staff have been relocated between external posts and the Central Administration and a high-performance communication network put in place.[20] But in spite of promising results, it seems doubtful that further progress can be attained by these methods alone. Limits have been reached, particularly regarding the diminishing number of staff compared to the increasing number of functions which the MFA is required to fulfil.

The ministry attempted to tighten the cohesion of its departments through the 1993 restructuring measures but also by increasing the authority of the Secretary General. The latter was assigned the specific task (not so much by a redefinition of status as by the minister's instruction), of ensuring the smooth operation of the Ministry, to strengthen linkages between the Central Administration and posts abroad and to settle possible internal conflicts of authority.[21] In doing so, the role becomes one of coordinator, being informed of all important mail, chairing interdepartmental meetings, receiving ambassadors and representing the minister, and he may be assisted by the two assistant Secretaries General.

The mission of French ambassadors abroad is comparable to that of the Secretary General. Diplomatic posts, especially the major posts, group representatives of several technical departments: financial, commercial, military, and agricultural, among others. At the same time, some ministries have tended recently to organize local representation outside the embassies. As is the case in Paris, a close coordination of their activities has had to be implemented to avoid disorganized and even wasted efforts. This is why the Prime Minister reminded all departments[22] of the 1979[23] decree that states that each ambassador is the sole representative, in his country of residence, of the President of the Republic and the French government. This confirmed the central responsibility of the heads of diplomatic posts in the implementation of foreign policy.

This reaffirmation of the role of the ambassadors also strengthens regular co-operation between French representatives and the diplomatic missions of allied countries such as NATO and EU member states and enables them to discuss problems of common interest. France encourages her diplomats to take part actively in this type of co-operation. In Abuja, for instance, the new capital of Nigeria, the French Government participated in the project of accommodating the embassies of EU member states in the same building in order to facilitate their mutual relations. However, for constitutional reasons, France does not consider it possible, for the time being, to maintain joint embassies with one or more states, as is the practice of some governments. Contrary to the opinion of some, the ambassador's role is as important today as it was in the past.[24] One might even say that, in some respects, it is more useful because of the growing complexity of the contemporary world.

The Quai d'Orsay also strives to multiply contacts with actors outside governments but which are significant and useful at an international level. This applies firstly to the media. The MFA Department of Information and Communications meets every morning with accredited journalists for briefing sessions on current issues. The Ministry also assists groups and individuals who can provide a better understanding abroad of various aspects of contemporary France. The MFA Department of Political Affairs and

Security has a mission to liaise with NGOs and can grant subsidies for their programmes. The Ministry has also created several associations which come under the supervision of the Department of Cultural, Scientific and Technical Relations and which are financed by it. For example:

- the French Association for Artistic Action
- the Association for a Better Knowledge of French Culture
- the Association for Welcoming Personalities from Other Countries.[25]

The first two organize events or conferences for writers, scientists, artists or other personalities abroad and the last one welcomes visitors to France.

However, outside action can only be effective if close coordination is maintained between all the departments involved. This is a question of avoiding policy clashes which could be detrimental to the coherence of external policy. Although the MFA has departments ready to take action on all international issues, they cannot, in most cases, intervene before consulting other ministries. Contacts between these ministries and the Quai d'Orsay are very frequent and generally informal, by mail or telephone.[26] In certain areas, where coordination is essential, the procedure is more elaborate and interministerial meetings are held, sometimes with the participation of the Ministry's Secretary General. Coordination may also be achieved through permanent commissions or organizations such as:

- the MFA's Archive Commission including members of the Ministries of Culture, Education and Defence;
- the office for teaching the French language abroad supervized jointly by the MFA and the Ministry of Co-operation;
- the Office of the Secretary General for Defence (SGDN) where all the ministries involved in defence and security are represented, in particular the Minister of Foreign Affairs;
- the Interministerial Committee for the export of equipment for warfare[27]
- the Interministerial Committee for questions of European economic co-operation[28] which includes all relevant departments.

As distinct from the first two organizations mentioned, the others are responsible to the Prime Minister and not to the Minister of Foreign Affairs. However, the latter is represented at the decision-making level and the MFA contributes to their staffing. As for the export of weapons, the MFA is, of course, particularly careful regarding the control of such operations and the need for compliance with strict regulations. In this area, the Ministry has had sometimes to make its opinion prevail over those of other departments less well-informed or less sensitive to the political risks existing in certain areas of tension such as the Middle East and Africa.

As far as the European Union is concerned, the MFA possesses the means of expressing its views when necessary. It does not usually intervene in the technical aspects of European co-operation and lets the different ministries act according to their competence and play their proper role in the various committees and task forces in which they are involved. But it remains responsible for the coordination of French European policies. In this capacity, the MFA has to keep up with all issues and plays, in most cases, a central role. As stated by a former director of the MFA's Economic Department: 'The more the community domain extends, the interaction develops, and the common policies multiply, the more the responsibility of the Quai d'Orsay increases.'[29] It is the permanent guarantor against possible risks of technocratic solutions to problems where diplomacy and realism must prevail. In the preparation of the French position as well as in negotiations within the European Union, its role is, in fact, not challenged. Besides, Paris is traditionally represented in Brussels by a diplomat and the Minister of Foreign Affairs is as a rule the only one to sit with the Head of State at meetings of the European Council.[30]

However, it must be pointed out that, until recently, there were problems with the present system as far as the MFA was concerned. The Ministry of Economy and Finance handles more than half the funds devoted to the state's international activities, whereas the MFA only about twenty-five per cent and the Ministry of Co-operation, its partner for Third World support, only ten per cent. Overall funds for departments other than the Quai d'Orsay comprise three quarters of the total. This is why a new measure assumed significance for the MFA. A Decree of 5 February 1994 created the Interministerial Committee for Co-ordinating the State's Means Abroad (CIMEE).[31] It is chaired by the Prime Minister and groups all members of the Government whose administrations handle foreign affairs, as well as a representative of the President of the Republic and the Secretary General of the Interministerial Commission for European Co-operation (SGCI). The deliberations of this new body are serviced by a Permanent Bureau chaired by the Government's Secretary General but whose spokesperson is the MFA's Secretary General. This Committee's mission is fourfold:

- to collect all information concerning the organization of the State's external network and all details regarding the use of funds for external action;
- to define policy concerning the location of offices in other countries;
- to propose measures for redeployment and rationalization of overseas activities;
- to produce yearly reports concerning the progress of France's overseas activities.

Placed under the authority of the Head of Government, this committee keeps abreast of all the means employed to pursue France's external policy goals. Although it is not dependent primarily on the MFA, the Ministry recognizes that it has a zone of influence here and prepares the committee's work. Even if it is too early to appreciate the significance of the CIMEE, it is, nevertheless, in charge of a task essential to the Quai d'Orsay whose mission, as has been already indicated, is to lead and coordinate French foreign policy.

CONCLUSION

Finally, what conclusions does this analysis yield? More specifically, what position may be assigned to the MFA within the governmental structure and the life of the country? For over four centuries now, the Ministry has been the tool of external policy, ensuring its continuity under all regimes. Over the years, it has undergone reforms to accommodate developments and changes in international relations, but its position and role within the state have not been questioned.

Only recently have questions arisen regarding its significance.[32] Politicians, journalists and diplomats themselves, have expressed doubts. In their opinion, since the MFA is no longer de facto, if not de jure, the only actor on the international scene, it will be pushed aside by other centres of power such as the Office of the Prime Minister or even the Ministry of Economy and Finance. Naturally, the MFA no longer has any pretence of acting alone, if such was ever the case, but its role remains essential. Organized and centralized management of foreign policy is necessary in all sovereign states and is all the more necessary since international relations have become increasingly complex, and interwoven with domestic policy, thus demanding more professionalism from those in charge.

The French example is typical of this situation. In this country, the transformation of international relations brought about a significant change in the approach to foreign policy. Now a collective effort is necessary and requires the participation of many Ministries. The change is irreversible. But the Quai d'Orsay remains at the heart of the decisionmaking system. It has been able by successive reorganizational measures, carried out over 30 years, to equip itself with the services it requires; its personnel have acquired a multifold experience and have proved their aptitude to acquire new techniques. It is the only body in France to have proven and diversified experience of external action, to maintain complete archives and to possess an up-to-date and effective communication network on a global scale. Finally its head is in direct contact with the Prime Minister and the President of the Republic.

As the polls indicate, the MFA's role is not really questioned by public opinion in France. In fact, more and more French people abroad avail themselves of its services. If the Ministry has a weak point, it resides in a lack of resources resulting from present economic conditions, whilst its activities are increasing. Because of its relatively modest budget, it feels more deeply than others, the limitations of its resources. If this continues, the situation could affect its role as the initiator, the leader and the body ensuring the coherence of external policy. But the recent creation of the CIMEE and the place that the MFA has within it, indicates that this will not be so.

The mission of the Quai d'Orsay is no less essential today than in the past, although it assumes other forms and demands new methods to achieve it.[33] Therefore, there is no question of the decline of the Ministry, only of its necessary and continuous adaptation to an environment which continues to change. Obviously, its complex tasks now require an even greater competence and vigilance.

NOTES

1   The reference work concerning the history and the organisation of the MFA is: Jean Baillou et al, *Les Affaires Etrangères et le Corps Diplomatique Français* (vol. 1 and 2), (Paris: CNRS, 1984); see also Keith Hamilton and Richard Langhorne, *The Practice of Diplomacy* (London and New York: Routledge, 1996), pp. 173–4.

2   Olivier Duhamel and Jean Luc Parodi, *La Constitution de la Cinquième République* (Paris: Presses de la Fondation Nationale des Sciences Politiques, 1985).

3   See also Pierre Gerbet, *La Construction de l'Europe* (Paris, 1983); Pierre Gerbet, La Naissance du Marché Commun (Brussels: Editions Complexe, 1984); Jacques Leprette, *Une clef pour l'Europe* (Brussels, 1996).

4   Documents diplomatiques Français (Paris, July 1954, Imprimerie Nationale); Charles R. Ageron et al, *Les Chemins de la Décolonisation de l'Empire Français, 1936–1956* (Paris: CNRS, 1986).

5   The Agency for Cultural and Technical Co-operation was created on 20 March 1970 in the course of a conference grouping French-speaking communities in Niamey: Michel Tetu, *La Francophonie, Histoire, Problématique et Perspectives* (Montreal: Guérin Littérature, 1987).

6   *Journal Officiel de la République Française*, Decrees 61–1058 of 15 September 1961 and 69–233 of 14 March 1969, 79–666 of 6 August 1979 modified by decree 81–187 of 3 November 1981 and 82–658 of 27 July 1982 modified by decree 85–445 of 17 April 1985.

7   *Journal Officiel*, Decree 93–1210 of 4 November 1993.

8   It is the result of successive reforms prepared by special ad hoc bodies (Commission Racine 1969, Commission Rigaud 1979, Commission Viot 1987, Commission Picq 1993).

9   Included are 300 Lycées and schools, 200 Alliance Française groups, 133 cultural centres and institutes and 30 research centres throughout the world: Jacques Rigaud, *Rapport au Ministre des Affaires Etrangères sur les Relations Culturelles Extérieures* (La Documentation Française, 1980).

10   *Les Archives du Ministère des Relations Extérieures depuis les Origines* (Volume 1 Histoire, Volume 2 Guide), (Paris: Imprimerie Nationale, 1984).

11   Jean du Boisberranger, *Domaines et Instruments de la Politique Etrangère de la France* (Notes et études documentaires No. 4254–56), (La Documentation Française, 1976).

12   For all information concerning MFA personnel please refer to: Daniel Lequertier, 'L'outil diplomatique français', *Revue Française d'Administration Publique* 69, January-March 1994, pp. 17–33.

13   Please refer to *Journal Officiel*, Decree 69–222, 6 March 1969. This has been modified several times, concerning the special status of diplomatic and consular officers.

14   The main reference work concerning the MFA structure and staff is *L'Annuaire Diplomatique*, published yearly since 1858.

15   For instance, the disagreement expressed in December 1985 by Prime Minister Laurent Fabius regarding the interview President François Mitterrand granted General Jaruselski. See: Jacques Attali, *Verbatim II* (1995).

16   This relationship of a personal character developed in function of presidents and ministers; it was more or less close according to periods, but it had existed since 1958 and it certainly contributed to strengthen the position of the Minister of Foreign Affairs in the Government. See Maurice Couve de Murville, *Une Politique Etrangère* (Paris: Plon, 1971).

17   On this point, however, the Minister for Co-operation in charge of part of the Third World Aid (namely, the aid to French- speaking African countries and to some others) has often been an exception for historical reasons.

18   The budgeted manpower of the Ministry. Must be added, however, local personnel, technicians and teachers abroad who depend directly or indirectly on the Ministry and the representatives of other administrations abroad. This totals an overall figure of approximately 30 000 employees, working outside France, two thirds of which are borne by the MFA.

19   More precisely, 15 033 844 835 French Francs (ordinary and capital expenditure).

20   Known as: Système Automatique de Routage des Télégrammes des Relations Extérieures (SARTRE).

21   As defined by 20 January 1920 and 2 November 1976 decrees. See: Baillou, *Les Affaires Etrangères* (Volume 1), pp. 381–671.

22   Circular of the Prime Minister dated 8 November 1993.

23   *Journal Officiel*, Decree 79–443, 1 June 1979; Circular of 8 June 1979.

24   For instance, the opinion of Professor Zbigniew Brzezinski, a member of the US State Department's Policy Planning Council in 1966–68 and an assistant to the President for National Security affairs in 1977–81.

25   Baillou, *Les Affaires Etrangères* (Volume 2, la D.G.R.C.S.T.), pp. 720–35: In French: Association Française d'Action Artistique, Association pour la Diffusion de la Pensée Française, Association pour l'Accueil de Personnalités Etrangères

26   For example, relations existing between:
     – the Department of Political Affairs and Security and the Ministry of Defence, concerning the participation of France in the UN Forces or the French Military Program for Nuclear Weapons and Arms Control. See a history of nuclear studies by Maurice Vaisse, *La France et l'Atome* (Brussels: Bruylant, 1994).
     – the Department of European Affairs and Economy and the Ministries of Economy and the Budget concerning the European Union.

– the Department of Cultural, Scientific and Technical Affairs and the Ministries of Education and Culture concerning French schools abroad and external audio visual action.

– the Department of French Citizens Abroad and Foreigners in France and the Ministries of the Interior, of Social Affairs and of Justice, concerning immigration and so on.

– On these questions also refer to Jacques and Xavier Delcros, *Les Institutions Administratives*, (vol. 1, Les Structures, vol. 2 Le Fonctionnement) (Paris: Presses de la Fondation Nationale des Sciences Politiques, 1984–6).

27   Comité Interministériel pour les Exportations de Matériels de Guerre (CIEMG).

28   Comité Interministériel pour les Questions de Coopération Economique Européenne.

29   Henri Froment-Meurice, 'La Diplomatie Economique', *Revue Française d'Administration Publique* 69, January-February 1994, p. 96.

30   Leprette, *Une clef pour l'Europe*: ch. 12, p. 159, the COREPER, ch. 13, p. 169, Le Conseil des Ministres des Affaires Etrangères, ch. 14, Réunion des Chefs d'Etat et de Gouvernement; J. F. Gaillard, D. Carreau and W. L. Lee, *Le Marché Unique Européen* (Paris: Pedone, 1971).

31   *Journal Officiel*, Decree 94–108 of 5 February 1994. This created the 'Comité Interministériel des Moyens de l'Etat à l'Etranger.

32   Hamilton and Langhorne, *The Practice of Diplomacy*, pp. 231–45.

33   Alain Plantey, *De la Politique entre les Etats, Principes de la Diplomatie* (Paris: Pedone, 1991): 'Le danger réside dans l'illusion que la modification des règles du jeu peut remplacer les principes diplomatiques classiques'.

5 Israel Succumbing to Foreign Ministry Declinism

Aharon Klieman

Approaching the half-century mark, the organizational history of Israel's Ministry of Foreign Affairs (IMFA) is dominated by the theme of institutional marginalization. This makes both Israel and the IMFA unexceptional, confirming the general declivity of foreign ministries worldwide. Within the first decade of modern Israel's establishment and the IMFA's formation, directors and professional staff members alike resigned themselves to subordinate status as a governmental agency exercising only a secondary decisionmaking role on national security and foreign affairs.[1] This 50-year pattern is virtually uninterrupted save for a few shortlived periods when a compelling case can be documented for the foreign ministry having participated directly in the formation of policy (as distinct from policy implementation) and for it having contributed in any truly meaningful way to major diplomatic initiatives.

Therefore the years 1993–6, although an anomaly, are especially noteworthy precisely because they represent the exception proving the rule – a recent and rare departure from overall foreign ministry decline. Indeed, never has the foreign ministry been closer to the centre in the shaping as well as the conduct of Israeli foreign affairs since its inception in 1948 than in those brief, heady years of assertiveness.

In the first instance, it would be hard to draw a sharper contrast between the start of the present decade and its later phase. At the beginning of the nineties, both the State of Israel and its foreign ministry were on the defensive, their energies and attention directed at what amounted to a rear-guard holding action aimed at preventing any further erosion in their respective external and internal positions. By mid-decade the picture had been transformed quite dramatically. Each in its own way had come to assume exceptional prominence: Israel, abroad; the foreign ministry, at home. And yet, in another sudden reversal, by 1997 an abiding sense of vulnerability to external pressures, regional and global, reasserted its psychological hold over policymakers in Jerusalem. The country's international position, although improved was once more challenged, while the IMFA again finds itself thrust into the bureaucratic shadows.

The larger patterns are clear and indisputable; less so the reasons for this sorry state of (foreign) affairs. To be sure, the two influences most often cited in the case of Israel by way of explanation for the waning influence of the foreign ministry, and its reversion to a marginalized status are certainly valid, although unconvincing in themselves. The first factor, pointing to 'the new diplomacy', argues its negative impact on the profession everywhere, thereby stressing a feature the IMFA shares in common with other foreign ministries. The second underscores instead Israel's distinctiveness by pointing to the severity of its unique security dilemma. According to this situational argument, a constant Middle East threat environment stemming from the unresolved Israeli–Palestinian conflict and Arab world hostility expresses itself, domestically as well as externally, in the sacrifice of international considerations to the imperatives of immediate, physical military defence.

My analysis attributes IMFA policy impotence to a different set of twin factors centring upon the domestic bureaucratic model. On the one hand, the IMFA has been badly outclassed by institutional rivals at once more powerful, more determined, better positioned and intent upon expanding their scope and authority at the foreign ministry's direct expense. On the other hand, the ministry, its interests, talents, collective experience and diplomatic perspective have not been particularly well-served by political appointees selected over the years to head the ministry.

THE IMFA AND ISRAEL AT MID-DECADE

In retrospect, therefore, the period between 1993 and 1996 represents a 'false dawn'. At the time there were grounds for expecting that the foreign ministry might distinguish itself in defying the larger professional trend toward obsolescence long underway among foreign ministries elsewhere, by actually reclaiming its rightful position of centrality in the decisionmaking process. What set those years apart, both from the preceding decades and the current relapse, were their distinguishing hallmarks. The first was Israel's vastly improved global standing; one no longer heard references to Israel as a 'pariah', an 'international outcast' or a 'rogue state' beyond the pale of the world community. Secondly, the heightened sensitivity shown toward moral, legal, commercial and diplomatic considerations in the larger calculus of Israeli national self-interest was quite pronounced. But for our purposes the third trend was the most important: the renewed – indeed, unparalleled – prominence of the Ministry of Foreign Affairs in most aspects of internal policymaking. I suggest these factors are not unrelated. In fact, the argument here is for a strong inverse causal relationship between the three variables. Respect at home for statecraft's contribution to the longer-term security and well-being of Israel, together with the state's rising global prestige, positive image and widening network of commercial, transnational, cultural and defence relationships, were themselves derivative; more effect than cause.[2] Both directly relate to the foreign ministry's emergence as a stronger, more assertive bureaucratic actor in the decisionmaking process. Suffice it to recall that the Oslo initiative which did so much to improve the country's political fortunes originated with the IMFA.

Given this ascendancy, until as late as the summer of 1996 the ministry's experience seemed to be running counter to that of most countries, challenging the strong pattern of receding foreign ministries in this era of the new diplomacy.[3] Comparative frameworks for evaluating (a) the status and (b) the role of foreign ministries in a changing world present a depressing picture of constricting professional foreign policy establishments eclipsed, among other things, by summit diplomacy, electronic communication and special emissaries.[4] However, in the instance of Israel, its external affairs ministry, if anything, gave the impression of being in the midst of a bureaucratic renaissance.

Signalling the IMFA's regained status and elevated role, in the mid-1990s top ministry officials were enlisted not merely in the technical and administrative execution of policy decisions but in designing and carrying out strategic policy initiatives. This uncustomary activism found expression in streamlined organizational restructuring; the agency's expanded agenda and performance; its enhanced prestige in the eyes of the Israeli public; and, not least, its own improved *esprit de corps*.

ORGANIZATION AND AGENDA

A visitor to the Kirya, since 1953 the 'temporary' foreign ministry compound within easy walking distance of the central bus station in Jerusalem's Romema neighbourhood, may be forgiven for not viscerally grasping the IMFA's indispensability. The physical setting – the modest, improvised and distinctly old fashioned staff quarters hammered together from a crowded warren of aging, single-storey huts of 1940s and 1950s vintage suggests, if anything, an unprestigious government agency left behind and frozen in time.

Operating from within these cramped quarters, and with the standard terms of reference of external affairs departments everywhere, Israel's IMFA is expected to formulate, implement and articulate the foreign policy of the government of Israel. Accordingly, ministry officials and diplomats represent the state vis-à-vis foreign governments and international organizations, most notably the United Nations, explain its stand on issues of the day, foster co-operation and promote economic, cultural and scientific relations. In addition, the IMFA assists in drafting legal agreements to which Israel is a party, while also safeguarding the rights of Israeli citizens abroad. Similarly, the regional, functional and administrative services departments of IMFA are straightforward and unexceptional. The one truly special dimension to its labours is the added mission of promoting ties with dispersed Jewish communities outside Israel. The physical plant aside, and wholly inconsistent with their impoverished circumstances, disproportionately small budget and staff, the IMFA and members of the career foreign service nonetheless have undergone significant internal administrative reforms better enabling them to exercise their competencies.

The reorganization programme implemented in 1993, extends to both IMFA structures and functions. It was one major factor contributing to the ministry's revitalization. It also mirrors this transformation. The burst of reformist measures had as its declared aims: modernizing operations; coping with the proliferating number of regularized, formal ties, bilateral and multilateral; regrouping for future missions; and repositioning the foreign office at the centre of government policymaking. Of the four goals only the first three have been achieved to any appreciable extent, and incorporated in IMFA *modus operandi*. It is, of course, the fourth, and most critical, objective that continues to elude the ministry. Which is precisely the point. After shaping themselves into a more efficient unit, IMFA staff remain more frustrated now than before 1993. They possess the institutional capabilities equipping them to be a leading actor, but without the political clout for doing so.

NECESSARY BUT NOT SUFFICIENT: THE 1993 REFORMS

The theme of linking political diversification and expanded relationships to internal specialization and improved operational procedures stood at the centre of the extensive reshuffling undertaken in May 1993.[5] In announcing the structural changes, Uri Savir, IMFA director-general and principal architect of the reforms, in effect signalled a two-fold message. While the USA was still the focus for Israeli diplomacy, henceforth other areas of the world, starting with the Arab Middle East, would be targeted for increased attention and investment. Bureaucratically, too, the IMFA would be acting on a much broader front in the future by improving its performance in a number of core functions.

Toward this goal of retooling for an era of global and regional peace, among the specific steps taken were: elevating units dealing with cultural and international cooperation to the status of divisions, and their chiefs to the rank of deputy director-generals; substantially increasing the paltry seven million shekel budget for international co-operation; assigning Turkey and Cyprus to the European desk; separating the department for Asia and Africa into two autonomous sections; bolstering activities on the information and media fronts; stressing trade diplomacy; creating a new international human rights section; and a greater emphasis on personnel training.

Echoing foreign minister Shimon Peres and deputy foreign minister Yossi Beilin, his immediate superiors, Savir emphasized the imperative for the IMFA to be at the cutting edge of world events – indeed, on getting out ahead of them – while at the same time meeting the demands of an accelerated Arab–Israel peace process. These responsibilities are now entrusted to an enlarged political planning staff for circulating in-house papers dealing with Mideast futures and peace agenda topics like regional transportation and telecommunications, agriculture, water, energy and tourism. Indicative of this new spirit, a paper drawn up by the director of the Political Research Centre, 'A Foreign Policy for the Year 2000', ambitiously redefined Israel's overseas objectives to underscore heightened involvement in concerted efforts at resolving conflicts and easing tensions, in extending humanitarian and technical aid, in multilateral frameworks for cooperation and fostering developmentalism in the Middle East and elsewhere, and in promoting democratization as a member in the 'club of democracies'.[6]

Incorporating these 1993 improvements, Table 5.1 charts the present overall organizational structure of the Ministry of Foreign Affairs.

Table 5.1   Ministry of Foreign Affairs Organizational Chart, 1997

A. REGIONAL DEPARTMENTS (DIVISIONS/FUNCTIONS)

North America and Disarmament Affairs
- United States and Canada
- Disarmament Affairs

Western Europe
- European Community members
- EFTA countries, Turkey and Cyprus
- European Community organizations, NATO, CSCE

Eastern Europe and Commonwealth of Independent States (CIS)
- Russia, Ukraine, Belarus, Moldavia, Baltic countries
- East European countries
- Central Asian republics

Asia and Oceania
- Southeast Asia
- Northeast Asia
- Oceania

Africa
- South Africa and Swaziland
- Sub-Saharan Africa

Latin America
- Central America and the Caribbean
- South America

The Middle East
- Peace Negotiations
- Egypt
- Israel-Arab Division

B. Functional Departments

Media and Public Affairs
- Press
- Public Affairs
- Information
- Public Relations

Economic Affairs
- North America, Asia, Africa, Latin America, Egypt, Turkey and Cyprus, as well as functional economic cooperation in such areas as tourism, aviation and shipping accords
- Economic relations with the European countries
- Commercial ties with Eastern Europe, plus questions of oil and the Arab boycott

International Organizations
- International organizations and specialized UN agencies
- United Nations affairs, peacekeeping forces, the International Red Cross
- Third World, UNCTAD, NGOs

The Political Planning Division

The Legal Department
- International Law Division
- International Treaty Division
- Maritime and Israeli Law
- Claims Division
- Consular Affairs

Cultural and Scientific Relations
- Promotion of cultural relations
- Bilateral cultural and scientific agreements
- The academic community, research and exchange programme

International Cooperation
- Aid to developing countries
- Diaspora relations with world Jewry
- Division for Inter-Religious Affairs

Protocol and Official Guests Department

The Centre for Political Research

The Situation Room

C. Administration

Department of the Inspector-General

- Personnel Division
- Training Division
- Personnel Services

Computer Services and Communications
- Registry Centre
- Documentation Division

Material Resources Department
- Property Division
- Diplomatic Mail Division
- Transport Division

Finances Department
- Salary Division
- Accounts Division

Several specific changes, however, are noteworthy for insight into the IMFA's, and Israel's, shifting priorities and agenda.

The Middle East and Peace Department

Sponsored by Peres, Beilin and Savir following the September 1993 Oslo accords they personally had engineered with the PLO, the reconstituted Department is meant to: 1) underscore the commitment by Israel to a peaceful, comprehensive settlement of the Arab–Israel conflict; 2) orchestrate the various formats that quickly emerged for meeting Arab interlocutors; 3) facilitate enlarging the Arab peace camp; 4) institutionalize the shared belief their initiative would enable Israel to integrate fully into a 'new Middle East' regional framework. The second rationale assumed particular immediacy since the Madrid (1991) and Oslo (1993) blueprints risked Israeli negotiators working at cross-purposes in the different parallel as well as overlapping diplomatic channels: bilateral and multilateral, official and unofficial, public and back-channel, civilian and military, technical and functional as well as political, interim and final status, with Arab representatives but also extra-regional governments and foreign investors. To the extent these forums and channels have remained active since then, the Middle East and Peace Department has been actively engaged in both tracks: a) the 'bilaterals' with Egypt, the PLO, Jordan and, to a far less extent, Syria, and in establishing step-by-step cultural, commercial and eventually full diplomatic ties with countries like Mauritania, Morocco and Tunisia; b) the 'multilaterals', where the five regional issues of arms control, confidence-building and security, of water, of refugees, of economic development and of environmentalism have been explored. The latter round table format also enabled IMFA officials seconded to the Israeli delegations to pursue their first hesitant encounters with other Arab League states like Algeria, Bahrein, the Gulf Emirates and Yemen. In addition, the Department at times has coordinated among the various government ministries on the bilateral and multilateral peace talks, and also negotiations with Yassir Arafat's Palestinian Authority.

The International Organizations Department

Commemorating the end of Israel's estrangement from the United Nations and many of its affiliated and specialized IGO and NGO agencies, the foreign ministry has reinforced both its permanent missions at UN headquarters in New York, Geneva and the Hague, and the staff in Jerusalem working on globalist issues like peaceful functional development. One immediate indicator is the expanding programme conducted by *Mashav*, the centre for international co-operation, first set up in 1957, which proved extraordinarily successful in building bridges to the newly emergent Afro-Asian countries. Maintained throughout the diplomatic depression years, the technical assistance programme had to be scaled down; nevertheless, over the next 25 years more than 65 000 foreign students participated in specialized training courses.[7] Renewal of ties with most of the developing Third World has made it possible to conduct these seminars on a larger scale. In the two-year period 1991–3, an additional 25 countries participated, including nationals from India, China, the former Soviet republics and Eastern Europe. By 1994 *Mashav* was sponsoring courses in Israel for 3214 participants from 113 nations, including 20 hold-outs as yet denying Israel full recognition.

The Political Planning Division

Flagship of the 1993–4 reform, the Division is ostensibly an 'in house' think-tank. By freeing a select group of staff members from daily operational responsibilities and charging them with defining the objectives of Israeli foreign policy (ranging from the short-and medium-term to longer-range projections), systematic thinking and originality – never exactly the hallmarks of bureaucracy – are being encouraged. In this sense and in one other the IMFA's Political Planning Division and Centre for Political Research possess deeper significance. First, Israeli international behaviour has long been characterized negatively: as *ad hoc*, defensive, reactive, short-sighted, and preoccupied with immediate security situations and crisis management. The post-1993 emphasis on strategic thought and planning are a serious attempt at rectifying this deficiency. Second, IMFA research and planning teams also correct a longstanding structural defect and functional asymmetry.[8] To the extent national strategic assessment and planning took place in the past, they were monopolized by the Israel Defence Forces (IDF), the defence agencies and the security services.

In effect, IMFA in 1993 dared to reclaim a role for itself in policymaking. If utilized by successor foreign ministers, then the Centre and Division – wedding the more passive, minimalist task of research to active planning and political advocacy – will have marked a major Israeli step toward avoiding the pitfalls of conformity and 'groupthink' by filling the need for policy pluralism through 'multiple advocacy'. In the interim, the Division has generated memoranda and position papers for high ministry officials, some of which were then circulated and discussed by the Cabinet, as well as in the Hebrew media.

The Situation Room

Too often in the past Israel found itself outpaced by events (the fall of the Shah, dissolution of the Soviet Union, Kuwait) and therefore a party, direct or indirect, to situations of crisis or near-crisis requiring immediate responses. The upgraded Situation Room represents institutional acknow-ledgement of Israel's fluid external environment, both regional and interna-tional. Fully operational seven days a week, it monitors televised news channels and foreign broadcasts, providing a continuous flow of information to and from the ministry. Staff members become responsible in a crisis for interdepartmental and interministerial coordination, enabling Israel to deli-ver a rapid but also appropriate response.

The Media and Public Affairs Department

Aside from policy initiation and advocacy, if there was one task in former years that the IMFA consistently failed to appreciate, or to claim as its own, it is *hasbara*, information. The strengthened MPA Department offers belated recognition of the need for sophisticated information campaigns on two distinct fronts: overseas, but also at home. Cross-cutting regional as well as functional lines, and touching every aspect of any external affairs ministry's work is that facet of public diplomacy directed toward informing and favour-ably influencing world opinion, while projecting the country's image as a constructive member of the international community. Yet, governed by an almost deterministic and Hobbesian worldview, Israeli foreign policy vir-tually abnegated this entire realm, abandoning the battlefield to Israel's enemies and critics. It is most encouraging, therefore, to find the Division redoubling efforts at disseminating publications and information about life in modern Israel along with explanations of government policy on Middle East peace issues and other political topics. Far more needs to be done by the IMFA, however, in winning over the other target audience, Israeli public opinion, by explaining the work of the ministry and its contribution to national security in the larger sense.

The Training Division

One final agency affected by the 1993 reorganization plan but easily overlooked deserves brief discussion for what it suggests about the ministry, its
programme and capabilities. As its name suggests, the Training Division is
responsible for recruitment and training of fresh entrants into the ministry
and diplomatic service. Beyond its formal duties, the recent experience of the
Division again illustrates the reorientation away from Israeli provincialism,
with its dismissal of the outside world as alien and hostile, in favour of
greater pragmatism.

Testifying to renewed interest in international affairs are the hundreds of
applicants, university graduates with military service behind them, sitting
each year for rigorous qualifying examinations and personal interviews.
IMFA thus has no difficulty filling its quota (in some years less than two
dozen openings).[9] Nor is the selection process as politicized as in former
years, when party affiliation and political patronage more often than not
determined admission. For all these reasons the close impression remains
one of professionalism and dedication among a younger generation of Israeli
diplomats on the whole better educated, more highly motivated and innovative than their predecessors.

Today, the new recruit enters an intense two-year internship run by the
Division involving language training, lectures by academic experts and senior
ministry and government officials, learning at first-hand about the functions
of each branch of the IMFA before being posted to one of the legations
abroad. Since its institution, the training programme has provided a higher
calibre of officials while meeting the unanticipated sudden increase in manpower requirements for staffing newly inaugurated consular and diplomatic
offices in such unfamiliar areas as the Maghrib, the Persian Gulf sheikh-
doms, the Baltic region, the Indian subcontinent and the trans-Caucasus,
where until recently Israeli emissaries were *persona non grata*.

One item of as yet unfinished business is to elevate the status of women in
the Israeli foreign service and to increase their representation. In 1995 the
ministry employed nearly 900 tenured people, but of the 235 senior positions
only 22 (9.4 percent) were filled by women.[10] However, that 23 of the 50 new
cadets admitted in 1996 are women offers encouragement.[11]

What organizational charts fail to convey is the dynamic nature of bureaucratic life, in contradistinction to Israel's first four decades, when relatively
few structural changes were made to the original 1948 design. For one thing,
there is an ongoing mixed pattern of fusion and fragmentation within the
IMFA. The tendency is to combine smaller offices, like those handling
different aspects of *hasbara*, commercial trade or assistance programmes,
within larger divisions and departments as a way of prioritising ends, and also
for achieving economies of scale. At the same time, the reorganization

fractionates what were loose, encompassing agencies, such as the former Africa, Asia and Oceania Department, giving each broad geographic and cultural region due attention and making possible greater area or country specialization. Important in themselves, these reforms reflected a still more profound ideological and attitudinal change in Israeli worldviews: entertaining peace prospects and pursuing normalization instead of assuming pure enmity and planning exclusively for war contingencies.

STRATEGIES AND RESPONSES

Formal blueprints aside, what explains this recent burst of IMFA energy in restructuring internally while reengaging abroad? Conversely, these welcome innovations notwithstanding, why has the ministry failed so abjectly since 1996 in converting these enhanced capabilities into permanent policymaking assets? Phrased differently, is the IMFA destined to revert permanently to being an auxiliary and strictly technical ministry limited to implementing dutifully policies determined by other, stronger agencies? Or might it yet be counted upon as an indispensable agent in crafting those very policies and in Israel's continuing struggle for legitimacy, security, normalization and peaceful commercial intercourse among the nations?

The questions no less than their answers are of more than passing historical interest. I submit they are the key to the foreign ministry's staying power as an organizational actor. In other words, even should 1993–6 appear to the present observer as a refreshing but only temporary respite from an otherwise irreversible decline instead of a genuine point of departure, nonetheless, there are important insights here for the domestic conduct of external affairs by Israel and for its behaviour as a Middle Eastern and international state actor in the future. A set of three principal determinants satisfactorily account for the IMFA's previous record, the two most recent turnabouts (the short rise and abrupt descent) and, ultimately, its future prospects. The ministry, its role and status are essentially hostage to (a) political forces far beyond its control, (b) bureaucratic politics only somewhat in its capacity to affect, and (c) what Henry Kissinger has aptly called the accident of personality.

The policy setting

The first factor underlines the existential primacy of Israeli security, physical and immediate, individual as well as collective. Arab enmity from the outset sacrificed diplomatic niceties, international legal formalities, political and commercial ties, prestige and respectability, and even morality to the argument of clear and present national danger. This shared threat perception was only further reinforced in subsequent decades by the anti-Israel stance of the Soviet bloc and the nonaligned camp alike.

Assuring reasonable perceived security with a fixity of purpose in the midst of a hostile external environment is the common denominator running from the Ben-Gurion era through the governments of Menachem Begin, Yitzchak Shamir and Yitzchak Rabin to that of Binyamin Netanyahu. This consensual and extremely narrow security prism also gave Israeli military experts a virtual free hand in undertaking coercive measures (cross-border operations, preventive strikes, counterterrorism overseas) outside accepted international legal norms and political conventions yet nevertheless deemed necessary for ensuring critical margins of safety. An imbalance in the handling of security and foreign affairs resulted. As one observer described the pre-1967 period: 'the success of the armies doomed the influence of the diplomats'.[12] Thereafter as well, sensitive military and intelligence operations on more than one occasion would be authorized without the knowledge, let alone prior consent of the foreign ministry or its foreign minister. According to this situational explanation a drastic improvement in Israel's security environment alone might enable the IMFA to redress the imbalance. Only in this present decade has Israeli–Arab reconciliation permitted restoring equilibrium and a sense of proportion between security on the one hand and foreign affairs on the other.

Bureaucratic politics

A second, related, factor in the IMFA's resurfacing as an influential actor similarly emphasizes impersonal forces. But in this instance it is the dialectic of the rise and fall of bureaucratic actors within an organizational rather than situational and geopolitical context. In effect one could argue that by the 1990s the 40 year decline of the ministry had reached such a low ebb that the only remaining course was for it to begin a gradual ascent. Israel has yet to incorporate institutional countervalence, suggesting approximate parity among semi-independent agencies, into the sphere of foreign affairs and security. Historically, the institutional price paid for national preoccupation with military security has been progressive subordination of an unassuming IMFA to bureaucratic rivals at once more resourceful (in both the material and the political sense), more authoritative and expansionist. And none more so than the MOD which stands at the head of an even larger and incomparably more powerful defence establishment.

Consistent with bureaucratic politics, the MOD used the situational constant of Middle East strife to arrogate unto itself added authority and functions from the IMFA, the otherwise logical candidate for maintaining relations with foreign governments and international agencies. By the present decade this had come to include the defence establishment's near monopoly over arms purchases and foreign military exports, overseas intelligence-gathering, policy assessment and planning. Also the conduct of negotiations with Arab belligerents, starting with the Egyptian and Syrian separation-of-forces agreements in the aftermath of the 1973 war.

Even successful foreign ministry initiatives like the leap over the wall of Arab hostility in the late 1950s and early 1960s in order to court the Afro–Asian nations were eventually coopted by an increasingly hegemonial defence network. This unequal IMFA–MOD rivalry was only further compounded by repeated interagency clashes over the years, particularly with the *Mossad*, represented by its '*Tevel*' branch entrusted with secret diplomacy toward estranged Arab and non-Arab countries, and also with the IDF and General Security (*Shabak*) intelligence services.

Illustrative are secret conversations with the Jordanians that eventually produced a major diplomatic breakthrough in 1994. Efraim Halevi acted as the *Mossad*'s contact person, travelling to Amman and back at Prime Minister Rabin's instructions. This, despite foreign minister Peres's career-long preoccupation with vindicating the Jordanian option and proving the wisdom in having waited patiently for Hussein. More recently, in reaching out for new ties, the foreign ministry advocated exploring informal contacts with North Korea, only to be blocked by the *Mossad*.[13] This appeared to be due not so much to fundamental differences regarding possible American reaction as the latter's claim to exclusivity in all such clandestine contacts.

Once these structural-functional inequalities became institutionalized in the first decade of independence, becoming more accentuated over time, the IMFA progressively found itself badly outclassed by the defence and the security intelligence establishments. This has particularly been the case whenever a sitting prime minister has also held the defence portfolio (for example, Ben-Gurion, Eshkol, Rabin), as happened following the Rabin assassination. When Shimon Peres moved to the Prime Minister's Office he opted to yield the post of foreign minister and to retain instead the more prestigious defence portfolio in the period from November 1995 to June 1996.

This asymmetry is reflected repeatedly in foreign ministry defeats in what would become increasingly rare instances of head-on interministerial confrontation: in military or civilian liaison with the UN mixed armistice commissions, for example; the Ben-Gurionist 'eye-for-an-eye' reprisal policy of the early 1950s;[14] or over arms transfer guidelines.[15] Not only did a docile IMFA fail in its responsibility to fulfil the role of counterweight, or, barring that, of devil's advocate, at critical times its presence was not even felt.

A late 1970s internal classified report indicates just how badly the IMFA was losing the bureaucratic turf wars. The main findings describe a government agency not functioning as an integrated operation but through isolated satrapies, deprived of authority as well as access to sources of information critical for carrying out its tasks and essentially irrelevant to major political issues like US–Israel relations. In the commission's view, the principal contributing factor was the absence of clear jurisdictional lines from above, making possible creeping encroachment by other predatory agencies. Above all, the defence ministry ran an independent foreign policy, abetted by intelligence operatives within the Office of the Prime Minister using covert channels and reporting exclusively to the prime minister.[16] In sum, the picture in 1977 showed a demoralized group of experienced and dedicated people in Jerusalem, understaffed, underpaid and unappreciated, while envoys despatched abroad to remote diplomatic posts felt isolated and uninformed by a home office itself ignorant of real government policies. More than a decade later the picture still remained essentially the same. Even as late as 1996 deputy IMFA spokesman Yigal Palmor confessed: 'in principle, the people of SIBAT [the MOD agency responsible for supervising and promoting defence exports] don't exactly take pains to consult with us. In practice they don't always keep the ministry in the picture. From this standpoint they operate pretty much independently. They have a very definite, and not flattering, opinion about the IMFA.'[17] Foreign ministry docility and the resultant growing disparity in organizational competencies are painfully apparent in standard indices measuring comparative bureaucratic power, especially budgets and job slots (Table 5.2).

Table 5.2   Basic Ministry Disparities

Foreign Ministry	Defence Ministry	Prime Minister's Office	
999.5**	2000*	561.5	No. of Employees
1.4	2.9	0.8	% Of total Government Employees
851 707	27 600000***	183 280	Budget (In Thousands Of N.I.S.)
0.49	16	0.11	% Of total annual Government Budget

* not including IDF personnel.
** out of the total pool of foreign ministry personnel, 557 are Israeli diplomatic representatives posted abroad.
*** includes the budget of the Israel Defence Forces.

The late 1980s were perhaps the nadir. But then the sliding curve began to reverse itself in accordance with the thesis presented here of a strong correlation between Israel's international standing and the IMFA's own institutional standing. Indeed, IMFA arguably was the prime (albeit temporary) bureaucratic beneficiary of the improved Middle Eastern and global climate in recent years. As of January 1997 bilateral relations numbered 160 and continued to rise. This, in comparison with the previous high of 98 countries recognizing Israel in 1967, which then plummeted to a low of 65 in the wake of the 1973 Yom Kippur war. The curve began to inch upward toward the end of 1986, when the figure reached 79.

Phase I began with the 1979 Egyptian peace treaty, followed in the 1980s by relations with Liberia, Zaire, Spain and others. During phase II (October 1991–September 1993) corresponding to the period between the Madrid and the Oslo peace negotiations, 34 more governments either established or re-established ties. Post-Oslo phase III shows an additional 34 states exchanging ambassadors in the years 1993–6.

Propelled by the sheer number of diplomatic exchanges and fresh openings, in effect extraneous developments dictated internal policymaking reforms. That the IMFA was not merely a passive beneficiary adds a certain poignancy. On the contrary, the ministry – or at least those speaking for it and working out of the Kirya – had a direct hand in creating the new external environment, and served as catalyst for the Oslo peace initiative which, in turn, then boosted its own fortunes as well as Israel's. In consequence, as the 50th anniversary for both approached, the IMFA gave promise – at least on paper – of becoming a more equal bureaucratic actor vis-à-vis its principal competitors.

Personality

A third school of thought attributes the IMFA's resurgence first and foremost to the personal impact of individual leaders – the 'high policy elite' at the top of the bureaucratic pyramid in contrast to the 'technical elites'.[18] Not the ministry but the minister heading it. Thus David Levy, recalling his previous term as political head of the IMFA (1990–2) observed: 'Although at the time it seemed like an impossible goal, I insisted that this ministry occupy a central position in the ongoing processes of thought and action, and I gave the ministry back its status'.[19] But if leadership at the top is the determining factor, then surely Shimon Peres's contribution to the IMFA reawakening must be acknowledged as well. A composite of the three qualities necessary for success at IMFA – statesman, but also administrator and politician, to a greater extent than Levy, Peres has left his personal stamp on the ministry.

This is somewhat ironic in that few individuals probably had as much to do with creating the fundamental MOD–MFA disequilibrium than Peres, who, in his previous bureaucratic career throughout the 1950s and 1960s and, even more, as minister of defence from 1974–7, basically outflanked the sluggish and recessive foreign ministry. Thus, it was he who seized the initiative in promoting Israeli clandestine military friendships; and later formed a Joint Planning Branch of the MOD and the General Staff, with reserve General Avraham ('Abrasha') Tamir as its head and directly responsible to Peres in matters of political strategy.[20]

During his two tours as Minister of Foreign Affairs (1986–8, 1992–5) the ministry benefited in particular from the strong political base Peres enjoyed as leader of the Labour party alignment, as well as his rise to international prominence. Years of survival in Israeli politics made him an articulate spokesman and a tough, experienced political infighter with honed skills for promoting his, and the IMFA's viewpoints. Secondly, as an administrator Shimon Peres encouraged brainstorming and initiatives within the IMFA. In micromanaging the ministry hierarchy he proved receptive to original ideas and broad conceptualization even as he insisted upon detailed position papers and staffwork. In addition, Peres came to acquire respectability as a senior international statesman, and helped put Israel and its policy positions in a favourable light by stressing moderation and the right themes; also, by capitalizing on personal ties with European, socialist, Third World and Jewish leaders.

Yet, Peres's record as foreign minister, particularly in his second stint, is a mixed one. True, Peres may have given permanent officials, department heads, middle-echelon experts and the ministry's rank-and-file considerable latitude in carrying out routine assigned tasks. Yet his preference for private initiatives and compartmentalization may only have improved IMFA's public image, while arguably even retarding its actual progress toward recovery from within. For example, it was his style and preference to concentrate particular relationships and issues exclusively in his own hands. Foremost, everything having to do with exploring Arab openings. Major initiatives (the 1987 London talks with King Hussein of Jordan) and diplomatic successes (the Oslo breakthrough with the PLO) took place entirely outside the ministry. Moreover, Peres and his most trusted advisers, Beilin and Savir, operated in strict secrecy, usually without the advice or cognisance of professional staff members, and often behind the backs of directly concerned ambassadors.[21]

However, the reasons Peres offers for this behaviour are what most prejudices IMFA's reputation. Echoing most statesmen, secrecy and elitist 'lone-wolf' diplomacy are justifiable, he would argue, on discrete grounds of national security. But, in addition, Peres chose to negate ministry capabilities, accusing IMFA officials of scepticism whenever bold policy departures like his visionary 'new Middle East' scheme were vetted, which for Peres confirmed his view of government bureacracies, civilian and military alike, as unimaginative and difficult to work with, but which, in turn, only alienated IMFA professionals.[22]

When some of Peres's more imaginative, albeit premature, ideas such as the League of Arab States converting to a 'Middle East League' and conferring membership on Israel, or a project for massive Arab world computerization, were met with derision or dismissed as impractical, he took immediate offense. By way of rejoinder, he was quoted as condemning 'those who are experts of the past but can't see the future' for their dismal record of 'not supplying the goods' in predicting world developments like the 1973 war, the Kuwait crisis or the collapse of the Soviet Union. Resentment by IMFA permanent staff members reached a peak in an unseemly public clash in early 1996. Several senior staffers openly attacked Savir, director-general and coordinator of peace-related efforts, with ignoring actual conditions in the Arab world, and for not utilizing professional experts in the Middle East talks themselves or in preliminary internal preparations, which they attributed to a desire by Savir (and by implication, his minister and deputy minister) to reach a premature peace settlement. To which Savir, a peace enthusiast, retorted: 'It must be decided exactly what is the ministry's role in the peace process – to emphasise obstacles, or to try and surmount them. The ministry ought to be that factor raising solutions and not merely pointing out the difficulties'.[23]

Whatever else, Peres's own agenda as foreign minister and his strained relations with ministry personnel do confirm the importance of personality, biography and interpersonal chemistry. This is especially true of an unsystematic Israeli foreign policy 'system' of rigid bureaucratization still easily circumvented by 'rogue operations', so-called 'kitchen cabinets', personal undertakings and informal arrangements, and through independent policy departures along secretive back-channels. The Pollard spy affair is cited as one example of a 'rogue operation', while the notion of the 'kitchen cabinet' traces to the late Golda Meir's preference on the eve of formal Cabinet sessions to consult informally at her Ramat-Aviv apartment with trusted Mapai party veterans and colleagues – meetings to which her foreign minister, Abba Eban, was not even invited. Again, strictly from a procedural standpoint, witness the entirely unorthodox Oslo private connection.

Yes, (Defence) Minister

A comparison of the 12 men and women serving as foreign minister since 1948 (Table 5.3) offers useful insights, while highlighting a triad of disturbing larger trends at the IMFA: politicization, militarization, personalization.

First, few foreign ministers assumed office with strong professional credentials or practical experience in high diplomatic posts (Sharett, Eban, Arens). Thus in 1977 Premier Menachem Begin's choice of Moshe Dayan from the Labour alignment opposition to serve as foreign minister in a Likud-led coalition, and Dayan's willingness to 'cross the aisle' might have taken the Israeli political system by surprise. Especially since the logic had little to do with foreign policy bipartisanship; even less with Dayan's schooling in diplomatic niceties or the fine points of international legal jurisprudence. Rather the move was meant to exploit Dayan's global military reputation, name recognition and *persona* in Arab eyes. Less appreciated,

Table 5.3 Israel's Policy Elite

FOREIGN MINISTER	DEFENCE MINISTER	PRIME MINISTER	YEAR
			1948–9
			1949–50
	David Ben-Gurion	David Ben-Gurion	1950–1
Moshe Sharett			1951–2
			1952–3
			1953–4
	Pinhas Lavon	Moshe Sharett	1954–5
			1955–6
			1956–7
			1957–8
	David Ben-Gurion	David Ben-Gurion	1958–9
			1959–60
Golda Meir			1960–1
			1961–2
			1962–3
			1963–4
	Levi Eshkol		1964–5
		Levi Eshkol	1965–6
			1966–7
			1967–8
			1968–9
Abba Eban			1969–70
	Moshe Dayan		1970–1
		Golda Meir	1971–2
			1972–3
			1973–4
			1974–5
Yigal Allon	Shimon Peres	Yitzchak Rabin	1975–6
			1976–7
			1977–8
Moshe Dayan	Ezer Weizman		1978–9
		Menachem Begin	1979–80
	Menachem Begin		1980–1
	Ariel Sharon		1981–2
Yitzchak Shamir			1982–3
	Moshe Arens	Yitzchak Shamir	1983–4
		Shimon Peres	1984–5
			1985–6
	Yitzchak Rabin		1986–7
Shimon Peres			1987–8
		Yitzchak Shamir	1988–9
Moshe Arens			1989–90

David Levy	Moshe Arens		1990–1
			1991–2
			1992–3
Shimon Peres	Yitzchak Rabin	Yitzchak Rabin	1993–4
			1994–5
Ehud Barak	Shimon Peres	Shimon Peres	1995–6
David Levy	Yitzchak Mordechai	Binyamin Netanyahu	1996–7

and yet what really made the Begin–Dayan working relationship possible was their ideological compatibility. On the central issue of the 1967 territories both men were determined anti-partitionists.

Second, politics were the criterion for selection: personal loyalty to the prime minister (Meir, Shamir), importance for coalition-building (Allon, Peres, Levy). Despite being the first prime minister with enhanced executive powers to be elected directly in nationwide elections, and contrary to his pledge to make cabinet appointments on the basis of professional excellence, in 1996 Binyamin Netanyahu's selection of David Levy as foreign minister was dictated by Levy's political standing and critical importance for forming a broad coalition. Students of Israeli politics well recall the strained relations between the two men dating back to the time when the positions were reversed, and Levy, in his earlier term at the foreign ministry, had Netanyahu's selection as deputy imposed on him by Yitzchak Shamir.

Striking, too, is how many ministers came to the IMFA schooled in the influence-by-force approach rather than the influence-by-persuasion approach after a previous career in the defence establishment: as senior defence ministry officials (Peres, Arens), IDF chief-of-staff (Dayan, Barak), or intelligence agency operative (Shamir). This has certainly contributed to militarization of foreign policy, its subordination to the defence establishment and to military definitions of national security at the expense of diplomatic considerations. Ehud Barak, rivalling Moshe Dayan as the most political Chief-of-Staff in Israel's history, provides the most recent illustration. After 35 years in uniform, as foreign minister in effect he doubled as unofficial government spokesman and military commentator during operation 'Grapes of Wrath' against the Hizbullah in southern Lebanon. His meetings with members of the diplomatic colony were more in the nature of military briefings.

Fourth, those who might have been eminently qualified were outclassed politically, or reluctant to fight for the ministry's interests and policy recommendations (Sharett, Eban). Fifth, ministerial success depended less on utilization of IMFA expertise and cumulative bureaucratic experience than interpersonal chemistry and confidences, almost always bad, in the triangular relationship between prime minister-foreign minister-defence minister (Ben-Gurion and Sharett; Meir–Eban–Dayan; Rabin–Peres–Allon; Shamir–Peres–Rabin; Rabin–Peres; Netanyahu–Levy).

The 'accident' or randomness of personality notwithstanding, our analysis of the Ministry of Foreign Affairs suggests that only in the three-year interval considered here does its experience run counter to the logic of institutional declinism. Threatened to the point of trivialization, in 1993–6 the IMFA managed to reverse its decades-long descent, gearing itself organizationally as well as psychologically for an era premised upon Israel's active engagement around the globe. Yet these IMFA successes are not to be exaggerated. A favourable prognosis is inappropriate simply because the ministry's deeper problems persist into the future. Here, attention is drawn to five particular constraints.

To an inordinate degree IMFA's ranking in the decisionmaking process remains hostage to the political process, and to the choice of foreign minister. His or her character and personality, political clout, worldview, leadership style, conception of office and personal agenda will affect the ministry's status and influence. Irrespective of the final choice, every changing of the guard also heightens uncertainty and emphasizes discontinuities.

Similarly, IMFA fortunes, much like its operational environment, are contingent on how the salient peace and security issue is going to be resolved. The country's new–found receptivity, its international standing, regional integration, trade ties and attractiveness for foreign investment are all conditional upon Israel being perceived as committed to liquidating the comprehensive Arab–Israel conflict. Should the 1999 timetable for Palestinian–Israeli reconciliation be set back, or the Arab–Israel security zone destabilize, with Israel perceived as intransigent and culpable, the goal of Middle Eastern and international normalization could unravel. This would be a double disaster: for Israel among the nations, as well as for the ministry's domestic input into national policymaking.

Politicization and militarization of foreign policy – putting politics over professionalism, and security considerations over diplomatic ones – are the third and fourth abiding cautionary signs. Illustrating the former is the problem of 'parachutists', those political appointees brought in laterally from outside. An agreement between the ministry executive and the staff committee permits eleven political appointments (the Washington embassy being foremost) on the grounds that sensitive posts should be filled by individuals with direct access to the prime minister or foreign minister, rather than working through regular ministry channels. Parachuting is an obvious source of contention, adversely affecting IMFA operating procedures; it is also demoralizing since these choice appointments to what are also singularly sensitive posts such as the UN, London, Paris, Moscow and Bonn, come at the expense of career diplomats and block the promotion process for junior officers.

Militarized foreign affairs symbiotically express themselves in two ways: further aggrandisement by various branches of the defence establishment in extending their spheres of competence at the IMFA's expense, and the consequent effect of key decisions being taken by the cabinet primarily on military as opposed to diplomatic considerations. The reaction of the military and intelligence establishments to the Oslo gambit by IMFA triumvirate Peres–Beilin–Savir is a classic case in point. Presented with a *fait accompli*, the MOD and IDF characteristically fought back by emphasizing their importance for implementation of all security provisions. And they quickly acquired a strong 'presence' on each bilateral and multilateral delegation, even chairing several, with Premier Rabin's acquiescence, whether because of second-thoughts, his own pro-military predisposition or suspicion of Peres.

As a matter of fact, the list of competitors actually threatened to increase in 1996 with incoming Prime Minister Binyamin Netanyahu's statement of intent to create an American-style national security council. Initial blueprints called for this NSC forum to brief the prime minister on the eve of visits abroad and provide the government with ongoing advice on issues broadly relating to national security, to oversee the government's various security arms, to mastermind the peace negotiations and, of particular note, to formulate Israeli foreign and defence policy through interministerial working groups comprised of the relevant agencies. As an earnest of his intentions, Netanyahu appointed the eminently qualified outgoing director-general of the defence ministry, David Ivri, to head the new agency.

This NSC panel would have been welcomed at the national level, and is certainly long overdue. The absence of mechanisms for presenting alternative assessments and policy options was one of the principal findings of the 1974 Agranat commission which investigated the 1973 Yom Kippur War intelligence failure. Its recommendation that independent bodies be set up within the different ministries, including the IMFA, was subsequently resisted, however, including by Moshe Dayan when he himself served as foreign minister in the late 1970s. Because IMFA in recent years had reclaimed for itself some of the above tasks, such as long-range planning and orchestrating an initiatory peace diplomacy, this council, if established, might have marked a setback for IMFA aspirations at regaining the high ground of policymaking. In the event it never materialized, but not because of IMFA objections. Rather, intense lobbying by a hegemonial military establishment unenthusiastic, to say the least, at prospects of yielding, or sharing, accustomed authority, plus the personal intervention of the new Minister of Defence, Yitzchak Mordechai, representing his ministry's interests, were what defeated Netanyahu's initiative at serious organizational reform.

Economic statecraft, rising to the fore, also inserts the Ministries of Finance and Industry and Trade more directly into the foreign policy process, along with private entrepreneurs and corporate interests. Nor can a quasi-state institution like the Jewish Agency, whose goals include providing material and moral support for Jewish communities throughout the world, encouraging immigration from the former Soviet Union and the West, increasing the Jewish diaspora's involvement in Israel and providing progressive Jewish education services, be omitted. All of these to some degree impact on Israel's external relations and impinge on the IMFA.

This multiplicity of bureaucratic actors, unfair division of labour and cumbersome policy apparatus, even without a strong NSC, is certain to aggravate policy coordination and consensus. In fact, the point is made embarrassingly clear by the first months of the Netanyahu government, when policy disarray and ineptitude plagued the new administration. The prime minister was forced to scale down the NSC plan; cabinet members were not made privy to Netanyahu's peace strategy; interpersonal friction and poor chemistry marked relations between the premier and both his defence and foreign ministers, but also with the heads of the intelligence services. Fully consistent with the thesis of a severely circumscribed IMFA, any really serious negotiation with the Egyptians, Jordanians, Palestinians and Americans was conducted on Israel's behalf either by Netanyahu and his lieutenants operating out of the Prime Minister's Office or by Defence Minister Mordechai and defence ministry personnel. IMFA's interagency competition and 'turf wars', in short, continue in accentuated form.

REMEDIAL MEASURES

The five constraints are certainly formidable, with some clearly beyond IMFA control. Nevertheless, this said, group dynamics within the Israeli system do allow greater room for manoeuvre than meets the outside observer's eye. In other words, the foreign ministry cannot be absolved of responsibility for its own bureaucratic fate. Instances of genuine co-operation with the defence ministry may be rare, for example, yet they are possible. In March, 1995 an initiative by the Disarmament and Arms Control Division of IMFA offering Angola, Mozambique and other strife-torn Third World countries assistance in dismantling and destroying anti-personnel land mines received the full support of both MOD and the IDF. Certainly in the past much depended on the the IMFA's own intramural errors, either of omission or commission.

One extreme definitely to be avoided would be a unifocal preoccupation with a single issue area. Equating foreign policy as synonymous with either the American connection or Mideast peace negotiations risks being oblivious to other relations and missing openings elsewhere. So, too, there is danger in the opposite extreme of allowing an expanding web of diffuse relationships to overwhelm and defy policy integration, leaving the ministry's own personnel to deal in isolation with matters nevertheless germane for other IMFA branches, possibly even at cross-purposes. In one memorable instance the failure to coordinate separate efforts toward Britain by the European desk and towards Argentina in the South American section proved embarrassing for Israel during the 1982 Falklands war. The Middle East Department's interest in a regional alignment with Turkey, for instance, is fraught with ramifications for Israeli–European ties because of Ankara's human rights record, and needs to be carefully calibrated. No less so, enthusiastic patronage by the MOD for the 1996 military pact with Turkey in the face of the Erbakan government's support for Islamic solidarity and defence ties with Iran.

No matter who serves as foreign minister, one thing is certain: the ministry itself will have to make do with little. As we have seen, IMFA was 'downsized' long before the term ever came into vogue. The ministry has problems enough just in fighting an uphill struggle to regain former tasks, maintain present staffing levels and budget allocation to dare contemplate substantial increases in personnel and budget commensurate with any further expanded responsibilities. Consequently, it will be asked to carry out its overseas missions despite being overstretched and faced with overload.[24]

While not offered as a panacea, one recommended IMFA response is to learn from the MOD and to work at cultivating its own client relationships. It is too easily forgotten that diplomacy involves addressing a domestic audience as well as an international one. Alliance formation, after all, is as much a feature of bureaucratic politics as it is of domestic and international politics. Unlike its defence ministry rival, but like all foreign ministries, the IMFA has no constituency at home – save to the extent foreign governments through their diplomatic envoys resident in Israel strongly voice such diplomatic arguments as UN support and economic carrots and sticks. Still, much can be done to heighten Israeli public awareness of the foreign service and its ceaseless if unsung efforts at promoting the national interest.

Domestic public relations *hasbara* requires lobbying for the backing of the Knesset and its Foreign Affairs and Security Committee. It also demands building bridges to special target groups: academics and research institutes, the media, business and corporate leaders with important investments, contracts and contacts abroad, and therefore with a stake in regularized, normal relations with the rest of the world. So, too, can this potential support system be widened to include ethnic emigre associations as well as Israeli activists and voluntary groups identifying with international NGOs. Surely refreshing is the palpable desire of younger Israelis for normalcy, to promote tourism and open borders, and for their country to be more involved in international relief operations and supranational organizations.[25]

CONCLUSIONS

There is much at stake in whether or not the Israeli foreign ministry does actually succeed in consolidating its improved institutional position independent of the personality factor, and the identity of its minister. At the national level, any reversion by Israel to its former insular, hard-line posture would indeed be tragic for the country's chances to integrate into emerging regional and other transnational frameworks. At the second, organizational, level, an outcast, 'pariah' state would have the attendant effect of devaluating the IMFA viewpoint that foreign relations do matter, and make the defence establishment's military stance all but incontestable. On the other hand, should the recent upward trend resume, due to some fortuitous blend of external, bureaucratic and coalition politics, it would require that the IMFA's traditionally negative stereotype be revised, for then the Ministry of Foreign Affairs would no longer be dismissed as a prestigious but secondary, inconsequential player.

The benefits are actually higher, considerably higher. For a more dynamic, fully engaged MFA in Israel could provide students of comparative foreign policies and the decisionmaking process with several timely object lessons. Firstly, MFAs retain a significant role in world affairs, but that role is neither automatic nor guaranteed. In order to survive, government agencies, like any living organism, must be capable of adaptation. In this instance, by foreign ministries learning from their cumulative experience and past mistakes such as neglecting their domestic political front or being delinquent in harnessing modern management techniques and technologies. Not to do so is to relapse into institutional decline and to face permanent obsolescence.

Second, adaptation, however, also implies fighting back. No matter how high-minded, foreign ministries are not exempt from political struggle. On the contrary. They are duty-bound to be fully committed and also fully engaged. Their very institutional staying power and role depend on the inevitable interplay of personality and setting but, above all, organizational politics – with the good and bad this implies.

Third, in role definition there is still a distinction to be made between a secondary and subordinate position as opposed to marginalization, which is where the IMFA once again threatens to find itself. The former status is, to be sure, unfortunate; the latter, not only unhealthy but unacceptable. Because of the longstanding structural and functional imbalances in Israeli security and foreign affairs, it is hard to imagine any return in the foreseeable future to a more healthy institutional equilibrium. Still, one can only hope these lessons are not lost upon Israeli patrons of the art of diplomacy who have the foreign ministry's interests, and the national interest, at heart.

NOTES

1   Surely one manifestation of its fall from grace is how little scholarly attention the foreign ministry has received. Such material as does exist is largely limited to collected documents and autobiographies. Useful guides to the workings of the Ministry and insightful personal memoirs include: Abba Eban, *An Autobiography* (New York: Random House, 1977); Gideon Rafael, *Destination Peace. Three Decades of Israeli Foreign Policy* (New York: Stein and Day, 1981); Moshe Dayan, *Breakthrough* (New York: Knopf, 1981); Shimon Peres and Arye Naor, *Battling for Peace. A Memoir* (New York: Random House, 1995).

Another genre are works that focus upon crisis decisionmaking at the expense of the routine execution of policy, and those interested in substantive issues and policies rather than the process of actually *making* policy. In a separate category are generalized treatments, often by outsiders far removed from the actual workings and informal group dynamics. One example from many is Chapter 5. 'Israeli foreign policy', in R. D. McLaurin, Mohammed Mughisuddin and Abraham R. Wagner, *Foreign Policy Making in the Middle East. Domestic Influences on Policy in Egypt, Iraq, Israel, and Syria* (New York and London: Praeger Publishers, 1977), pp. 169–218, of which a mere two pages are devoted to policy*making*. The author has sought to correct this oversight. Aaron S. Klieman, *Israel & the World After 40 Years* (Washington: Pergamon-Brassey's, 1990), especially Chapters 5–7, dealing with policy formulation, coordination and implementation.

2   This attitudinal sea-change in public and official views on the question of Israel's place in world affairs is analyzed in Klieman, 'New directions in Israel's foreign policy', in Efraim Karsh ed., *Peace in the Middle East: The Challenge for Israel* (London: Frank Cass, 1994), pp. 96–117.

3   Eban, *The New Diplomacy. International Affairs in the Modern Age* (New York: Random House, 1983).

4   A good place to start in tracing the evolution of diplomacy and the changing role of institutionalized foreign ministries are Sir Harold Nicolson's two surveys: *The Evolution of Diplomatic Method* (London: Constable & Company, 1954), and *Diplomacy* (New York: Harcourt, Brace, 1939). On the more recent phase, see: Paul Gordon Lauren, *Diplomats and Bureaucrats* (Stanford: The Hoover Institution Press, 1976), and James Der Derian, *On Diplomacy* (Oxford: Basil Blackwell, 1987). In analyzing diplomacy's geneology, he refers to 'anti-diplomacy', 'neo-diplomacy' and 'techno-diplomacy'. More readable is Keith Hamilton and Richard Langhorne, *The Practice of Diplomacy* (London and New York: Routledge, 1995). After reviewing diplomacy's evolution, theory and administration, the authors entitle their concluding chapter 'Diplomacy Transformed and *"Transcended"*'. (Italics mine).

5   Details of the Ministry's plans for an immediate shakeup were presented by Director-General Uri Savir at a press conference, and reported in *Haaretz*, 5 May 1993. Supplementary material on the previous arrangement and on the phased reconstruction of the IMFA's outmoded apparatus is drawn from *The Israel Government Yearbook*, (Jerusalem: The Government Printing Office), for the years 5750/1990 (July 1991), and 1993–4 (1995).

6   Contents of the policy paper appeared in the *Haaretz* daily edition of 25 February 1994.

7   *Haaretz*, 12 February 1993.

8   A study of national security decisionmaking carried out at Israel's National Defence College in the mid-80s notes 'The IDF has at its disposal the most sophisticated and efficient staff system, far outweighing the staffs of the Prime Minister, the Foreign Ministry and the Defence Minister all put together, and as a result it exercises virtually exclusive power over strategic and tactical questions.' Cited in Yehuda Ben-Meir, *National Security Decisionmaking: the Israeli Case* (Tel-Aviv: the Jaffee Center for Strategic Studies, 1986), p. 71. In a later expanded version, the IMFA does not even merit entry as an Index item by Ben-Meir, himself a former Deputy Foreign Minister in the years 1981–4. *Civil-Military Relations in Israel* (New York: Columbia University Press, 1995).

9   In 1991, for example, only 25 candidates were selected from among over 800 applicants. This was an increase of 15 compared with the year before. *The Jerusalem Post*, 6 March 1992.

10   Tamar Hermann and Gila Kurtz, 'Prospects for democratizing foreign policy-making: the gradual empowerment of Israeli women', *The Middle East Journal* 49: 3, Summer 1995, p. 458. As of 1995, only five out of 97 heads of diplomatic delegations were women i.e. 5.1 per cent. But four of them had been appointed that year (see p. 461).

11   *Haaretz*, 25 January 1996. The official figures were provided by the Deputy Foreign Minister, Eli Dayan.

12   Martin Mayer. *The Diplomats* (Garden City, New Jersey: Doubleday & Company, 1983), p. 341.

13   *Haaretz*, 18 March and 31 May 1996.

14   These and other episodes from the first decade of Israeli diplomacy are recalled by the first director-general of the IMFA, Walter Eytan, in his personalized account, *The First Ten Years* (New York: Simon and Schuster, 1958). A recent scholarly investigation of the policy of retaliation during the 1950s is Benny Morris. *Israel's Border Wars, 1949–1956* (Oxford: Clarendon Press, 1993).

15   On marginalization of the IMFA in so important an area of external relations as military transfers, see Klieman, *Israel's Global Reach: Arms Sales as Diplomacy* (Washington: Pergamon-Brassey's, 1985). On the Ministry and its plight in the early 1980s, see Mordechai Gazit, 'The role of the foreign ministry', *The Jerusalem Quarterly* 18, Winter, 1981, pp. 3–14.

16   The report and findings of the Gur-Arye 'Commission to Study the Organisational and Operational Structure of the Foreign Ministry' are presented and discussed in the Hebrew-language daily, *Maariv*, 15 July 1977.

17   The IMFA spokesman is quoted in the weekly supplement to *Haaretz*, 3 May 1996. The issue of uncoordinated arms sales arose in the context of an alleged supply relationship with Nigeria.

18   The distinction between the two sets of policy and technical elites is drawn by Michael Brecher in his extensive study, *The Foreign Policy System of Israel* (New Haven: Yale University Press, 1972). Also useful for his enquiry into the organizational model of decisionmaking is Graham T. Allison, *Essence of Decision* (Boston: Little, Brown, 1971).

19   From remarks during the transition ceremony at the Ministry on 19 June 1996. Emphasis added.

20   Avraham Tamir, *A Soldier in Search of Peace* (London: Weidenfeld and Nicolson, 1988).

21   The story is told when the tables were reversed. In 1988, IMFA Director-General Avraham Tamir was seen on the streets of Moscow in the course of an uncoordinated 48-hour visit (actually, at the highest level since the rupture of relations in 1967), to which other embarrassed top ministry officials

expressed surprise and outrage. All Foreign Minister Peres could do was promise the matter would be clarified upon the errant Tamir's return. *The Jerusalem Post*, 28 November 1988. On the 'prominence' of secretive meetings and contacts in Israeli foreign relations, see Klieman, *Statecraft in the Dark. Israel's Practice of Quiet Diplomacy* (Boulder: Westview Press, 1988).

22   *The Jerusalem Post*, 23 May 1996, p. 13.

23   The accusation and counter-accusation are reported in *Haaretz*, 8 March 1996.

24   Despite recruitment having trebled in the rush to fill junior posts necessitated by the opening of so many new political and trade relationships, the IMFA as a whole remains understaffed. Also underfunded, with the cost for maintaining a diplomat abroad estimated at well over $70 000 a year, according to *The Jerusalem Post*, 'The "greening" of the world map', 6 March 1992.

25   That public support can be gained in Israel for civilian and humanitarian involvement through the UN and other agencies is demonstrated by the endorsement given the IMFA's plan to send a field hospital and medical team to Rwanda in 1994, and then 30 police officers to Haiti, in lieu of military personnel, but as part of international peacekeeping efforts. *Haaretz*, 2 August, 12 and 14 September 1994.

6 Japan
Towards a More Proactive Foreign Ministry
Kyoji Komachi

Following Japan's opening up to the outside world, the Foreign Ministry was established in 1869. The Meiji Restoration of 1868 had ushered in a completely new environment: a Japan which until then had been peacefully secluded from the rigours of colonialism engulfing Asia was suddenly exposed to the harsh reality of European-dominated international relations. However, Japan's international profile gradually increased and, in the years leading up to World War II, the Foreign Ministry came to occupy a prestigious position within the Government. For example, the budget of the Foreign Ministry accounted for roughly one percent of total government spending on average. This was no small figure, given the military's huge share of overall government spending. However, all the achievements came to nothing with World War II.[1]

After World War II, the Japanese foreign service was initially busy dealing and liaising with the American occupation forces. It was not until 1950 that it reappeared in the international arena through the opening of its liaison offices in New York, San Francisco and elsewhere. However they had to wait until the signing of the San Francisco Peace Treaty in 1952 and the recovery of full independence before anything approaching fully-fledged diplomatic activities were resumed. With the re-establishment of diplomatic relations with the Soviet Union in 1956 and Japan's accession into the United Nations in the same year, the Japanese Foreign Ministry truly regained its place in the world.

Japan's acceptance through membership of the UN into the international community in 1956 marked a watershed in the country's post-war rehabilitation. Exuding new hope, the Japanese Foreign Ministry published its very first diplomatic Blue Book and announced the three principles underlying foreign policy of the 'new' Japan:

a) placing importance on the ideas and activities of the United Nations;
b) co-operation and policy coordination with the Free World;
c) retention of Japan's identity as a member of Asia.

However, in the harsh reality of the Cold War, it was not always feasible to honour the first principle. This, in real life diplomacy, meant more emphasis on the second principle, in particular on our relations with America, as well as on the third principle. Moreover, on political and security issues, Japan maintained a very low profile due to the legacy of World War II. This allowed the foreign service to focus its efforts primarily on integrating a battered Japanese economy into the Bretton-Woods system by way of accession to the General Agreement on Tariffs and Trade (GATT), the International Monetary Fund (IMF), the Organisation for Economic Co-operation and Development (OECD) and other relevant economic organizations.

After the GDP of Japan exceeded one hundred billion US dollars, thereby ascending to third place after the USA and West Germany, Japan was welcomed into virtually all major economic and trade organizations of the world. 'Economic recovery and prosperity' was the slogan and goal of post-war Japan. It was not at all surprising, therefore, to find in the 1960s and 1970s the extraordinary emphasis placed by Japanese foreign policy on its economic and trade relationship with the West. In the mid 1960s, Japan overtook West Germany by the sheer size of its GNP to occupy the position of number two economy in the Free World. The first oil crisis of 1973 was instrumental in making Japan more globally oriented as it led to Japan's acceptance as a member of the G-7 Economic Summit.

However, the Japanese foreign service was not well-equipped to deal with the rapid upward rise in Japan's international status. The Japanese Foreign Ministry suffered very much from drastic cuts in its budget and personnel after the war. For example, in the immediate post-war years the Foreign Ministry budget languished at under 0.1 percent of overall government spending, compared to the 1 percent level it reached before the war. Such a lamentable situation did not last long due to Japan's quick economic recovery. Today the Japanese Foreign Ministry is probably one of the very few government departments which enjoys a preferential allocation of resources both in terms of budget and personnel. Currently the Japanese foreign service has a network of 191 missions subdivided into 113 bilateral embassies, 7 permanent representatives and 71 Consulates-General protecting the interests of Japan. It had 2006 staff working in Tokyo against 3159 in overseas missions totaling 5165 in the course of the 1998 fiscal year. This can be compared with the staffing levels of other advanced countries:

UK	7 287
France	12 569
Germany	9 396
Italy	5 295
US	24 011

CHALLENGES

As the economic might of Japan grew beyond traditional and natural bound-aries, the scope of its diplomacy also widened. Its budget in 1996 reached the level of US$7.5 billion – almost half the size of the US State Department budget. The oil crisis of 1973 revealed an inherent weakness of the foreign service in its failure to maintain close contact with such non-traditional partners as the oil-producing countries of the Middle East. This crisis trig-gered the increase in training of Arabic-speaking diplomats. The G-7 sum-mit, hosted for the first time by Japan in 1979, demonstrated the mismatch between the prestige and status accorded to Japan as a G-7 member and the poor infrastructure of the foreign service in conducting appropriate diplo-matic activities. This prompted the Foreign Ministry in 1979 to launch a six-year programme to increase the number of staff from the level of 3400 to 5000, which would put the Japanese foreign service on a par with West Germany and Italy, at least in terms of staff numbers. The main focus of the programme was directed towards strengthening Japan's mid- to long-term policy planning capability, the bilateral geographical desks and such new areas of diplomacy as development assistance and consular work to cope with the rapid expansion in the number of Japanese working abroad.

In 1983 the report on administrative reform of the Japanese Government emphasized the need to strengthen the coordination function of the Prime Minister's office and recommended the establishment of three offices: inter-nal affairs, external affairs and security affairs. In parallel to the above efforts, and in the same context, another attempt was made to improve the quality of overall policy planning of the Foreign Ministry. As we have seen, designating additional resources to the policy planning function both for overall diplomacy and for bilateral relationships was one of the main features of the 5000 strong foreign service programme of 1979. In 1984 the Bureau for International Information Analysis and Research was established within the Foreign Ministry to support and feed sophisticated analytical material for policy planners. This step has to be seen also in the context of the above report.

As the profile of Japan as an international player of significance rose, the Prime Minister's role in diplomacy increased. The 1983 Williamsburg Sum-mit confirmed the security of the West as indivisible, thus anchoring Japan firmly in the Western Alliance. This added momentum to the drive to establish external affairs as well as security affairs offices reporting directly to the Prime Minister. This was heralded by some as a move away from a very traditional bottom-up approach to a bolder and more initiative-oriented style of leadership from the Prime Minister.

Decisions on these changes were taken as a result of serious discussion and directed first and foremost at efforts to face up to new diplomatic challenges, including political and security related challenges. The international community no longer condoned Japan's role as a traditional but very taciturn economic giant (the second largest economic power in the West since 1964).

The need for redirection away from economic issue-oriented foreign policy towards a more balanced approach started to be felt as early as the late 1960s. This led in 1970 to the restructuring and merging of geographical desks which had existed side by side in the same Ministry and had dealt with either bilateral economic issues or bilateral political issues exclusively. In 1979 the Latin America Affairs Bureau was established which completed the organizational process towards a comprehensive, geographically equipped foreign service.

The reforms of the 1980s were based on the concepts outlined in the report on administrative reform of 1983, which primarily called for the streamlining of the number of layers in government departments, thereby strengthening the coordinating role of the Prime Minister's office to cope with the rising budget deficit. This report also emphasized the increasing linkage between domestic and external affairs, and proposed a new line-up of offices to advise the Prime Minister, including the above-mentioned office of external affairs together with the office of security affairs. These offices were supposed to function as a secretarial headquarters to organize ministerial-level meetings hosted by the Prime Minister to coordinate the external activities of various government departments and to deliver one single coherent policy, including foreign policy.

All these administrative reform efforts were in areas of both external affairs and security matters and were sparked by the deepening of global interdependency among nations, not only in economic and trade issues, but also in the security area. This process also reflected the increasing number of players at home involved with setting the foreign policy agenda. The question is, who is really setting the agenda? Due to the bitter experience of pre-war diplomacy, where the military acted on its own agenda separate to that of the foreign office and brought the nation haphazardly to the brink of war, foreign policymakers after the war made a very clear stand against double-channel diplomacy.

This tenet has never been challenged by successive governments and has resulted in the emphasis being placed upon the coordination of a coherent foreign policy among the various ministries. During the 1960s through to the early 1980s, when the Japanese economy was more regulated than it is today, there was a well-known tug-of-war under way between the Foreign Ministry and other ministries, in particular the Ministry of International Trade and Industry (MITI) and the Ministry of Finance. It related to different emphases between ministries, the Foreign Ministry leaning towards less regulation with MITI and the Ministry of Finance favouring regulation to protect the Japanese economy. Moreover, the tug-of-war particularly reflected the process whereby both MITI and the Ministry of Finance tried to reach agreements with their counterparts by bypassing the Foreign Ministry. This raised within the Foreign Ministry the above-mentioned fear of double diplomacy, such as had been practised before the war. However, as the Japanese economy became increasingly deregulated, this difference began to disappear rapidly.

The second question concerns the global trend towards the transfer of decisionmaking power, particularly on economic and trade issues, to such international organizations as GATT, IMF and OECD. More recently the Asia Pacific Co-operation forum (APEC) has adopted a leading role as an Asia–Pacific coordination forum for economic and trade activities. This poses a similar challenge to the Japanese foreign service to that faced in European capitals. However, the depth and degree of the transfer of power by Japan to these international institutions is not at all comparable with the situation facing EU nations. Therefore the Japanese foreign service has been spared the challenges many European counterparts are facing in the unification process.

A more pressing issue for Japan is the ongoing soul-searching on what Japan's new role should be. We have been rather cautious since the end of the war, given the serious concern by some neighbours about the role to be played by Japan. It was only in the late 1950s that a serious discussion took place regarding the security issue relating to the new constitution. From that time on, predominantly pacifist ideas reigned over the country until the Iran–Iraq war of the 1980s brought into focus the question of whether there was any auxiliary military role for Japan to play, including the dispatch of minesweepers to the Gulf. This did not materialize and did not lead to any change in the Government's position. However, the Gulf War of 1991 left Japan no option but to extend a huge financial contribution totaling US$13 billion as well as to dispatch Self Defense Forces minesweepers to the area at the end of the war[2].

The most unforgettable episode for many Japanese in the context of the Gulf crisis was not so much the lukewarm reception for its US$13 billion contribution by the world media nor the division of public opinion concerning the dispatch of troops, but the glaring absence of Japan in the list of countries to which the Kuwaiti Government expressed its appreciation via an advertisement in *The New York Times* at the end of the war. It was now recognized that money was not a panacea for all issues. This left many Japanese pondering whether a country the size of Japan could continue to carry on without a security-related contribution in the future. Here the trauma of the Gulf War stimulated a far-reaching discussion going back to the basic question of how to interpret the Article 9 of the constitution.[3] One of the offshoots of this was the conscious drive by the Government to pursue permanent membership of the Security Council of the United Nations.

In summary, the challenges for the Japanese foreign service since the war have been threefold: first, to increase the sheer number of staff simply to cope with the increasing, multi-faceted requirement of the foreign service as a result of the rising profile of the country. Second, in a similar vein, to play the crucial role in building a single coherent foreign policy and not to repeat the pre-war mistake of double-channel diplomacy. Third, to identify a new role for Japan in response to the rapidly-changing environment surrounding the country and the rising expectations in the rest of the world concerning Japan's global role. All these three challenges were closely interrelated but the first two were easier to comprehend and more readily attracted consensus.

A 5000-strong foreign service was achieved in the course of fiscal year 1996, albeit after a ten-year delay. The share of the budget for the foreign service bounced back from 0.1 percent in the immediate post-war years to the 1 percent level of the total government budget in the 1995 fiscal year. The budget has been increasing at an above-average rate. This achievement has to be discounted somewhat due to the fact that more than half of the budget is eaten up by the ever-increasing overseas assistance budget, which in other countries is allocated to other, independent government agencies.

One important effect of the Gulf War syndrome was the attempt to review the basic premises for Japanese official development assistance (ODA); one being a humanitarian concern for the victims of poverty and famine, the other comprising a recognition of interdependence among the nations of the international community, whereby the stability and development of poorer countries is indispensable to the peace and stability of the entire world, including Japan. In April 1991, the Japanese Government announced that it would pay full attention in the implementation of its ODA to:

- trends in military expenditure by recipient countries
- trends in the development and production of mass destructive weapons by recipient countries
- trends in export and import of weapons by recipient countries
- efforts to promote democratization and introduce market-oriented economies as well as respect for basic human rights and freedoms on the part of recipient countries.

This was the first step by Japan since it had started extending assistance in 1954 to introduce a more political element to its ODA policy.

In June 1992, the Japanese Government adopted the ODA Charter, which reflects and develops the above principles. It is a comprehensive statement of Japan's ODA policy setting out basic concepts, principles and priority areas from a long-term perspective. It embraces the following four points:

1) humanitarian considerations;
2) recognition of interdependence among nations of the international community;
3) conservation of the global environment;
4) support for self-help efforts of recipient countries.

Expanding this basic philosophy, the following principles will be given consideration as constituting the core of the ODA Charter:

• compatibility between preservation of the environment and development;
• avoidance of the use of ODA funds for military purposes which could
  inflame international conflicts;
• monitoring of military spending of developing countries, their activities of
  developing and producing weapons of mass destruction, and the level of
  export or import of weapons;
• monitoring of activities in promoting democratization in developing countries, as well as their efforts to introduce a market-oriented economy and
  to protect basic human rights and freedoms of their citizens.

Of course, the third challenge – that of identifying a new role for Japan – is
the toughest because it could shake the very premises that post-war Japan
has tried to keep untouched.

STRATEGIES AND RESPONSES OF THE FOREIGN MINISTRY

The Gulf War brought into focus and tested Japan's role on the world stage.
The question many Japanese asked themselves after the war was whether or
not Japan had passed the test. The verdict was a very close one. Under the
actual circumstances of the Gulf crisis, Japan was viewed by the other
countries as not having rapidly and comprehensively fulfilled its duties as it
should; the Japanese response was often being characterized as 'too little,
too late'. As expected, the resulting gap between Japan, which considered it
had done everything possible under the existing domestic constraints and the
international community, which regarded Japan as having shirked yet again
its share of responsibility commensurate with its actual power, led to harsh
criticism of the way the Foreign Ministry had coped with the crisis and to a
push for a review of the existing foreign service organization.[4]
    This review was conducted partly in the belief that there may have been
some structural shortcomings in the Japanese foreign service system, which
had not been successful in providing timely policy options on the basis of
appropriate information. Six months later, after the end of the Gulf War, the
Foreign Ministry commissioned a group of eminent persons chaired by Mr
Seshima to compile a report (the so-called Seshima report) on this issue,

which was completed in December 1991. The report, emphasizing that the international community was still groping for a new order following the end of the Cold War and that active involvement in that process would itself contribute to Japan's national interests, urged the Foreign Ministry to take the lead in establishing the specific direction of Japanese foreign policy. The report concluded that:

- the Foreign Ministry should formulate coherent foreign policy options and conduct a crucial role in coordinating and building consensus on these options within the Government;
- the Foreign Ministry should intensify and deepen its liaison with the Prime Minister's office;
- the Foreign Ministry must activate consultation with other ministries at deputy-minister level. Personnel exchange between the foreign service and other Government departments should be encouraged;
- the Foreign Ministry should implement the following organizational reforms as quickly as possible:
  - (a) the establishment of a policy coordination bureau to formulate coherent foreign policy within the Ministry itself;
  - (b) the establishment of an international information bureau to collect and analyze information upon which to base policy options;
  - (c) the strengthening of its crisis management capacity to cope with terrorism, hijacking and the protection of Japanese nationals exposed to large-scale accidents or national conflicts;
  - (d) the building of an appropriate framework to promote international co-operation;
  - (e) the strengthening of its overseas diplomatic establishments;
  - (f) an increase in staff numbers and improvement in training of staff recruited;
  - (g) seeking understanding by, and support from, public opinion and channelling into diplomacy the existing wealth of experience and knowledge held in various quarters outside the foreign service;
- the foreign service should increase its staff by about 1000 to carry out the above reforms;
- the separate Foreign Service examination should be continued, but more emphasis should be placed on interviews to identify appropriate foreign service recruits, with a reduction in the volume of written tests;
- in appointing ambassadors, efforts should be made to recruit the best available human resources, including those from other ministries as well as from the private sector.

The summer of 1993 saw the realization of the key components of the proposed reforms, namely the establishment of the Foreign Policy Bureau and the International Information Bureau. In the process, the United

Nations Affairs Bureau was merged with the all-powerful Foreign Policy Bureau. This bureau proved instrumental in forging policy options within the Government on such delicate issues as how to react to the North Korean Nuclear Development Programme as well as to the 50th anniversary of the end of the war.

As indicated above, the Foreign Ministry is one of the very few growth industries in the entire Japanese Government. This is eloquently demonstrated through the ever-increasing budget and staff numbers from stagnant overall government resources. What Parliament and public opinion are asking for through the media is not, unlike in the case of some G-7 countries, a slim foreign service but one which is strong and capable of leading the country with clearly-defined policy initiatives. If the public were only seeking value for money out of the foreign service, it would not have been so liberal towards the recent build-up of the Foreign Ministry.

The real strategies of Japan can be summarized in the following components as propounded in the article from *Gaiko Forum* by Foreign Minister Kohno of 5 January 1995:

• to promote international co-operation for strengthening the foundation for democracy. In this connection note should be taken of the four principles underlying the disbursement of ODA, already mentioned above, which militate against the provision of assistance to countries with increasing military expenditures and to those not promoting democracy and a market economy at home;
• to facilitate disarmament and non-proliferation. Japan joined the EU in establishing the UN Register of Conventional Arms in 1991;
• to participate in peacekeeping operations. Since the International Peace Cooperation Law was enacted in 1992, Japan has dispatched Self Defense Forces personnel to Cambodia, Mozambique, Zaire and Syria (Golan Heights).

From these ideals emerge the following foreign policy priorities to be pursued: first, Japan–USA relations remain the cornerstone of Japan's foreign policy.[5] The Japan–USA Security Arrangements are also a source of stability in the Asia–Pacific region in the post-Cold War era. Against this background, extending cooperation with such neighbouring countries as China and Korea is crucially important for Japan. Second, there is an urgent need to promote Asia-Pacific regional cooperation, building upon APEC. Japan espouses the concept of open regional co-operation as opposed to the restrictive regionalization pursued elsewhere. Third, Japan is more than ready to enhance the level of global co-operation through the G-7 forum and the UN. Also, in this context, there is the important issue of intellectual exchange. This is particularly relevant at this juncture of history when the Asia–Pacific region is coming out of a long dormant period with all the accompanying problems such as pollution, energy shortages, urbanization and crime. In this context Japan is the only country straddling the Asian and Western worlds and has a great deal to contribute. All in all, one of the key points encompassing all these components is the need to move away from a passive, reactive foreign policy to a more proactive one. This is the result of the long and natural process of healing the wounds inflicted by the war.

Summing up, it would be appropriate to illustrate a couple of points of comparison vis-à-vis European foreign services. First, unlike the situation in Europe, Asia-Pacific regional co-operation is not so deep as to be able to influence the functions of the foreign service in the member countries. There is neither an Asia-Pacific parliament nor a Brussels-like Commission or Council. To put it simply, there is no equivalent of the Maastricht Treaty. Nor is it anticipated that APEC will move in this direction. The APEC process is a more gradual one.

Second, the Japanese foreign service is still enjoying the benefits of a preferential budgetary allocation. The challenge here is how to expand the foreign service so that Japan can conduct a coherent and effective foreign policy. The Foreign Ministry is confident of being able to continue increasing its staff numbers as well as to receive reasonable increases in its budget in the future. So in Japan, the Foreign Ministry is not a declining but a growing industry. However, the Japanese and European foreign services have in common such problems as how to modernize the foreign service in the age of information technology. It has now introduced a Windows-based e-mail system in all workplaces in Tokyo. The embassies in Washington DC and London are already part of this system and other embassies will follow shortly.

Third, the difficulty for the Japanese foreign service is, unlike those in Europe where integration is the way forward, to set a new agenda for the Japanese role in global diplomacy. This has to be faced up to in the absence of a consensus like that in Europe.

RELATIONS WITH OTHER MINISTRIES

To recap, the first and foremost lesson from pre-war diplomacy was not to repeat double-channel diplomacy. Therefore, for successive leaderships of the Japanese foreign service the number one task was to ensure one-channel diplomacy through the Foreign Ministry. There have been instances where this principle has not been strictly observed, but the Japanese foreign service insisted on having only one governmental overseas establishment, whether that be an embassy or consulate-general. Thus a conscious effort was made to integrate and conduct foreign affairs under one roof. The idea was for the Foreign Ministry to play an active coordinating role in forging foreign policy options within the government and to carry out the enunciated policies abroad through one consolidated government establishment.

With advances in technology and the more sophisticated nature of trade-related dealings, it has become possible to refer more directly to each responsible government agency but the essence of foreign policy is conducted through one channel. However, the devil is in the detail, and the foreign service gets involved with details when they threaten to become diplomatic issues. Therefore the Japanese foreign service has felt the need to bring in specialists in various fields which were neglected in traditional diplomacy. There are now more staff seconded, for example, to the UN, OECD, GATT, the International Energy Agency, the UN Office of the High Commissioner for Refugees, and the World Health Organisation, to name but a few. These efforts will continue and are under way in response to the trend, particularly prevalent since the mid-1980s, whereby domestic departments have tried to develop their own capacity for international activity. The issue of coordination among Government agencies has always been the number one priority for the Foreign Ministry. Various attempts have been made to improve coordination, for example through the establishment of the Prime Minister's external affairs office in 1986 and then of the Foreign Policy Bureau of the Ministry in 1993. Of course these efforts are being continued. Fortunately for the Foreign Ministry, there have been no serious attempts to merge government agencies into one gigantic body for international trade and foreign affairs, as has been the case in Australia. Moreover, the fact that the director of the Prime Minister's external affairs office is always seconded by the Foreign Ministry has helped the latter to retain the coordinating role. One may still sometimes witness haphazard cases among government agencies concerning external policies. Such cases will invite severe public criticism, given the public's strong anti-bureaucracy mood at present.

ROLE OF PUBLIC OPINION

Public opinion is crucial in any country in the conduct of foreign policy, but it is vitally important for Japan at this critical juncture of its history, when it is trying to decide what kind of role it is going to play in the international community. The central issue concerns the constraints imposed by the constitution. The discussion was sparked by the Gulf crisis of 1990–1 and continues. There have been several opinion polls conducted by major newspapers which reveal that the Japanese people are not afraid of an open discussion of the issue. This change may have been brought about by the recognition that the constitution has played a decisive role in post-war Japan in bringing prosperity and peace but 50 years on there are aspects of it which do not necessarily correspond to the reality surrounding Japan.

It does not come as a surprise to many, to find that the 1995 polls conducted by the *Yomiuri* and *Mainichi* newspapers showed 50.4 per cent 37 per cent respectively in favour of a review of the constitution. Even the most liberal newspaper, the *Asahi*, revealed 74 per cent in support of the dispatch of Self Defense Forces for peacekeeping operations by the UN.

RESPONSES TO GLOBAL ISSUES

As Japan became a more integral part of the West in the 1980s, it began to state more unequivocally that it shared Western values, including recognition of the importance of human rights. In 1982 Japan was enrolled into the membership of the UN Commission on Human Rights. This forced Japan, which had previously taken a rather ambiguous position, to face up to this issue. In 1984 the Foreign Ministry established a new division responsible for human rights and refugee affairs, and a full division for disarmament was established in 1984 after the Williamsburg Summit of 1983. A new division dealing with global issues including environmental issues, was also set up in 1993. These organizational changes in the Japanese foreign service not only provided resources to cope with emerging issues but had the effect of extending on-the-job training to the Japanese foreign policymakers, who had to think hard about these delicate issues from a global perspective and made them more aware of the need to base foreign policy on Western values.

The Tiananmen Square incident of 1989 brought into sharp focus the position of each government, including Japan, in relation to the international community. Japan showed no hesitation in disavowing the abuse of human rights. Recently Japan fell neatly into line with the Western countries in condemning human rights violations in Myanmar. However, in these human rights abuse cases Japan has been advocating the policy of engaging each of the countries in dialogue so as not to isolate them from the international community. This position of Japan has little to do with so-called Asian values, as proclaimed by some countries. Rather, it is based on a realistic calculation of how to influence the policies of relevant countries in a direction which we would like to see, through more exposure to chilling international public opinion.

RELATIONS WITH BUSINESS AND NGOS

As Japanese business extended its worldwide operations, top business leaders began to assimilate an international frame of mind. After all, when one's company has to locate – as in the case of Toyota, for example – more than 50 per cent of its production abroad, one has no choice. This has provided a natural framework for the foreign service and business community to come closer and compare notes on the various issues and challenges they both have to face. Unlike an earlier era when business leaders had to consider only their business at home and they did not have to go beyond meetings with policymakers of domestic ministries, they now accept regular meetings with the foreign service both at home and abroad as a routine part of contemporary business life.

With this in mind, a future challenge for the foreign service may be whether it will feel comfortable in arranging an Anglo-Saxon type link between the Government and business. This was most eloquently demonstrated by a 1996 British delegation to China, where a 270 strong group of business people accompanied the Deputy Prime Minister. So far, under the legacy of pre-war practice, when allegedly formidable conglomerates called 'Zaibatsu' wielded a strong influence on politics, the Japanese Government has taken a very puritanical stance towards that kind of idea.

Concerning NGOs, one has to bear in mind the basic difference which existed in the past between Western Christian societies and Japanese society. The tradition of NGOs is very weak in Japan: people have looked more to the Government to extend various social services, whereas in the West it would have been more natural for NGOs to carry this out. Economic achievements and the resultant additional resources have provided extra room for NGOs to flourish, as evidenced during the tragic Kobe earthquake of 1995. One characteristic of Japanese NGOs is that many of them originated abroad and associated themselves with humanitarian activities in poverty-stricken areas. This very Japaneseness of NGO history was linked to the start of the programme called 'grass-roots grant assistance' in 1989, which was the catalyst in closing the gap between NGOs and the foreign service. Thanks to this new programme, now totalling about US$45 million a year, the horizons of development assistance policy have been greatly widened and the effects of such policy have started to reach out more directly to people in need. Similar ideas are now being explored at home. Moreover, for the purpose of supporting projects undertaken by Japan's NGOs, the government established a system of subsidies for NGO projects.

CONCLUSION

Fifty years on after the war and as we approach the twenty-first century, the Japanese foreign service is at a critical juncture. As pointed out, unlike in some West European countries, the Japanese foreign service is still a growth industry and many look to the Foreign Ministry to take the initiative in diplomatic matters. Its budget and staff are continually increasing and are expected to grow in the future. People want a more proactive foreign policy.

There are several influences at work here, not all tending in the same direction. First, the future of the internal alignment of political forces is very difficult to predict. As we have seen, public opinion no longer shirks from a discussion of Japan's global political role or of security related issues. However, public opinion is clearly divided over the nature of the security role that Japan should perform, in particular concerning the dispatch of Self Defense Forces abroad even in the context of collective security arrangements. This division is reflected in the positions of the major political parties both in power and in opposition. To forge a consensus may require a very long process. In the meantime, the Foreign Ministry is expected to find policy options which necessarily touch upon this question. This will be the toughest challenge of all. Connected to this, the question of permanent membership of the UN Security Council is another challenge facing the Foreign Ministry.[6]

Second, as the only G-7 country straddling Asia and the West, the Japanese foreign service will come under constant scrutiny from both Parliament and the media as to which direction it is going to take. For policymakers in the Ministry it is a foregone conclusion that Japan shares and believes in Western values. This is self-evident from post-war history; Japan has built today's peace and prosperity upon these values. It is also an absolute pre-requisite for Japanese diplomacy to take the initiative in bringing about co-operation and integration in the Asia-Pacific region. The emphasis that Japanese diplomacy places on open regionalism relates somewhat to this recognition. The real test for the foreign service in this regard is still to come. Third, at the same time, in spite of the above division over which role to play, public opinion will probably ask for a more proactive foreign policy. This is in part a contradictory request, since whether Japanese diplomacy can be proactive or not depends greatly on the above two elements. The demands of public opinion can be a very tall order in any country.

Against this background the Japanese foreign service has to cater for various demands at the same time. Unlike the European foreign services, where the agenda is clearly set in terms of the Atlantic alliance and EU integration, the situation is more fluid for Japan. For the Japanese foreign service the challenge has always been and will continue to be how to keep playing a crucial role in the process of coordinating policy formulation. One positive fall-out of the recent global deployment of business activities is that both the MITI and the Ministry of Finance are becoming more and more internationally-minded. This is making the coordination process easier than before when these ministries were primarily preoccupied with the protection of their constituent industries and business activities.

Conversely, the increasing interdependency of global economic activity and its complexities pose more formidable challenges to traditionally minded diplomats. For the foreign service to survive with renewed strength into the twenty-first century, it will be necessary to make constant efforts to modernise itself while keeping the comparative advantage of commanding a far-reaching network and gathering information on foreign countries. The recent decision by the foreign service to abolish the nationality clause which required foreign spouses of diplomats with Japanese nationality to become Japanese nationals during the course of five years is a small but important step in this direction. If the foreign service continues to move in a similar way, its future should be increasingly bright.

NOTES

1   Edwin O. Reichauer, *My Life between Japan and America* (New York: Harper Row, 1986), pp. 161–295.
2   For an historical overview of Japan's post World War II security policy see Yakio Satoh, *The Evolution of Japanese Security Policy. Adelphi Paper 178* (London: International Institute for Strategic Studies 1982).
3   For the view of the Japanese Government on the Self Defense Force and the constitution see: *Defense of Japan* (Tokyo: Defense Agency of Japan, 1995), pp. 61–5.
4   For a view supporting a more active foreign policy and a necessary review of the internal decisionmaking process see: Ichiro Ozawa, *Blueprint for a New Japan* (Kodansha International, 1993), pp. 33–4. An interpretation and discussion of Mr. Ozawa's argument can be found in: 'Reforming Japan', *The Economist*, 9 March 1996, pp. 19–21.
5   For a comprehensive account of the ongoing discussion on Japan's role see: Kenichiro Sasae, *Rethinking Japan-US Relations. Adelphi Paper 292* (London: International Institute for Strategic Studies, 1994).
6   For the views of the Foreign Ministry on the course of Japanese diplomacy after the Gulf War see *Japan's Post-Gulf International Initiative* (Ministry of Foreign Affairs, August 1991).

7 Malaysia
Change and Adaptation in Foreign Policy: Malaysia's Foreign Ministry
Zakaria Haji Ahmad

The core concern of any foreign ministry is to safeguard by acts of diplomacy the sovereignty, integrity and territory of the political entity to which it belongs – in short, the national interest – in an asymmetric and predatory world of nation-states. This statement may well be challenged by those who identify changes in the international system arising out of trends in regionalism, multilateralism and globalism.[1] In addition, rapid advances in communications and information technology (IT) have resulted in the world becoming a global village or indeed, a 'borderless world',[2] suggesting a reduced role for foreign ministries and their functionaries.

Viewed against the preceding parameters, it can be asked if Malaysia's Ministry of Foreign Affairs – better known as *Wisma Putra* – has suffered a decline in its role or if it has had to shoulder more onerous responsibilities in responding to the challenges of rapid change characterized succinctly by former UN Secretary-General Boutros Boutros Ghali as 'the acceleration of history'. Since its inception in 1957, *Wisma Putra* has played a sterling role in Malaysia's diplomatic efforts, but its biggest challenge in the decades of the 1980s and 1990s has been to forge an instrumental role in the conduct of foreign policy of a Third World polity led by a strong and iconoclastic political executive.[3] At the outset, it can be stated that *Wisma Putra* had not been unmindful of the rapid changes in the international arena and in the shift away from bipolar politics as the Cold War receded into history. Nonetheless, its more pressing concern essentially has been the primacy of its role in foreign policy decisionmaking as Malaysia, since 1981, began to assert itself as a spokesman for the South, engaged in high profile diplomacy and developed a global role.

To be sure, a dynamic foreign ministry such as *Wisma Putra* has not been oblivious either to changes in the international system or the imperatives of its political masters and the domestic political context. But in doing so, it has also kept close to – one might say has been jealous of – its custodial role as upholder of the national interest in the regional and international contexts,

117

ever mindful of the parameters of Malaysia's position in Southeast Asia and the world. In this regard, it may even be possible to assert that *Wisma Putra* has been more proactive in the formulation and implementation of Malaysian foreign policy than might otherwise be surmised. Indeed, *Wisma Putra*'s record in this regard should not be overstated, but in retrospect, to cite one instance, Kuala Lumpur's push for the 'neutralization' of Southeast Asia in 1971, set against the region's then turbulence, was a regional diplomatic overture of remarkable stature.

Has *Wisma Putra*'s role declined because of international change and Malaysian Prime Minister Dr Mahathir Mohamad's emphasis on geoeconomics? Has the need for specialization in an increasingly multilateralized environment at both regional and global levels meant a downgrading of traditional diplomatic conduct? Additionally, has a new mandate in foreign policy allowed for an usurpation of *Wisma Putra*'s duties by other agencies (especially the Ministry of International Trade and Industry)? Is the arrest of the purported decline to be answered by subservience to political authority in the conduct of foreign affairs? These questions set the stage for understanding the change and adaptation of *Wisma Putra* as an agency buffeted by both domestic and external challenges in the last two decades, but not unmindful of its main mandate of protecting and enhancing Malaysia's national interests.

A useful caveat to note is whether Malaysia as a 'developing' country would have the resources to implement its foreign policy objectives in the light of the rapid changes alluded to. Without a resort to force, it might be argued that Malaysia's ability to perform its foreign policy goals would depend more on the quality of its diplomats and its ability to garner all its national resources in order to implement a cohesive and unitary foreign policy. That very theme of 'paying attention to the next generation of diplomats' was underscored by one of its outgoing senior diplomats, Tan Sri Razali Ismail, who had served as President of the UN General Assembly in 1997 when he said: 'We must run away from the belief that we only need glorified protocol people to take care of VIPs at airports.'[4] Nevertheless, short-staffed as it is, *Wisma Putra* currently (at mid-1997) operates in 79 missions abroad with a staff strength of only 279 officers and about 500 home-based support staff. Its most pressing need at this juncture, indeed, is to find persons with the correct aptitude, training, skills and inclination to fill some 50 available vacancies in the officer category.[5]

To some extent, the decline of the 'traditional' diplomacy of the 1960s and 1970s did mean a need for adaptation to the so-called international context of geoeconomics (as distinct from geopolitics) of the 1980s and 1990s. But what was more crucial for *Wisma Putra* was for it to sustain a legitimate role as the purveyor of external concerns even as the locus of foreign policy decisionmaking itself shifted away from it to that of the Malaysian Prime

Minister's Office – in particular, after the accession in 1981 of Dr Mahathir Mohamad as Prime Minister. In this process, *Wisma Putra* initially resisted the shift in locus but gradually took on the role of willing partner (detractors might want to use the term 'able sycophant'), in pursuit of what has been called 'high profile' diplomacy. In doing so, the mid-90s has seen, perhaps, a re-emergence of *Wisma Putra*'s pre-eminence in the conduct of foreign policy which it believed it held after independence in 1957 through the 1960s, but which declined or took on a secondary character as the country focused more on domestic or national development issues in the decade of the 1970s. It is likely that this pre-eminence may become more consequential as Malaysia enters the next millennium which some tout as the Pacific Century.[6]

In assessing the changing nature of the response of *Wisma Putra* to the evolving global and regional contexts, it should be remembered that the Malaysian case is that of a Third World country transforming into a rapidly-developing country (with concomitant economic restructuring), of a country that is highly stable but with authoritarian political leadership in a quasi-democratic polity,[7] of a country that is multi-ethnic but relatively unscathed by ethnic unrest, of a country that is being pushed to achieve 'developed country status' by the year 2020.[8] Some argue that Malaysia should be regarded as a 'middle power',[9] but even more important is that Malaysia's foreign policy has been to pursue the position of an international actor out to achieve a more equitable global order and thereby redress former or existing inequities in the international system. At the same time, this high profile diplomacy has an 'Islamic orientation' that is difficult as yet to gauge (though not without domestic ramifications in Malaysia itself) and it can be observed that Malaysia is intent not merely to comment and critique but to translate words into action (as opposed to earlier instances elsewhere of Third World rhetoric that in the main were simply the stating of shibboleths).

ORGANIZATION AND CONTEXT

Modelled on the Westminster system of government, *Wisma Putra* is the ministry within the public bureaucracy charged with the conduct of Malaysia's foreign policy. The bureaucrats who man *Wisma Putra* are drawn from the Civil Service establishment but generally form a closed cadre, and since 1970 have been perceived as junior to the Home service sector. The Foreign Affairs Ministry is led by a Minister who is a member of the government.[10] Below the Minister is the bureaucratic apparatus headed by the Secretary-General (previously known as Permanent Secretary).

Within the bureaucratic structure, *Wisma Putra* is not regarded as a major or central agency (unlike the Treasury, the Public Services Department or the Prime Minister's Department), but the Secretary-General in some instances has exercised clout in the high councils of national decisionmaking. This was particularly so during the period of Tunku Abdul Rahman, the first prime minister. 'The Tunku', as he was popularly referred to, was also the Foreign Minister during his tenure of office (1957–70). '*Wisma Putra*' (House of the Tunku), in fact, is named after the Tunku ('*Putra*' meaning 'prince', since the Tunku was a scion of the Kedah state royal household).[11]

During the period of the Tunku, which was also the first decade or so of independent Malay(si)a, *Wisma Putra* enjoyed a status of importance in national decisionmaking. Looking back, Malaysia's own survival – as a newly-independent state and against a hostile regional environment (especially Indonesian *Konfrontasi*, 1963–6) and challenges within (for example, the insurgency mounted by the Communist Party of Malaya, CPM) – highlighted *Wisma Putra*'s role in matters of state. But equally important was the role of the political chief executive, a factor that also looms large in the present administration of Dr Mahathir Mohamad.

Although Dr Mahathir is not Foreign Minister, a lot of foreign policy initiatives have derived since 1981 from the prime minister himself – indicating that the locus of foreign policy decisionmaking is effectively in the hands of the political chief executive. The role of the Foreign Minister in the era of Dr Mahathir seems to have been eclipsed and some perceive this post as a 'junior' appointment in Malaysia's system of cabinet government. On the other hand, given the wide publicity within the country concerning external initiatives, Foreign Ministers can be judged in terms of their competence and loyalty to the Prime Minister and can derive considerable mileage in terms of their standing in the domestic political establishment.[12] But thus far, the only real impact in terms of novel or distinctive foreign policy initiatives from a Foreign Minister was during the tenure of Tan Sri Ghazali Shafie.[13] This is not to say that other incumbents did not have a say in foreign policy formulation, but rather to indicate the difficulty of identifying their distinctive contribution.[14]

As part of the overall Malaysian Civil Service (more correctly the Malaysian Administrative and Diplomatic Service or PTD) *Wisma Putra* is composed of well-educated civil servants whose *esprit de corps* has remained intact in the 40 years of Malaysia's post-colonial indigenous rule. Although the Diplomatic Service began as an independent service when Malay(si)a gained independence in 1957, in 1970 it was merged with the rest of Malaysia's elite civil service (that is, together with the 'Home Service' sector), a move that was ostensibly designed to tap the talents of a larger, amalgamated civilian bureaucracy.[15] By and large, however, there have been very few instances of lateral transfers between the Diplomatic and Home sectors of the PTD, suggesting that the amalgamation of the two is only putative. Some such transfers were attempted in the early 1980s, but in the main the

Diplomatic Sector has remained a 'closed service'. There has been relatively better success in Diplomatic Officers going over to the Home sector, but again the number is very small and involves only senior officers.

'Elitism' in *Wisma Putra*, it can be argued, is an ingrained element in the socialization of its officers, and some might say has led to hubris on its part in relation to the rest of the PTD. This posture signifies the closed nature of the Diplomatic Service and has also meant the exclusion of other Malaysian talents in *Wisma Putra*. Even political ambassadorial appointments have not been entirely welcomed. But even more surprising, perhaps, is that the non-inclusion has been steadfastly adhered to even during times when *Wisma Putra* had felt severe shortcomings in its personnel make-up and in meeting the tremendous demands made on it to realise Dr Mahathir's initiatives.

Wisma Putra's *esprit de corps* is also attributable to the particular breed of officers who were trained in the 'Ghazali Shafie mould'. Tan Sri Ghazali Shafie was a long-serving permanent secretary during the Tunku period; after the May 1969 racial riots he joined the government and then served also as Foreign Affairs Minister and as Minister of Home Affairs. Popularly referred by his adherents as 'King Ghaz', Ghazali Shafie's impact was more than a matter of style and has had an indelible effect reflected in the current leadership of *Wisma Putra*. Some might even attribute Malaysian foreign policy initiatives before Dr Mahathir's period to the brilliant leadership, intellectual quality, elegance and substance of Ghazali Shafie and his coterie of able officers, although this has been rebutted by one of his detractors.[16]

More important than formal structure and context, it is apparent that personalities have a huge impact on foreign policymaking in Malaysia. This is reinforced by the nature of the political system with a strong chief executive and the centralized nature of national decisionmaking. These elements of the political milieu of *Wisma Putra* appear to be more pronounced since 1981 with the advent of Dr Mahathir. Dr Mahathir's impact contrasts greatly with that of his predecessors who, while also exercising executive writ in decisionmaking, were quite willing to allow *Wisma Putra* bureaucrats to advise, counsel and even present initiatives. Some argue that Dr Mahathir's style is due to the fact that he was not previously a civil servant, whereas his three predecessors came from the ranks of the bureaucracy and therefore understood the nature of ministerial responsibility *vis-à-vis* the civilian bureaucrats.

In the case of Dr Mahathir, the locus of foreign policy decisionmaking has effectively shifted from *Wisma Putra* to the prime minister's office. Some might even argue that such a shift in locus has affected the whole machinery of government; his critics even assert that the present administration is a one-man government. In the case of foreign policy, although prime ministers in Malaysia have always exercised certain prerogatives, it might be said that

Dr Mahathir's style was causing *Wisma Putra* to act on his advice rather than vice versa as heretofore.

This style is not inconsistent with his manner of operation on domestic matters, but one related development in the foreign policy arena was the establishment of the Institute of Strategic and International Studies (ISIS) in 1983–4. Although ostensibly a private think tank, ISIS's creation was possible because of a substantial infusion of government funds as well as Mahathir's personal interest.[17] The exact position of ISIS in foreign policymaking is not known, but tensions are said to have existed with *Wisma Putra* in its formative period. It is significant that ISIS's research mandate also covers domestic issues, and it has played a key role in advancing Mahathir's ideas, including the 'South' initiative through the establishment of the South Commission. Indeed, at certain periods ISIS has been regarded by some as the 'other' foreign ministry. ISIS's role as a sounding board for leadership initiatives in both foreign and domestic policy cannot be discounted, but obviously it cannot supplant the role of *Wisma Putra*; nor does it complement it in functional terms.

It is also believed that Mahathir has made more extensive use of a little-publicized government unit known as the 'Research Division' located within the Prime Minister's Department (JPM). This unit's frame of reference is unclear, but it came into existence after the May 1969 riots, and it is believed in some quarters that its purpose is to ensure the 'Malay character' of the regime and government. Its operatives have both a domestic and external mission that is combined with political and intelligence functions, and they usually serve in diplomatic posts abroad alongside regular foreign ministry appointees. Whatever their mission, their role in foreign policy cannot be discounted, and their use after 1981 has probably been enhanced.[18]

Just as importantly, Dr Mahathir has introduced a new dimension to his foreign policy initiatives by his exhortation that Malaysia must develop businesses abroad. On practically every visit overseas, Dr Mahathir is accompanied by a business delegation; other ministers seem to have adopted this style, in particular the Minister of International Trade and Industry. Viewed as part of the need to develop the economy, Malaysian business investment abroad is part of going global. Seen as a partnership of diplomacy and business, one observer remarks: 'As he makes his global quest, Mahathir wears two suits: the first the armour of the Third World knight, promoting "South–South" cooperation and coming to the aid of the downtrodden – particularly the Muslim; and the second, the engineer's overalls, as he scours for technology bargains that will kick-start a high-value manufacturing industry in Malaysia.'[19] The speed of Malaysian overseas investment is quite impressive, though it has also earned opprobrium and critical comment from some quarters.[20] In 1995, Malaysian external investment totalled 7 billion ringgit or US$2.8 billion.[21] But what is important is not so much the investment abroad but that it is an outcome of Dr Mahathir's diplomatic forays in the world. In post-1993 Cambodia, interestingly, Malaysia is probably the only country whose citizens are allowed entry visas gratis – a situation arising out of Malaysian investment there as well as a recognition of Malaysia's gestures and demonstration of assistance.

It is probably the case that 'trade follows the flag' in Mahathir-led Malaysian foreign policy, but as noted by Razali Ismail, it is also a case of translating rhetoric into substance: 'we are not simply posturing and talking, we back it up by trying to do something on the ground.'[22] According to Razali, 'Our private sector has been able to compete with some of the biggest companies in the West. In Zimbabwe, we outbid the British firms for the power contract. In South Africa, we joined hands with an American company to do telecommunications.'[23]

It is possible to view the marriage of diplomacy and external investment as one stratagem to overcome trade protectionism in established markets in the developed world, or even to use economic factors to exact diplomatic advantage,[24] but it is likely that the challenge contemplated by Dr Mahathir is more to promote Malaysia's economic standing in an increasingly competitive environment. In this respect as well, it is noteworthy that Malaysia has pushed for the formation of the East Asian Economic Grouping (EAEG) so as to create a platform for the articulation of views of the East Asian countries against a complex international trading regime when it was felt that the GATT mechanism would not survive the Uruguay Round. The EAEG proposal, however, still remains to be realized even though the ASEAN countries have agreed they could act as a caucus (and hence the name change to that of an East Asian Economic Caucus, or EAEC) within the APEC (Asia-Pacific Economic Co-operation) grouping. The EAEC, which includes the ASEAN countries, China, the two Koreas and Japan has not yet been formally launched.

Another feature of Dr Mahathir's global outlook and his understanding of the necessity for Malaysia to be on the global grid in a fast changing world has been Malaysia's latest project in the development of the Multimedia Super Corridor (MSC) in a new development belt extending from Kuala Lumpur to the new administrative capital of Putra Jaya. In the MSC, foreign IT firms have been invited to set up shop under liberal conditions for the free exchange of information and trading access. The MSC is an indication of how Malaysia under Dr Mahathir has been latching itself onto the global grid of the highway.

What is less clear, however, is whether these initiatives spell the decline of *Wisma Putra* as Malaysia's external relations are forged in non-traditional areas, especially as the key issues are less concerned with government-to-government or inter-state relations and diplomatic contacts. Dr Mahathir's emphasis on economics was essentially spelt out in instructions to *Wisma*

Putra to go beyond traditional diplomacy and 'sell' Malaysia. The interrelationship between economics and politics in inter-state relations seemed clear enough: in the mid-1980s already it was found that Malaysia had a high trade dependence of 79 per cent; in terms of manufacturing export performance, by 1970 it had achieved the distinction of being one of the world's top twenty producers of manufactured goods.[25] The importance of these economic realities is underscored by the inclusion of economics as a core subject in the curriculum of the Institute of Diplomacy and Foreign Relations (IDFR) for all foreign service officers undertaking courses there.

The IDFR, established in 1991, was a signal in many ways of the need to marry traditional diplomacy with the changing and complex nature of the international environment. According to Tan Sri Ahmad Sarji, then the Chief Secretary to the Government, he had proposed that the IDFR be established to enhance the professionalism of government officers as Malaysia began to play a larger international role. Tan Sri Ahmad Sarji writes:

> In early 1991, I passed a memorandum to the Prime Minister stating the reasons for the establishment of IDFR as follows:
>
> (1) to provide systematic training for Government officers, especially those who are responsible for the nation's overseas interests;
> (2) to provide training programmes that are specifically tailored to improve knowledge and skills in this area, and to inculcate the right attitudes in consonance with their roles and responsibilities;
> (3) to undertake research, studies and reports on diplomatic issues and foreign relations;
> (4) to provide consultancy services to Government and non-Government agencies on economic, political and security issues relevant to Malaysia's overseas interests; and
> (5) to improve co-ordination between Government and non-Government agencies involved in promoting the nation's interests overseas.[26]

The functions of the IDFR are spelt out further in the curriculum as explained by Tan Sri Ahmad Sarji:

> Among the important subjects which are given emphasis by the Institute are protocol and the niceties of diplomacy, etiquette, attitude training, the art of effective communication, the art of negotiation, global political and economic trends, trade regimes, and practices and laws of countries. The Institute also lays emphasis on language training, especially English. This is carried out with the co-operation of the National Institute of Public Administration (INTAN). The main target groups of this Institute are officers of the Ministry of Foreign Affairs, trade commissioners from the Ministry of International Trade and Industry, officers of the Malaysian

Industrial Development Authority, directors of tourism and officers from the Ministry of Primary Industries who are serving overseas.[27]

This indicates that IDFR's establishment was and is a recognition of the expanding areas of diplomacy and the need to involve other agencies in international matters, apart from *Wisma Putra*.

Thus far, nonetheless, the emphasis on new areas of Malaysia's external relations (economic interdependence, gender, the environment, and so on), has not resulted in other ministries usurping *Wisma Putra*'s position. On the other hand, the new emphases of Malaysia's high profile diplomacy has meant a need for some specialization by other agencies, though still allowing for *Wisma Putra* to play a lead role in policy coordination at the working level. Other agencies, as indicated, have appeared which seem to challenge *Wisma Putra*'s intellectual role in foreign policy formulation but the style of Dr Mahathir indicates that he is receptive to a wide variety of sources for his foreign policy ideas as well as Malaysia's development strategies. The political chief executive is still the final arbiter of policymaking and the initial impetus in foreign policy formulation.

It is also pertinent that thus far there has been no suggestion for a major reform of *Wisma Putra* or that foreign affairs should be a privatized activity. Indeed, because foreign relations are a central prong of Dr Mahathir's interests, *Wisma Putra* officers have been accorded better recognition than before and the appointment in 1996 of Halim Ali, a senior *Wisma Putra* official as Chief Secretary to the Government, is a coup of sorts for the Foreign Ministry in terms of Malaysia's bureaucratic politics setting. (It is understood that normally this post is the preserve of senior Home Service officers.)

STRATEGIES AND RESPONSES

It is a moot point whether Malaysia's Foreign Ministry has been in decline as a result of the changing international environment, if by 'decline' is meant *Wisma Putra*'s inability to implement its roles or meet national goals in the external environment. While it is true that the foreign decisionmaking locus has shifted to the prime minister's office, *Wisma Putra* has had to assume a large number of functions and duties in carrying out 'high profile diplomacy'. Thus, *Wisma Putra*'s own response to the changing international environment is akin to that which transformed the German and French foreign ministries at the onset of the twentieth century from traditional diplomatic roles,[28] though perhaps not at the same pace or with identical outcomes. The responses of *Wisma Putra* have put a high premium on resources and manpower which, whilst lacking in the initial stages, may actually result in better endowment in the future. That response, as well, has been fashioned and catalyzed as a result of prime minister Dr Mahathir's international agenda whose impact coincides with the changing environment of international relations.

It is not clear if *Wisma Putra* itself has responded to these circumstances with perceptions of its own corporate interests either being preserved or promoted, although it was probably mindful that any inability to meet the 'new' goals of Dr Mahathir's policy would have resulted in its status and role being diminished. As mentioned earlier, there had been attempts by the central bureaucratic agencies to have 'Home Service' officers assigned to diplomatic posts but more ominous was the establishment of the IDFR in 1991. Tasked to train diplomats, IDFR is an agency under the Prime Minister's Department, not *Wisma Putra*, and *Wisma Putra* officers assigned to it are 'on contract'.[29] This indicates as well a recognition of the centrality of foreign policy in Dr Mahathir's Malaysia. However, apart from training – a function deemed as less critical than the need for 'on the job' experience – *Wisma Putra*'s own structure has grown to accommodate the more complex issues of foreign policy and specific international issues. In the 1980s and 1990s, apart from the Department of Political and Economic Relations (the latter part of the title was added once 'economics' was defined as important) which shouldered the bulk of *Wisma Putra*'s duties at headquarters, a separate department was created to deal with 'International Organizations and Multilateral Economics'. Throughout its existence, one can note the burgeoning character of *Wisma Putra*'s headquarters organization and overseas representation, and as indicated, its overseas diplomatic missions (including consulates-general and liaison offices), now number close to 80.[30]

Structural re-ordering may be discerned in the organizational charts of *Wisma Putra* for 1967 and 1993 respectively in Figures 7.1 and 7.2. It is apparent from the organizational charts that equal emphasis is paid to political and economic issues and that bilateral relations are as important as multilateral ones in the contemporary period, in contrast to the more mundane concerns of diplomacy during the first decade of *Wisma Putra*'s existence.

Largely in response to Dr Mahathir's leadership style with its emphasis on commitment and results, the top hierarchy of *Wisma Putra*'s officials have responded with a 'political' commitment rather than the role associated with neutral civil servants in the classic Westminster mode. The instances of such commitment to meet Dr Mahathir's foreign policy goals, including that of the minister in charge (especially Abdullah Badawi) are not unnoticed in the Malaysian context and certain personalities stand out (such as Tan Sri Razali Ismail at the UN – 1997 President of the UN General Assembly; and former Secretary-General Ahmad Kamil, now serving as 'Special Envoy of the Prime Minister'). What is interesting is that these very top officials have more or

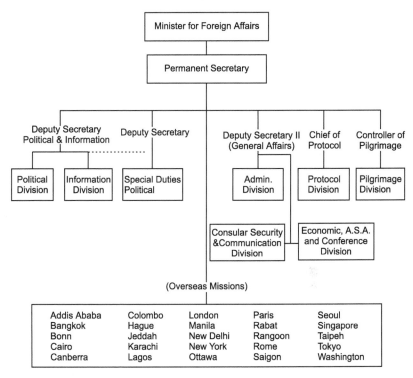

Figure 7.1   Ministry of Foreign Affairs, 1967

Source: Malaysia, *Organization of the Government of Malaysia* (Kida Lumpur: Penchetak Kerajaan (*Government Printer*) (1967), P. 90

less subscribed to the ideas of Dr Mahathir and have not hesitated to speak out with enthusiasm going beyond normal diplomatic reserve. Nonetheless, there is a large number of outstanding ambassadors (serving and retired) not named here, and mention of the more publicized personalities should not disguise the fact that many of *Wisma Putra*'s accomplishments are also due to instances of 'quiet' diplomacy.

In this respect, such vocal representation, accompanied with the usual diplomatic leg work is the manifestation of a 'proactive' style in inter-state relations. This style embodies, outwardly, the views of Dr Mahathir so that the interests of the South can be expounded and that the North can be 'pressured'.[31] Such proactivism is perhaps the opposite of passivity. As articulated by Ambassador Tan Sri Razali Ismail: 'We cannot do it alone. A foreign policy that is passive is not a foreign policy. Just to follow and put up your hand is not enough. We must do more.'[32]

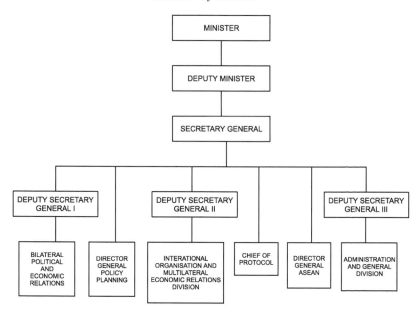

Figure 7.2 Organizational Sturcture Ministry of Foreign Affairs, 1993

Source: Dealing with the Malaysian Civil Service (Kuala Lumpur: Malaysian Administrative Modernisation and Manpower Unit, p. 739

This heightened sense of role-playing by *Wisma Putra*'s representatives suggests a great degree of professionalism. It is also in character with that of the elitist strain in *Wisma Putra* officers, a quality inculcated at the beginning of a diplomat's career and regarded as that which distinguishes the Malaysian Foreign Service officer from his other civil servant counterparts in style, elegance and substance. More importantly, this quality has brought forth a sense of urgency in meeting Dr Mahathir's expectations and the changed nature of international relations. Indeed, such a setting is a window of opportunity for *Wisma Putra*, not a signal of its lesser importance.

In yet another important sense, in spite of Dr Mahathir's high profile diplomacy and anti-Western rhetoric, his championing of the rights of the South and his rebukes at the excesses of the North, *Wisma Putra*'s own importance is understood, even sustained, below the level of conceptual substance in Malaysia's relations with other countries. This suggests that the role of traditional diplomacy is still important in securing support and agreement for Malaysia's ideas and initiatives, an area of activity no other agency can come close to in terms of results. For all the new initiatives and a more complex world, it is still the number of missions abroad, staffed by the

Wisma Putra officials, that can help to realize Malaysia's external interests. This indicates that the *Wisma Putra* officer is still the man or woman at the front line defending or promoting Malaysia's national interests, and not therefore playing a diminished role in the changed international circumstances.

CONCLUSION

In the Malaysian case, the response of the foreign ministry to the rapid transformation of international events, especially since the end of the Cold War, has not been so much a question of ability or inability to react but more that of striving hard to play a competent role in enhancing Malaysia's external interests in an asymmetric world dominated by the Big Powers. In this respect, *Wisma Putra* had basically been tasked to carry out the foreign policy initiatives of Malaysian Prime Minister Dato' Seri Dr Mahathir Mohamad, whose high profile diplomacy thrusts became evident with his accession to the premiership in 1981. It can be said that *Wisma Putra*'s role has been more that of accommodating the intrusion of Dr Mahathir's ideas in foreign policymaking and interpreting these ideas through the conduct of diplomacy in the various regional and multilateral fora. As compared to the pre-Mahathir period, it might also be said that *Wisma Putra*'s tasks since 1981 have essentially been to promote Malaysia as a voice of the Third World/the South and as a leading activist in international affairs (especially in reforming existing international conventions).

In the process, *Wisma Putra*'s role has perhaps been 'subordinated' in the foreign policy decisionmaking process, but on the other hand, in the interest of self-preservation it has also secured its existence as a competent agency. Moreover, given the multifarious demands arising out of a complex and increasingly interdependent world, *Wisma Putra* has managed to ensure its primacy in the conduct of Malaysian foreign policy through its lead role in coordinating other agencies involved in specialized and technical areas of Malaysia's overseas interests.

In the context of a political system dominated by a strong chief executive and more answerable to the plurality of diverse constituencies in the domestic arena, *Wisma Putra*'s success in not sinking into decline while responding to both international change and challenge from its own political master(s) is an indicator of strength and resilience. Indeed, it may be hypothesized that, in the Malaysian case, the more prime ministerial imperative intervenes in foreign policymaking, the greater the opportunity for *Wisma Putra* to locate a window of opportunity in terms of sustaining, or even expanding its role. *Wisma Putra*, in other words, has not been submissive to the winds of change, but has been able subtly to assert itself as the agency responsible for the conduct of Dr Mahathir's foreign policy.

It needs to be remembered that in the context of change, the fundamental element of the national interest, in terms of territorial integrity and sovereignty, continues as a given of foreign policy. In the case of Malaysia, under a strong political chief executive in the form of Dr Mahathir Mohamad, its foreign policy in the last two decades has undeniably taken on a more assertive thrust, but the primacy of national interest remains uppermost. In short, inasmuch as prime ministerial imperative has been substantial, what has happened is that the business of foreign policy has become as much a question of and for the state as it is a question of the representation of Malaysia's interests in the traditional processes of inter-state diplomacy. In this context, rather than being in decline, Malaysia's *Wisma Putra* has in fact found a new lease of life in the ever-evolving context of rapid transformation in the international arena.

NOTES

1   For an elaboration of these issues, see Paul R. Viotti and Mark V. Kauppi, eds, *International Relations Theory, Realism, Pluralism, Globalism*, 2nd edn (New York: MacMillan, 1993).

2   A major proponent of this thesis is Kenichi Ohmae. See his *The End of The Nation State* (London: Harper Collins, 1995). Mr Ohmae's ideas, incidentally, have been a source of inspiration to Malaysian Prime Minister Dr Mahathir, and the former served as a full-time adviser to the Malaysian government in the mid-1980s.

3   For one account of Dr Mahathir Mohamad's role, see Johan Saravanamuttu, 'Malaysia's foreign policy in the Mahathir period, 1981–1995: an iconoclast come to rule', *Asian Journal of Political Science* 4:1, June 1996, pp. 1–16.

4   Anis Kamil, 'Our activism pays dividends', *New Straits Times*, 26 November 1997.

5   Information made available by the Secretary-General, Ministry of Foreign Affairs, Malaysia, to the author.

6   Dr Mahathir has argued that the twenty-first century should not be that of the Pacific but should be a 'global' one. See his 'The Asia century – a Malaysian perspective', delivered at the Beijing Dialogue, 26–7 August 1996. Reproduced in *The Edge, Survey and Guide* (Kuala Lumpur: ASLI, October 1996), pp. 41–5.

7   See Zakaria Haji Ahmad, 'Malaysia: quasi democracy in a divided society', in Larry Diamond Juan Linz and Seymour Martin Lipset, eds, *Democracy in Developing Countries, Volume 3: Asia* (Boulder: Lynne Rienner, 1989), pp. 347–81; Zakaria Haji Ahmad and Sharifah Munirah Alatas, 'Malaysia in an uncertain mode', in James Morley, ed., *Driven by Growth* (New York: M. E. Sharpe, 1997).

8   Dr Mahathir Mohamad, 'Malaysia: The Way Forward', a speech outlining Malaysia's goals of a 'developed nation' by 2020 (Kuala Lumpur: Centre for Economic Research and Services, Malaysian Business Council, 1991).

9   See David Camroux, *Looking East . . . And Inwards: Internal Factors in Malaysian Foreign Relations During the Mahathir Era, 1981–1994* (Brisbane: Griffith University Australia-Asia Paper No. 72, 1994), and J. Saravanamuttu, 'Manoeuvrings for middle power,' *Trends* 48 (Singapore: Institute of Southeast Asian Studies)

10 Normally, ministers are elected politicians. However, ministers can also be appointed in the Malaysian context.

11 Any appellation using 'Putra' in Malaysia today is specifically in honour of Tunku Abdul Rahman.

12 This appears to be the case of the present incumbent, Dato' Abdullah Badawi who in the 1996 UMNO (United Malays National Organization) General Assembly election garnered enough votes to also become a party Vice-President. In the 1993 Assembly, he lost his vice-presidency though was still retained on the UMNO Supreme Council. UMNO is the dominant partner of the ruling coalition, the Barisan Nasional (National Front).

13 The definitive work on Ghazali Shafie's contributions is yet to appear, although his many speeches bear testimony to his thinking.

14 A counter-thesis to this view, in arguing for multi-faceted sources of foreign policy formulation is found in Mohd. Azahari Karim, 'Malaysian Foreign Policy', in Mohd. Azahari Karim, L. Howell and Grace Okuda, eds, *Malaysian Foreign Policy, Issues and Perspectives* (Kuala Lumpur: INTAN, 1990), pp. 3–16.

15 On the technicalities, see Norminshah Sabirin, 'The merger between the Malayan Civil Service and the External Affairs Service to form the Malaysian Home and Foreign Service', Diploma in Public Administration Project Paper, University of Malaya, 1969/70.

16 See Abdullah Ahmad, *Tunku Abdul Rahman and Malaysia's Foreign Policy, 1963–1970* (Kuala Lumpur: Berita Publishing, 1985). This was never stated in the book, but the unstated underlying reason may be surmised to the fact that Dato Abdullah Ahmad, then a Deputy Minister, had been jailed when Ghazali Shafie served as Home Affairs Minister in 1966–8. Dato Abdullah is presently Malaysia's Special Envoy to the United Nations.

17 The idea of such a research institute based on the lines of Jakarta's Center for Strategic and International Studies (CSIS) had been in the offing since 1974.

18 Zakaria Haji Ahmad, 'Malaysian foreign policy and domestic politics: looking outward and moving inward?' in Robert A. Scalapino, Seizaburo Sato, Jusof Wanandi and Sung-joo Han, eds, *Asia and the Major Powers* (Berkeley: University of California Institute of East Asian Studies, 1988), pp. 266–7.

19 'From logs to lotus', *Far Eastern Economic Review*, 12 December 1996, p. 64.

20 'From logs to lotus', *Far Eastern Economic Review*, 12 December 1996, p. 64–9.

21 'From logs to lotus', *Far Eastern Economic Review*, 12 December 1996, p. 64.

22 Kamil, 'Our activism pays dividends'.

23 Kamil, 'Our activism pays dividends'.

24 See Soh Chee Seng, 'Economic issues in Malaysia's foreign policy' in Mohd Azhari Karim, L. Howell and Grace Okuda, *Malaysian Foreign Policy*, pp. 53–62.

25 Zakaria, in Scalapino, Sato, Wanandi and Han, *Asia and the Major Powers*, p. 268.

26 Ahmad Sarji, *The Chief Secretary to the Government, Malaysia* (Petaling Jaya: Pelanduk Publications, 1996). p. 212.

27 Sarji, *The Chief Secretary to the Government*, pp. 212–13.

28 See Paul Lauren, *Diplomats and Bureaucrats* (Stanford: Hoover Institution Press, 1976).

29 This author was privately asked to study the 'model' for the establishment of the IDFR by a Home Sector civil servant. Several institutes relevant to foreign service or international relations training in the US were visited for the purpose but in deliberating on the findings, it was clear that a principal issue was whether IDFR would be a part of *Wisma Putra*. As indicated by then Chief Secretary Tan Sri Ahmad Sarji (see note 22), the IDFR was seen as central to Dr Mahathir's objectives and therefore the IDFR was to be part of the Prime Minister's Department.

30 For a glimpse of the expanding number of overseas missions, see Appendix 1 in G. K. A. Kumaraseri, *Professional Diplomacy and Foreign Affairs Management: The Malaysian Experience* (Petaling jaya; Pelanduk Publications, 1992), pp. 347–51.

31 See Saravanamuttu, 'Malaysia's foreign policy'.

32 'Tough job for our man in the UN', *The Star*, 25 January 1996.

8 Mexico
Change and Adaptation in the Ministry of Foreign Affairs
Andrés Rozental

The rapid process of change undergone by Mexico and its institutions to keep pace with recent developments in international affairs has had a major impact on the organization, structure and operation of its Ministry of Foreign Affairs.[1] As is the case with its sister bodies around the world, the *Secretaría de Relaciones Exteriores* (SRE) has had to adapt quickly to new challenges and opportunities – often with little or no additional resources – and faces a vastly more complex international environment than ever before. Although historically equipped to respond to traditional diplomatic tasks, Mexico's transition from a relatively minor player into an important actor on the international scene has meant that its primary foreign policy instrument – the SRE – has had to keep up with dizzying and often contradictory events. It has also had to implement a complex and continuing stream of modifications to update its structure, composition and operation.

Although many of the changes outlined in this empirical study are still in the experimental stage, it seems clear that in principle they are here to stay and will determine the parameters within which Mexico's foreign policy will be conducted in the years to come. Some will require further refinement with the benefit of experience, while others will prove to be ill-advised and may be dropped as impractical or unnecessary.

In this summary analysis of the massive transformation that has taken place over the past 15 years, I have chosen to concentrate on three major aspects of *the Secretaría's work*:

- organizational structure and relationships with other foreign policy actors;
- recruitment, selection, advancement and renewal of career diplomats;
- the role of information technology (IT).

Each of these has been the subject of profound change during successive government administrations over the last 30 years.[2] This is especially true when developments are measured against the very conservative, highly institutionalized history of the SRE since its establishment in 1821, just as

independence from Spain was being consolidated and the new nation was
building its capacity to interact with the world around it.

A BRIEF HISTORY

The Foreign Ministry has been present on the political scene since Mexico
became an independent nation.[3] Charged with obtaining full international
acceptance of Mexico's separation from Spain and recognition of its territorial integrity, the Foreign Ministry was among the first agencies established by
the new government as one of four Departments, along with Justice and
Ecclesiastical Affairs, War and Navy, and Treasury, organized to share the
initial burdens of government. Until 1836 the functions of Foreign Relations
and Interior were combined in the same ministry.

Achieving diplomatic recognition was the first foreign policy priority,
requiring the development of strategies and posting of diplomatic agents to
the major powers of the time, as well as to neighbouring countries. During
the first half of the nineteenth century however, several major events pitted
Mexico against an array of foreign threats, the most important of which
ended in the dismembering and loss of over half of Mexico's territory as a
consequence of invasion and war with the United States (1846–8).

Historically, the Ministry of Interior and Foreign Relations ranked first in
importance and in its original form, had many duties to perform. It handled
matters pertaining to foreign relations, to the building and upkeep of minor
roads, highways, post offices, as well as communications. Its official jurisdiction embraced every part of the Republic, and it maintained an official
liaison between the Federal Government and both States and Municipalities.
From 1835 to 1844 – and then again in 1917 – the administration of justice
was also in the competence of the Ministry of Interior and Foreign Relations.

The history of the first decades of independence largely determined the
principles under which Mexican foreign policy were to be conducted. Having
suffered at first-hand the meddling of the major powers in Mexico's internal
affairs and the violent aftermath of numerous armed invasions, Mexicans
became especially attached to the principles of non-intervention and self-
determination. Although the Foreign Ministry and its diplomats were not
able to prevent the loss of half of the country's territory to the USA, at least
they succeeded in avoiding the disintegration of Mexico as an independent
nation. During this period the Foreign Ministry faced frequent changes of
Foreign Secretary and a serious lack of resources to support its diplomats
abroad, most of whom came from the upper classes of Mexican society and
therefore had sufficient family means to maintain themselves.

By the 1860s, the Foreign Ministry also had to deal with civil conflict
within Mexico's own borders. The confrontation between Conservatives

and Liberals led to both forces vying for diplomatic recognition abroad and ended with Maximilian's arrival to head the Second Empire.[4] By then a Marine and Foreign Affairs Secretariat had been established to replace the earlier Department of Internal and Foreign Affairs. It was efficiently organized along the European model, with court-like protocol, uniforms and a highly-structured elite diplomatic corps. In 1867, a republican regime under Juárez came to power, by which time Mexico took the first steps that would eventually lead to its consolidation as a modern nation-state and with it, a new stage in the Foreign Ministry's development.

The 1910 Revolution once again set the scene for a period of domestic conflict in Mexico. Foreign powers took advantage of the turmoil to obtain political and economic gain, while the Foreign Ministry acted as an important vehicle in the struggle to defend the country's sovereignty. At this time several Mexican foreign policy doctrines were expounded which reflected the historic experiences of the nation in its dealings with its neighbour to the north and the major European powers of the time. One of these, the *Doctrina Estrada*, has been a tenet of Mexican diplomatic practice to this day.[5]

The end of the revolutionary period in Mexico marked the beginning of the State's consolidation process. The current form of government was established by a Constitution which took effect in 1917.[6] The political and social stability in which post-revolutionary governments evolved enabled them to focus their efforts on Mexico's economic and social well-being. Nevertheless, Mexico was living in complex international times. The threat to peace from two world wars; the disintegration of the great colonial empires and the consequent proliferation of newly independent states; the Cold War and the threat of nuclear conflict, all influenced Mexico's increasingly active participation in the international arena.

The SRE played a crucial role in most of the key events during Mexico's turbulent history. Thus it is not surprising that the career foreign service[7] and its work abroad on behalf of Mexico has led to its well-recognized role as a defender of the country's national interest and sovereignty, a reputation which in subsequent years would result in constant conflicts with other government departments and often within the presidential Cabinet itself.

ORGANIZATION AND AGENDAS

Mexico's government is organized as a federal system, with executive, legislative and judicial branches at both the national and state[8] levels. The President of the Republic[9] is constitutionally vested with the power to conduct foreign policy and the SRE is the administrative body entrusted with its implementation. The SRE is headed by a *Secretarío*, freely appointed and removed by the President, without the advice and consent of Congress.[10] Foreign policy responsibilities are by and large similar to those in other independent countries (that is, treaty making, appointment of diplomatic agents, accreditation of foreign emissaries, and so on). In order to carry out its work, the SRE has a hierarchically organized career foreign service, complemented by an indeterminate number of political appointments at the head of mission level, named by each President for a limited period of time usually not exceeding his administration.[11]

As the lead government agency in charge of foreign policy, the powers, functions and duties of the *Secretaría* are set out in Article 28 of the Organic Law of the Federal Public Administration (LOAPF).[12] Included among its responsibilities are those of securing the coordination of all federal government departments and entities on foreign policy matters, and participating in the negotiation and approval of treaties, agreements and covenants to which Mexico is a party. As will be seen later, this coordinating role has only been partially exercised by the SRE, often becoming a source of conflict between it and other ministries.

The powers and duties of Congress in the foreign policy arena are assigned to the Senate. They relate to the approval of ambassadorial and consular appointments – both career and political – and the ratification of treaties. In recent years, largely through practice rather than in law – and with the executive's acquiescence – the lower house of Congress has also had the opportunity to question the Foreign Minister and senior officials on a variety of foreign policy issues.

The Foreign Ministry is one of nineteen Departments[13] making up the executive. It ranks second in the Cabinet, but the LOAPF specifically states that no one agency has precedence over any other. The high ranking of the *Secretaría* relates to the date of its establishment and not to its relative importance, which depends on each President's own priorities. The law also states that the *Secretario* carries out duties according to instructions issued by the President. It provides for a common organizational structure for all *Secretarías*, with a certain number of *Subsecretarios* (Deputy Ministers), a Chief Clerk, Directors-General and so on. In the case of the Foreign Ministry, *Subsecretario* responsibilities and other hierarchical divisions have changed over time. At present the SRE has three Deputy Ministers, one charged with overseeing Mexico's bilateral political relationships, another for multilateral economic matters and international organizations, and a third dealing with cultural and co-operation issues. During the De la Madrid administration, a fourth *Subsecretario* with responsibility for bilateral and global economic affairs was eliminated for budgetary reasons.[14]

With economic relations playing an increasingly important role in foreign policy and more departments and agencies becoming involved, problems of coordination and institutional rivalry arose over responsibilities in the non-traditional areas of diplomatic activity. As foreign policy was no longer the sole preserve of the Foreign Ministry, the SRE was faced with the task of modernizing itself and its activities so as to successfully compete with other agencies, at the same time as it defended its traditional role as guarantor of the national interest and sovereignty. This often put the Ministry at odds with sister *Secretarías* who were much more interested in advancing their narrower objectives and had little patience for what they saw as the consistent conservatism and bureaucracy of the diplomats. In addition, a failure to recognize the importance of a multi-disciplinary approach within the Foreign Ministry had led to most of its officials being generalists, with little or no knowledge of economic, financial or trade issues and scant technical expertise to bring to bear on policymaking. This was particularly exacerbated when President López Portillo became the first chief executive to come from the ranks of the financial technocracy rather than from the more traditional political *Secretaría de Gobernación* (Interior), or from elected office.

CURRENT STRUCTURE

Today Mexico's Foreign Ministry has some 4000 employees, of which 1352 are career members of the Foreign Service that represent the country in 134 embassies, permanent missions and consulates.[15] A notable feature of the Foreign Service is that it is the only true civil service in the country. Mexico maintains diplomatic relations with 177 nations. Sixty-nine embassies assure resident representation in as many countries, with the majority in the Americas and Europe. Seven separate permanent missions to international organizations,[16] 61 career consulates – mostly in the USA – and 130 Honorary Consulates[17] in cities and countries where permanent representation is not feasible, make up the rest of Mexico's mission network abroad. The foreign service is supported by additional representatives from the ministries of trade, finance, tourism, army/navy and justice that are neither paid by, nor administratively subject to, the SRE.[18]

Unlike some other governments, responsibility for foreign trade policy and promotion in Mexico lies with a separate Ministry of Trade and Industry. Frequent differences arise between trade negotiators and foreign policy operators which cannot be resolved within a single ministerial structure and require arbitration at a higher level. The problem is more acute in the field, where trade offices separate from embassies have a tendency to operate on their own, rather than under the overall supervision of the Foreign Ministry.

The *Secretaría* is divided into functional and geographic departments, with administrative bureaux providing additional support. At the functional level, current structure reflects the priority given to the new issues on the international agenda: human rights, narcotics, environmental affairs and women's issues. A further functional priority relates to the protection of Mexican citizens abroad, primarily through the consular network in the United States.

On the substantive side, in addition to directorates responsible for cultural, technical co-operation, legal and consular affairs, the SRE has five geographic bureaux,[19] regional and global multilateral directorates to cover Mexico's membership in international bodies[20] and offices for regional economic affairs. New departments[21] have been created over the past decade to reflect transformations taking place around the world and the evolving priorities of Mexican foreign policy.

FORCES FOR CHANGE

Beginning in the early 1970s, Mexico's international agenda underwent a major change. From a mainly reactive diplomatic presence, foreign policy objectives became considerably more proactive. Already during the Echeverría administration, the SRE was suddenly confronted by new challenges, from the presidential decision to establish a leadership role in the developing world, to the utopian idea of sponsoring the abolition of the veto in the UN Security Council. Parts of this new agenda were successfully achieved, while others fell by the wayside, mostly because they lay outside the country's traditional scope of international activity or because they had not been adequately thought through.[22]

Within the new agenda several important foreign policy objectives clearly emerged. Relations with the USA needed to be put on a more balanced footing by simultaneously diversifying political and economic ties with the rest of the world. Mexico needed to play an increased role in the international organizations to which it already belonged, as well as to join new ones.[23] Foreign policy would have to actively support the nation's development priorities, adding new issues such as economic affairs, trade promotion and private sector relationships to the traditional diplomatic agenda. Mexican culture, language and technology would need to support more aggressively foreign policy, including a *rapprochement* with the large community of Mexicans living in the USA and recognition of the emerging hispanic influence on that country's political scene.

All this was taking place at the same time as major changes in the external environment forced Mexico to re-define its traditional foreign policy goals. The emergence of a united Europe, the end of the Cold War, the break-up of the former Soviet Union and the arrival of democracy and stability in Latin America all had consequences for the country's strategy, while the North American Free Trade Agreement confirmed Mexico's association with the world's largest economy and sole remaining superpower.

Major political and structural domestic reforms also played a significant role in this process. The emergence of non-governmental watchdog groups, increased representation by opposition political parties and a vociferous media all pushed the Foreign Ministry, together with the rest of the government, to re-define its relationship with the citizenry. Together with Mexico's new foreign policy objectives, these changes joined time-honoured principles – already enshrined in the Constitution – as the framework within which the *Secretaría* has been operating since the early 1970s and set the scene for the opportunities and challenges facing the Ministry and its diplomats. Under pressure from rapidly evolving events and constantly shifting priorities, the bureaucracy was forced to respond by reshaping its image and adapting itself to a situation for which it was not totally prepared.

CHALLENGES TO THE FOREIGN POLICY ESTABLISHMENT

Four major areas of the Foreign Ministry's work have dominated change in the conduct of foreign policy:

- the Ministry's role within government;
- the synergy between foreign policy decisionmaking and outside interest groups;
- the profile of diplomats;
- the use of information technology.

Each of these in turn has been the subject of efforts to adapt the Foreign Ministry and Mexico's diplomatic service to present requirements, without losing the respected traditions that characterized the nation's diplomatic history over the last century.

The Ministry's role within government

The single, most complex challenge to the foreign policy establishment relates to the interaction between the decisionmaking process within the Foreign Ministry and outside national interests. Once the preserve of the career diplomatic corps, international affairs can no longer be conducted within the confines of the SRE. Other government departments have entered the foreign policy arena by handling their own affairs abroad and by creating specialized bureaux of international affairs[24] which often compete with the Foreign Ministry and its generalists. Almost all are staffed by non-diplomats, trained in their technical specialities and given wide briefs to establish international contacts, travel, sign agreements, commit resources and otherwise interact abroad. They often do so without notifying the Foreign Ministry, and occasionally even hide their activities from Mexican diplomats.

Thus today's SRE has to assimilate the proliferation of foreign policy actors at all levels of national life while attempting to ensure a minimum coordination of their activities and varying interests when interacting with other countries. Within the Cabinet, as with any such role assigned to one of several peer institutions, the SRE has had mixed results in exercising this function. Interinstitutional rivalries, personality conflicts and clashing interests contribute to undermine the 'single voice' concept in Mexico's dealings with the rest of the world.

Technically, there should not be any problem. The law is very clear in giving the President exclusive responsibility for the conduct of foreign policy, with the Foreign Ministry as the main implementing instrument. Article 28 of the LOAPF states that the Foreign Ministry's role is to coordinate all Federal government departments and entities 'without prejudice to the exercise of their attributions', an impossible task when in practice each department has equal access to the President and Ministers often find it difficult to reconcile conflicting interests among themselves. Some recent Presidents have been forced to undertake this role directly, while others have created commissions and sub-cabinet groups to streamline government coordination and facilitate policymaking. Miguel de la Madrid organized sub-cabinet groups along policy lines, including an economic cabinet. These became more active during the Salinas administration, with the addition of specialized cabinets for foreign policy and national security issues, both of which included the Foreign Ministry. But none of these groups and committees are permanent. They are often created or meet for a specific issue and rarely produce a written document. When the participants are unable to reach a consensus, the group usually disbands or fades away, to be replaced with yet another coordinating body.

Government decisionmaking in Mexico is highly centralized. In foreign policy the President, Foreign Ministry and Congress are the lead institutions, but of these the President is clearly the main player and the centre of process. Although in theory relying on the Cabinet team as a whole to formulate and implement policy decisions, Ministers do not meet regularly and collectively with the President who often prefers to deal with the Cabinet individually on problems pertaining to each department's area of responsibility. This encourages competing pressures on the chief executive and can often lead to conflicting implementation actions. In extreme cases, the Minister who gets to the President's ear last can often sway a major interinstitutional policy issue his way and consequently 'score a victory' over colleagues.

This problem becomes especially acute in foreign policy negotiations because other governments and interlocutors generally expect a unified, well-defined position to which they can react. Often however, they quickly find that depending on which Ministry they are talking to, postures can vary considerably thus giving them the ability to play one department off another, which inevitably results in a divided and weakened negotiating situation.

Mexican Presidents have found different ways to manage the conduct of diplomacy, mostly according to the personal interest of the Head of State in international affairs. Echeverría created a parallel foreign policy team within his own office to supervize – and often contradict – the Foreign Ministry, which he basically mistrusted. He was convinced that the traditional diplomatic establishment would be unable to follow his own 'modern' diplomacy and therefore entrusted real authority to his advisors in *Los Pinos*.[25] Whenever a particular policy decision failed or was delayed, Echeverría blamed it on the Ministry's career service, while successes were quickly attributed to his own team of aggressive, young go-getters who paid little attention to the niceties of diplomacy. Direct contacts bypassing the *Secretaría* were encouraged and the President travelled extensively encompassing dozens of capitals at a time. The Foreign Minister at the time was the first in a string of political appointments made by Mexico's last five presidents, although in many instances they had to be replaced at some point during each *sexenio*[26] by a career diplomat.

Decisionmaking and Outside Interest Groups

The second change has to do with civil society and the emerging nongovernmental community in Mexico. Whereas in the past Mexico's foreign policy was normally discussed and decided within the confines of the executive, it is now increasingly subject to congressional scrutiny – especially by the Senate – and by a host of interest groups all demanding a say in the decisionmaking process. Today the Foreign Ministry has to take many new and often divergent opinions into account when formulating policy, as well as to explain its decisions to the legislature and public opinion in general. This is not easy for those traditional diplomats who tend to defend their positions on the basis of a 'this is the way it has always been done' perspective, rather than by being receptive to new ideas and methods. It is curious to observe that this problem is equally prevalent among younger foreign service officers, as with veterans who view any change with suspicion.

Mexico's participation in major international conferences or bilateral talks must now be discussed and negotiated beforehand with dozens of NGOs that deal with such matters as the environment, human rights, and women's issues, which did not even exist ten years ago. Congressional observers from all political parties routinely demand to be included in official delegations travelling abroad, and the NGO community attends UN-sponsored international gatherings alongside governmental delegations. If a Mexican position is not previously discussed and generally agreed with the main groups, they effectively can, and often do, pressure the government to change its mind. Sometimes they even undermine the work of the official delegation by launching media campaigns back home criticizing Mexico's stance on any of these issues.

Other major constraints on foreign policy decisionmaking have emerged. The media play their role by constantly questioning and examining foreign affairs, often with the benefit of reports from journalists abroad portraying other countries' interests on a particular issue. It is not unusual for a newspaper to attack a particularly sensitive diplomatic strategy on the basis of information obtained outside Mexico, pushing the Foreign Ministry to publicly defend itself at the expense of confidentiality and discretion. This has led the *Secretaría* to become much more open in the conduct of foreign policy, calling for more frequent contacts with the press and costly public relations efforts where none were needed before.

On the broader administrative front, a growing Mexican population required the Ministry to decentralize by providing its services in all major cities, as well as throughout the nation's capital. A simplification of administrative requirements was also introduced so as to make the *Secretaría* more accessible to those who need its services. Each of Mexico City's boroughs now has a passport office which issues travel documents, while provincial SRE branches function in many of the country's state capitals and larger cities. These are connected on-line to the Ministry's central computer and can issue passports on a same-day basis, as well as legalize signatures and perform most of the functions assigned to the SRE by Mexican law. They also serve to liaise with State governments, many of which are themselves becoming increasingly active on the international stage.

The Career Foreign Service

Image has often influenced the way in which Mexican presidents have approached the country's career foreign service. Often characterized as elitist and privileged, the individuals who made up the SEM were at first unable to project the dynamism of their younger technocrat colleagues in government. While economists, bankers and politicians easily broke into the national bureaucracy as a consequence of rapid generational change, diplomats still needed 20 or more years to climb painstakingly the hierarchy and reach top positions. This in effect meant that directors and *Subsecretarios* in the SRE were generally much older than their counterparts in other ministries, and consequently more prone to caution and tradition. If to this inherent imbalance one adds the fact that most career diplomats up until 1970 were lawyers trained in the *minutiae* of their profession, it is easy to understand the clash that arose between them and their colleagues. Popular imagery had diplomats standing around at cocktail parties, drinking champagne and dancing in their tuxedoes in faraway foreign capitals. No one thought diplomats good for much else than reporting home on gossip gleaned in spy-like encounters, or helping obtain hard-to-get tickets for the theatre.

So it became imperative for the diplomatic service to change its image. Echeverría used one peculiar method by naming a dozen young economists fresh out of university as ambassadors to several Latin American, European and Asian capitals, equipping each with an attaché case filled with brochures and samples of Mexican products which were to be promoted abroad. Their instructions were to sell Mexico and their performance was measured by whether bilateral trade statistics increased or not. In addition, a new Foreign Trade Institute opened offices in dozens of major cities around the world – many in capitals where embassies were also present – with huge budgets and representatives who earned more than the country's top diplomats. Conflict was inevitable. Career foreign service officers felt displaced and ignored; disparities in income and office luxury led to frustration, which in turn undermined the effort to have trade promoters and diplomats join forces and work together. Coordination in the field was non-existent and institutional rivalry back home promoted an adversarial relationship between ministries.

Similar problems occurred in Mexico City. The Foreign Ministry, traditionally under-budgeted and out of the modernization mainstream, remained tied to old working methods, outdated technology and a highly-centralized bureaucracy. While other agencies managed to pay better bonuses and expenses to their officials, the SRE had to make do with basic civil service salaries for diplomats who were posted in Mexico. The image of highly-paid – in attractive foreign currencies – Mexicans abroad was consistently used as justification for refusing increases to match jobs in the public and private sectors. This was to lead to a most serious consequence for the Foreign Ministry: the inability to compete with other government agencies in the recruitment of the best and the brightest job entrants.

Another serious difficulty faced by the *Secretaría* in the recruitment process related to the length and difficulty of the career process. A young *attaché* in his or her early twenties was faced with the daunting prospect of slowly climbing the career ladder, perhaps to reach the enviable position of Counsellor or Minister by the age of 45. From then on, political influence and contacts determined further promotions and every step of a diplomat's career was pegged to time in service rather than to merit, intelligence or productivity. In contrast, young *pitufos*[27] quickly rose in the ranks of other government agencies, were better paid and often reached top positions within a single *sexenio*. Although they did not have the permanent job security enjoyed by members of the SEM, the short-term attraction of rapid promotions and higher remuneration often blurred worries about the future, which Mexicans in any case prefer not to think too much about.

The task was clear: the *Secretaría* had to transform radically both the image and reality of the career foreign service if it was to survive in the environment described above. Above all it meant changing the profile of Mexico's diplomats, giving them the tools required to function in that environment, and making the members of the SEM fully competitive within the government bureaucracy and the business community.

Information and Diplomacy

Traditionally, diplomats were trained to obtain as much information as possible, while giving out as little as they could get away with. This is no longer the case and contemporary foreign services need to take an entirely different approach to the flow and use of information in the conduct of foreign policy. For a start, foreign ministries and diplomats today are inundated with information. In addition to the traditional reporting by embassies and missions, there is instantaneous access to television, radio, facsimile and the Internet. Foreign ministries are often better informed about international events than other government departments, but the chances are that most senior officials throughout government have access to 24-hour news programmes, on-line financial links and press reports from around the world. They are as well informed as their diplomat colleagues and often have more specialized data at their disposal.

In addition to being highly informed, diplomats are often better equipped to discriminate, analyze and work with abundant information because of their training and background. This cannot be accomplished, however, with outdated hunting and gathering techniques, which brings us to the fourth major challenge faced by the *Secretaría*: modernizing the dissemination, collection and analysis of information in the entire Mexican foreign service system.

A final significant change affects the way information moves between ministries at home and posts abroad. Where once diplomatic pouches and tedious cipher telegraphy were the rule, this is an age of instant communication. Often given as a reason to dispense with diplomacy in general, the larger consensus is that the new technology allows foreign ministries to become more effective and significantly increases the information flow to and from their offices abroad. The challenge, however, lies in being able to use these developments in such as way as to become more efficient rather than just better informed, especially since the flood of information currently available is impossible to digest without efficient management and clear guidelines.

STRATEGIES AND RESPONSES

Mexican diplomacy has gone a long way towards meeting the challenges outlined above. Through a carefully designed plan for modernizing the foreign service and using state-of-the-art technology, the *Secretaría* and the SEM have undergone a profound transformation, one which hopefully gives today's diplomats the tools they need to operate in the changed domestic and global environment. How have the challenges been dealt with, to what extent have the changes been successful and what further measures are required to complete the process?

The Coordinating Role

Although the Foreign Ministry has not been completely successful in ensuring total coordination of government actions that impact on foreign policy, mechanisms have been established which at least help the SRE know what is going on and thus allow it to play an increased role in policymaking. A new law on treaties was passed several years ago which requires Foreign Ministry approval for every international governmental agreement, whether a formal treaty, so-called executive agreement, memorandum of understanding or simple exchange of letters. Any document not vetted by the SRE has no legal standing and therefore does not obligate the Mexican State. This allows the Ministry to ensure that all such agreements conform to international law and practice, as well as to the national interest. In addition, the Senate has strictly interpreted its constitutional prerogatives in treaty-making by requiring congressional approval of *all* international covenants, including executive agreements not previously subject to legislative scrutiny.

Inter-ministerial coordinating bodies have been created under the chairmanship of the Foreign Ministry. One such group regularly gathers *Subsecretarios* from several government departments to discuss and harmonise policy on Mexico's relations with the United States, an especially complex set of issues that involves the entire Cabinet. Another administrative measure designed to keep the SRE informed is a presidential decree requiring that any official trip abroad by a senior government employee needs prior notification to the SRE. Although in practice it has proved difficult to fully implement, this mandate now gives the Ministry advance warning of most government visits to other countries. Other successful coordinating efforts have been at the level of broader institutional contacts between government departments below the *Secretario* and *Subsecretario* levels, and frequent seminars on foreign policy issues with senior officials from other ministries.

A final novel approach to fostering understanding between agencies has been to encourage diplomats to take leave of absence for temporary secondment to other government agencies and to bring senior officials into the *Secretaría* from ministries whose work is foreign policy-related. This can now be done without losing seniority or the right to be promoted within the SEM.

Once diplomats themselves recognize that they and their foreign ministries are no longer able to exercise a once-sacrosanct monopoly over the conduct of international affairs it becomes easier to adapt structures and personnel profiles to the new situation. This has now been accomplished by Mexico's SRE, although not without difficulties or resistance from the establishment.

Foreign Policy, Media and Civil Society

The relationship with the media and civil society is a key feature in the changes that have taken place, not only at the Foreign Ministry but in government as a whole. On the media side, it has become necessary to increase significantly contacts between representatives of the press and Ministry officials. The position of spokesman was established to ensure direct access to the *Secretaría* by journalists who cover foreign affairs. The Ministry has had to multiply the number and increase the detail of press releases and frequent press conferences are held – on and off the record. The Foreign Minister, as one of the members of Cabinet with the highest media exposure, now has to worry about his and the Ministry's image more than ever before.

The foreign service has managed to adapt to this new media relationship. Most larger diplomatic posts have specialized press officers who maintain close contact with Mexican journalists at home and abroad, and with the media in their jurisdictions. Many are career diplomats with specialized language abilities who have been trained in media relations. They are extremely important to the daily functioning of an embassy or consulate as they constitute the direct link between Mexico's outside image and those who report on it.

As a result of these changes, the *Secretaría* has become much more open in the conduct of its business. Secrecy and discretion are still the key to the work of diplomacy, but equally important is the image that the Ministry and foreign service project on the national and international scenes. Better communication, the general availability of foreign policy information and lively public debates on Mexico's position on international issues have gone a long way towards demystifying the conduct of diplomacy.

But the greatest change has been in the relationship between the foreign policy establishment and the numerous NGOs that have emerged in Mexico over the last decade. Where originally the Ministry was deeply suspicious of NGOs – often seen as external *agents provocateurs* – it now has a daily working relationship with the principal groups dealing with human rights, the environment, narcotics and women's issues, among others. Most are firmly established in Mexico and represent national interests, although some are affiliated with wider international groupings. In almost all cases they comprise concerned members of Mexico's civil society.

A case in point is the preparatory process that takes place prior to major international summit meetings such as the 1986 Rio Conference on the Environment, the Vienna gathering on human rights or the Cairo population summit. NGO representatives now join governmental delegations and participate fully in the drafting of position papers and conference documents. They exercise a considerable degree of influence on the official Mexican position, often paying for costly campaigns in the national press so as to make known their views. Now the Ministry has a co-operative rather than an adversarial relationship with the NGO community and is fully conscious of the important role the latter plays in ensuring a consensus on foreign policy questions. This is a major change from the past.

The Foreign Service

The immediate task was to change the image and reality of the foreign service by reforming the law governing the SEM and bringing it in line with modern international civil service practice. The recruitment process was opened up to university graduates from all academic disciplines, rather than just from the social sciences as was the case before 1988. Instead of testing prospective diplomats solely on their knowledge of law, history and languages, the selection mechanism was changed to incorporate new subjects of greater relevance to Mexico's new foreign policy agenda. Economics, trade, finance, general culture and consular protection were introduced as test subjects.

Candidates are now required to have full proficiency in either English or French, while a working knowledge of a major second foreign language is mandatory. Writing and thinking ability are also measured. Another change allows applicants to be tested outside Mexico City and at embassies abroad. This permits the service to broaden its recruitment throughout the Republic and to allow students in foreign institutions, or other residents abroad, to take parts of the examination without travelling to Mexico.

Other changes were introduced which affected those already in the foreign service. An annual mandatory rotation programme now ensures that diplomats serve in Mexico and abroad in a more balanced and predictable way. Geographic and thematic specialization is encouraged. Ongoing training and education has become an important part of career development, which is now based both on time served *and* merit. Promotions are obtained in transparent, annual competitive examinations and an expanded Foreign Service Personnel Commission meets more regularly. Written evaluations are required every six months and are seen by the person being judged. In a controversial, but important reform to the old tenured system, failure to obtain a promotion after three attempts leads to automatic dismissal.

Lateral entry into the foreign service – often the bane of career diplomats – is now understood as a necessary tool for enhancing the Ministry's role in government. By allowing experienced mid-career officials from other departments to join the diplomatic service, and having foreign service personnel temporarily seconded to other parts of the government – including the legislative branch and State bodies – the SRE is able to play a better coordinating role. It also promotes understanding of the diplomatic service and of the Ministry's perspective on foreign policy issues. Finally, a one-year Master's degree programme was created in the diplomatic academy for those applicants who pass all the entrance examinations, allowing complementary education in subjects not normally covered in conventional studies and further evaluation of the candidates before they are formally accepted into the service. An accelerated fast-stream programme has been created to encourage bright young diplomats by abbreviating the early stages of their career development.

These far-reaching changes have now been in operation for six years. Several hundred new entrants have joined the career foreign service under this system, while almost all veteran officers have participated in one or more advancement competitions and ongoing education programmes. Although not everyone is entirely satisfied with the new system, most believe that it is a considerable improvement over the past.

Information and Diplomacy

Electronic mail, networking and the Internet have become basic tools in the management of information within Mexico's foreign policy institutions, in addition to the computerization of the Ministry and most major posts abroad. Resources previously dedicated to secretarial work have been re-directed to substantive tasks. Foreign service personnel are now required to handle computer hardware and software, both as a condition for entrance and during career development. Networks allow documents, messages and information to flow freely throughout the system. Posts abroad can communicate directly among themselves, breaking the long-standing monopoly on the central office as the sole authorized conduit. Future projects include a secure video conferencing facility that will allow meetings to take place without physical travel, and real-time access to central office computers from the field. Many documents already move via secure e-mail and are commented on, revised and distributed at the touch of a button.

Press releases, information sheets, speeches and other public domain documents are disseminated through the Internet, reducing costs. This not only gives missions access to a wealth of information previously unavailable to them on a timely basis, but also provides similar possibilities for individuals in Mexico and beyond. Direct communications have also been set up between the Ministry – and its missions – and other government departments with which day-to-day business is transacted. The Interior Ministry's Immigration Service now authorizes visa issuance to Mexican consulates through e-mail, and the Federal Electoral Commission keeps missions informed of voting results during national and state elections. Finally, voice and facsimile communications between and among offices have been upgraded and rationalized. Through the use of a virtual private satellite network (VPN), the Ministry enjoys secure voice and written contact with any mission in a matter of seconds.

CONCLUSIONS

As is clear from this analysis, a major attempt has been made in Mexico to meet many of the key challenges affecting contemporary foreign ministries and diplomacy. Changes which in recent years have affected the content, methods and style of modern diplomacy call for an increasingly efficient apparatus to cope with the new challenges. Although modernization efforts have included novel methods for relating to the rest of the federal government and the reorganization and modification of the Foreign Ministry's organic structure, the main change has come from within the body of men and women who make up the foreign service.

By transforming and constantly adapting to evolving circumstances, the Mexican Foreign Ministry hopes to continue to give the country justifiable pride in the conduct of its foreign policy. For its part, the diplomatic service is committed to support this effort by becoming as efficient and effective an instrument of that policy as possible. That is the challenge for present and future generations of Mexican diplomats, and one that will surely be met in the years to come.

NOTES

1   The author is indebted to Alicia Buenrostro, First Secretary at the Mexican Embassy in London, for her invaluable support in researching and assisting in the preparation of this study.
2   This study covers the administrations of Luis Echeverría (1970–6), José Lopez Portillo (1976–82), Miguel de la Madrid (1982–8) and Carlos Salinas de Gortari (1988–94), during which the author personally participated in and implemented many of the reforms described in this chapter.
3   Mexico formally declared its independence from Spain on 15 September 1810, but it was not until 1821 that the process was completed with the Plan de Iguala and the formal handover of power by the Spanish Viceroy to Iturbide.
4   The war of reform lasted for three years. During that period, the US, UK, Spain and France all had grievances against Mexico, mostly dealing with unpaid loans borrowed by both sides to finance their campaigns in the Civil War.

5   According to this doctrine, named after Genaro Estrada, Foreign Minister from 1928 to 1932, Mexico does not use diplomatic recognition of other governments as an instrument of foreign policy, limiting itself to maintaining diplomatic representation, or not, as the case may be. A previous and equally important milestone in Mexico's foreign policy was the so-called Doctrina Carranza named after President Venustiano Carranza (1917–20), enunciated in 1918 as a response to the pressures of foreign oil companies on the Mexican government to protect their interests. This doctrine embodies the principles of non-intervention and self-determination.

6   Although often amended and added to, the Mexican Constitution of 1917 remains as one of the oldest in Latin America.

7   The *Servicio Exterior Mexicano* (SEM) is highly regarded in international circles and is considered one of Latin America's premier civil service institutions.

8   Mexico has 31 states and a Federal District, which is the nation's capital. Beginning in 1997, the *Distrito Federal* will have many of the attributions of a State, including direct popular election of its Mayor.

9   Mexico's Chief Executive is elected by direct, popular vote for a single period of six years. He can serve only a single term.

10   This is in contrast to the US system, under which the President requires the advice and consent of Congress for major government appointments, or the parliamentary system as practised in the UK where Ministers are Members of Parliament and also serve at the pleasure of the Head of Government, although they are responsible to Parliament for their actions.

11   In recent years, successive Presidents have amply used their prerogative to name ambassadors and consuls general from outside the career foreign service, sometimes reaching over half of all heads of embassies abroad.

12   *Ley Organica de la Administracion Publica Federal* (LOAPF), published in the *Diario Oficial* on 21 February 1992.

13   The inner Presidential Cabinet comprises 17 *Secretarías* and two Attorneys-General, one with federal responsibilities and another for the nation's capital. A second, 'outer' Cabinet adds the heads of major government agencies.

14   Although cost-cutting was given as the reason, other government departments dealing with financial and trade issues had strenuously lobbied against the SRE having a high-level economic role which they viewed as 'trespassing' on their briefs. The new *Subsecretarío* for Economic Affairs had barely been established in 1980, and was considered at the time an important 'turf victory' for the SRE.

15   Mexico's public sector is made up of over one million *burocratas* who serve on short-term contracts, mostly within a single six-year presidency. Although in practice many government employees make a career of public service, often moving from department to department with their superiors, there is no legal framework to protect their employment at mid-level and senior positions. Only the lower echelons are unionised and hold more or less permanent *plazas* and consequent job security. The armed forces and diplomatic service are the only government institutions that have legal frameworks ensuring continuity, hierarchy and career development over a professional lifetime.

16   United Nations (New York), Organisation of American States (Washington DC), UN Specialised Agencies (Geneva), World Trade Organisation (Geneva), OECD (Paris), International Civil Aviation Authority (Montreal) and UNESCO (Paris).

17   These are usually non-Mexican citizens who provide essential consular services for Mexican citizens abroad, in addition to supporting the SRE in business contacts and trade promotion.

18 In theory they work under the coordination of each ambassador or consul general, as the case may be. In practice some operate on their own and do not always keep the Head of Mission informed of their activities.

19 North America, Latin America and the Caribbean, Europe, Asia-Pacific, and Africa/Middle East.

20 United Nations System, Organisation of American States and the inter-American system, and the OECD.

21 In one case, a decision was made in 1986 to merge the former Western and Eastern Europe divisions into a single unit covering Europe from the Urals to the Atlantic long before the fall of the Berlin Wall or the break-up of the Soviet Union. A Pacific Basin Bureau was created in 1989 to support Mexico's efforts to reinsert itself into that area of the world and take advantage of the growth and increasing geopolitical importance of the Asian economies.

22 An example of a 'mission impossible' thrust on the SRE by President Echeverría was to push for Spain's expulsion from the UN as a result of the Franco regime's repression and murder of five Basque separatists.

23 During the Salinas Administration, Mexico became the first new member of the OECD since the mid-1970s, a founding member of the European Bank for Reconstruction and Development (EBRD), helped establish the Association of Caribbean States, entered the Asia Pacific Economic Conference (APEC) and the Pacific Economic Co-operation Council (PECC), in addition to signing new trade and co-operation agreements with the European Union, the US and Canada (NAFTA), Chile and several other Latin American governments.

24 Almost every Ministry has a *Dirección General de Asuntos Internacionales*. At best they are small, coordination units set up to assist the department in its relations with similar agencies in other countries and to plan trips abroad by senior officials. At worst, they are large, well-financed offices that constantly conflict with the Foreign Ministry and often seek to displace it. A recent study undertaken by the *Secretaría de Relaciones Exteriores* found that the total staff and financial resources assigned to these bodies throughout the federal system was similar to the total of SRE employees, and exceeded the SRE's budget by 20 per cent!

25 The official presidential residence and office complex in Mexico City.

26 The six-year presidential term in Mexico.

27 A derogatory term applied to young, aggressive technocrats in government.

9 Norway
The Foreign Ministry: Bracketing Interdependence

Iver B. Neumann[1]

The literature on the Norwegian Ministry of Foreign Affairs (MFA) is dominated by the comparative foreign policy writings of Maurice East and his associates. It explores the implications of growing interdependence in world politics and focuses on what they see as a puzzle: how is it that the MFA does not modify the organization and its interface with other administrative bodies so that it maintains an optimal measure of control over Norwegian foreign policy decisionmaking? This paper postulates a clash of cultures between East on the one hand and the MFA on the other. It explores the MFA by looking synoptically at its historical interfaces with Norwegian society, with the MFAs of other countries, with Norwegian domestic ministries and with Norwegian politicians. The introductory section presents East's pre-empirical presuppositions and suggests that, as long as one formulates research puzzles without taking into consideration how the MFA is seen by the people working in it, one cannot adequately explain those puzzles. The two following sections present two clusters of empirical material which are part of the horizon of people working in the MFA: organizational trajectory and discourse on reorganization. The conclusion suggests that more of MFA behaviour can be explained by starting with the question of MFA identity rather than with the systemically global characteristic of interdependence, as does the comparative foreign policy literature.

East and his colleagues postulate that a change at the level of the system of states, interdependence, necessitates 'an examination of how foreign policy-making systems adapt organizationally'.[2] The reasons for focusing on MFAs are that they are traditionally the most important organizational units in these foreign-policy systems, that 'the single most significant effect of interdependence seems to be the reduced influence of foreign ministries in foreign policy-making systems', and that the management of this challenge 'is of intrinsic interest since it anticipates a complex process of managing decline in the organization rather than expansion or growth'.[3] Due to the nature of interdependence, which tends to relativize the role of MFA-to-MFA relations in world politics by shifting the action to multilateral organizations, ministry-to-ministry relations, society-to-society relations and the like, all of the expected adaptive strategies are to do with coordinating activity with other ministries and establishing better rapport with society at large.[4] One way of managing decline is to outsource tasks, but East is sceptical of this strategy, mainly because it will 'cut the foreign ministry out of the network, and this severely reduces its capability to monitor or coordinate activities in the area'.[5]

The alternative strategy advocated by East and associates is an increase in coordination of foreign activities. The metaphor of the network seems to cover what they have in mind: a shift in strategy away from being at the apex of a hierarchy of domestic ministries from which one can deal direct with other MFAs, to being a node in the interdependent network which is world politics.

One notes immediately that East and his co-authors formulate the question in a way which lays itself open to the kind of critique advanced by Brian Hocking in the introduction to this volume. By using as their baseline a representation of MFAs as all-powerful gatekeepers of the interface between the inside of a nation-state and the outside of the international environment, they lay themselves open to Hocking's charge of being ahistorical. After all, MFAs are a relatively recent phenomenon in the forms which we know them. Their origins lie in a gradual dismantling of a unified administrative structure which did not distinguish between domestic and foreign policy, and conflict between foreign ministries and a variety of rival agencies with external concerns has been a continuing feature at least since the late nineteenth century.

However, I want to focus on another problem. East found that his respondents recognized a growth in interdependence and the challenge it posed. However, there was also 'a general consensus in the organization that coordination problems are not among the highest priority items on the action agenda'.[6] Indeed, often the question of wanting coordination 'was not even mentioned at all until mentioned first by the interviewer', and 'Virtually all felt that [the MFA] had both sufficient access to information and resources and expertise to carry out coordination in a particular case *if [the MFA]* made it a high priority matter'.[7] Furthermore, the research done by East's team confirmed that this was indeed the case.

If coordination was clearly not the mechanism which might explain why the MFA acted like it did, then why did not East begin the hunt for some other explanatory mechanism? Why did he not take into account the representations of their own work offered by MFA personnel? East was told that much of the international activity of the specialized ministries which he saw as a competitive threat to MFA activity, was peripheral, since it was not really foreign policy, defined as actions binding on Norway. Thus, East was confronted with something which his interdependence framework told him should not exist, namely a representation of policy as being divided into 'low' and 'high' politics. East reacted by not validating this representation, and insisted that 'issues with "significant" foreign policy aspects'[8] were indeed settled by these specialized ministries – that is, that 'low' policy was not 'low' and thus could not be ignored.

In my view, East's associate, Efjestad, demonstrates convincingly that other ministries sometimes do take decisions which the MFA would have liked to influence or veto, had they only known about them in time.[9] This finding, however, tells us nothing about why MFA personnel act as they do. Of the three explanations which East does present: lack of interest in organizational questions, lack of clout due to a culturally conditioned disability of the MFA to lead, impaired possibilities for leadership at the time when the research was carried out, only the second begins to suggest a fully fledged explanation. But it does so in terms of the domestic political culture inside which this particular MFA operates, not in terms of the systemic conditions of interdependence which are postulated as the framework for the operation of all MFAs and which form the foundation for the entire project.

An alternative explanation should be able to explain, firstly, why MFA personnel insist on representing politics in terms of 'high' and 'low' and, second, why they are not particularly interested in inter-ministerial coordination. It should also go some way towards addressing the following issues:

a) the lack of correlation between rational factors such as the seeming importance of a task as measured in terms of the attention given to it by the political leadership and public opinion, its economic importance to the country (for example, energy), the possibility it offers for attracting additional funds to the MFA (for example, concrete aid projects) on the one hand, and the attention actually given to it by MFA personnel on the other.

b) The repeated involvement of MFA personnel in tugs-of-war with both the political leadership (particularly with leaders who themselves lack experience as serving diplomats) and the Ministry of Commerce and Industry over questions which had to do with the exclusive right to be under a legal obligation to accept posts abroad (flytteplikt), to be administered by personnel who were themselves flyttepliktige, and to insist that the way to become flyttepliktig should be by attending the MFA in-house academy. It will be demonstrated that previously attempted explanations cast exclusively in terms of porkbarreling and prestige are inadequate. A pattern will be identified wherein the MFA personnel insist strongly on maintaining overall, direct and preferably exclusive right of command vis-à-vis Norway's foreign missions, and the right to man them.

c) The lack of overt and prolonged resistance of the kind repeatedly shown vis-à-vis the Ministry of Commerce and Shipping when the Prime Minister's Office took over vital aspects of the coordination of EU matters in the early 1990s.

d) Finally, why the 'no' in the 1972 referendum on Norwegian membership of the EC came as such a shock to the MFA.

I want to start with the representations put forward by MFA personnel themselves, and not, as does East, with a postulated systemic trait like interdependence. For me, the MFA has the status of shaper of its own reality, not simply reacting to systemic change. I now want to investigate what this status is by focusing on its organizational trajectory.

ORGANIZATIONAL TRAJECTORY

When Norway broke away from the union with Sweden in 1905, one of the issues which had been posed by the preceding nation-building efforts was that of the organization of the diplomatic service. As a result of great power dispositions at the end of the Napoleonic Wars, Norway had been carved off from Denmark and become the weaker part of the United Kingdoms of Sweden and Norway. During the nineteenth century, it was a non-entity in just about all spheres of international life save that of shipping. Sweden, on the other hand, was one of Europe's middle powers, and that was a status which mattered in an era where, alongside the six great powers of Germany, Great Britain, France, Austria-Hungary, Russia and Italy, only Turkey, Spain, Denmark and Sweden could make such a claim.[10] The major differences between the historical trajectories of the two nations and states made for very different outlooks upon the outside world in general, and diplomacy as an institution in particular. In Sweden, where diplomacy had been a major concern since the Thirty Years War and there was an aristocracy from which to recruit diplomats, the Foreign Service was routinely and unquestioningly treated as a major concern by all layers of society.

In Norway, whose state apparatus was historically weak and where the very few aristocrats in residence were not strong enough to maintain social hegemony, there was little or no understanding of the institution of diplomacy as such. Interest in the world focused on practical matters. Specifically, Norwegian shipping needed assistance once it found itself in trouble in foreign ports. Thus, in the 1890s, when the demand for a separate Norwegian state began to be heard, it took as one of its major forms an attack on the local bureaucracy, which was seen as anational. Specifically, there was an attack on the closed and aristocratic diplomatic world of which Sweden was represented as a major exemplar, and a call for the upgrading of the consular services afforded to Norwegian ships. When the Norwegian MFA was established in the summer of 1905 it took the form of an upgrading and separation of what had been the Foreign Department (Udenriksavdeling) of the Ministry of Commerce and Shipping. Only two people left the diplomatic corps of the United Kingdoms to help establish a Norwegian one.

There are three reasons why an examination of the Norwegian Foreign Ministry in the 1990s should hark back to its formative period a century ago. First, and most importantly, from its very inception the Norwegian diplomatic service had a legitimacy problem vis-à-vis the society it was supposed to represent. In everyday Norwegian, the words diplomati, diplomat and diplomatisk are used to denote an approach to mediation of conflicts, and not as a term for a profession and its practitioners. When used in the latter sense, they have the feel of technical terms. The second and the third concerns may be clearly linked to the first. The social tensions surrounding the diplomatic service impinged on the question of how to organize the service and inaugurated an ongoing tug-of-war over how to mesh matters of commerce and shipping with those of politics. Thirdly, just as 'diplomacy' has not entered into everyday Norwegian, 'diplomat' is not a recognized status. Instead, the self ascription most commonly used is 'civil servant working in the MFA' (UD-tjenestemann), and the most frequent way to refer to a diplomat is to say that he or she is 'working in the MFA'. Thus, the identity of a diplomat is something which must be constantly reaffirmed not only vis-à-vis society at large, but most particularly vis-à-vis other civil servants as well as politicians. Thus in Norway, diplomacy and diplomats are rather indeterminate concepts, regardless of whether they are investigated on the societal, organizational or personal levels.

The Norwegian MFA emerged at a point in time when MFAs throughout Europe were growing rapidly. If, at the end of the nineteenth century, the MFAs of the great powers employed only somewhere between 50 and 100 people, by World War I numbers were pushing 200. Whereas the MFA of Sweden–Norway had 19 employees in 1905, by 1918 the Swedish MFA had 88.[11] Once the Norwegian MFA became properly instituted in the spring of 1906, it employed 16 civil servants and seven secretaries. Following strong domestic opposition, its organization was fashioned after the Swedish and European standards of the day, with two departments each consisting of two divisions, and an archival detachment. The Foreign Service, which was kept separate from the MFA, consisted of six missions in Europe, one in Washington and one in Argentina. In the early years, the minister to London was informally considered to be its primus inter pares.[12] The Consular Service, which was also kept separate, administered 20 salaried Consuls.

In 1913, the shipping portfolio was moved from the Ministry of Commerce to the MFA, only to be moved back again three years later. A law passed in 1922 merged both the Foreign and the Consular services with the Ministry under one secretary general, established an in-house training academy and made one corps out of the disparate groups of personnel by insisting that every employee accept a legal obligation to fill posts anywhere in the world on a similar level to the one already held (that is, subject to flytteplikt, literally a duty to move). The MFA also incorporated questions of commerce in their more general work, launched a charm offensive aimed at the business world, and actually succeeded in winning them over to the idea that there was not necessarily a contradiction between general diplomatic and specific commercial work. At the time of the German occupation in April 1940, the MFA had won the respect of most Norwegian elites.

The MFA sat out World War II in Britain with a staff of only seven people, while the archives were moved to neutral Sweden. When the MFA was reorganized in 1945, it had 156 employees, and was organized in a general, a political and an economic department as well as a temporary one for questions to do with reimbursements in the wake of the war. The law passed in 1948 regulating the MFA's organizational and administrative practice gave way to a rather similar one in 1958, which is still in force.

Like other MFAs of industrialized countries, the Norwegian MFA added some delegations for multilateral work to its foreign service during the first half of the Cold War (there are now nine of them). There was also a modest increase in the number of embassies.[13] As a result of the disintegration of the Soviet Union as well as Yugoslavia, in the early 1990s there was yet another increase, to 60. A number of these are manned by only two diplomats, typically an ambassador and a first secretary, as well as an administrative officer. Mainly as a result of the international reorganization of the shipping trade in the 1970s, the number of professional consulates is now only 13, although Norway still maintains 405 honorary consulates.

Where the nature of functions was concerned, a major change concerned aid and development to developing countries. Together with other likeminded countries such as Sweden, Denmark and The Netherlands, in 1978 Norway decided to heed the UN's call to allocate one per cent of GNP to such projects, and the work was organized under the MFA's umbrella.[14] From 1961 to 1978, the foreign affairs budget multiplied fourfold, and at the end of the period almost 90 per cent of the total was in the area of foreign aid! The rest of the MFA also grew, but not enough to keep up with the average growth rates of other ministries.[15] Foreign aid left the MFA portfolio to be organized in a separate ministry in 1984, only to be reincorporated as part of a major organizational overhaul six years later (see below).

As of 1994, the MFA's budget was NK 10.7 billion and its payroll consisted of 297 senior and 426 junior personnel, 343 secretarial staff and seemingly as many as around 600 people who are recruited and paid locally. These are technical categories, however; the number of bona fide diplomats, that is those under a legal obligation to accept postings abroad (flyttepliktige), is 605.[16] To put these numbers in perspective, the total state budget for 1994 was around NK 400 billion and the number of professionals working in Norwegian ministries around 3500.[17]

The referendum on EC membership held in 1972 was a benchmark year for the Norwegian MFA. The reason has less to do with the beginning of organizational change than with the greatest upheaval in Norwegian politics during the Cold War. This issue once again injected parts of society with a solid dose of scepticism towards diplomats and diplomacy. Throughout the 1960s Norway consistently followed in the wake of Britain on issues concerning European integration, being among the founding members of EFTA, applying for membership of the EEC in 1962 and reactivating that application in 1967. On both occasions, the issue was treated mainly as an economic one by both the administration and public opinion, to the extent that it was handled by the Ministry of Commerce rather than the MFA. At the end of the 1960s, however, the impact of the Vietnam War, the student unrest throughout American and European universities as well as the burgeoning interest in the environment resulted in a growing radicalization, particularly within student and youth movements.

The particular Norwegian flavour added to this standard concoction was a revival of the anti-establishment, anti-urban and anti-elitist tendencies which had animated Norwegian nation-building in the latter half of the nineteenth century. Once the debate about EC membership got under way in earnest around 1970, it became the focal point for a lot of political activity. Since the Labour government made extensive use of MFA personnel in order to publicize the (positive) consequences of Norwegian membership, the MFA widely came to be seen as representing the Norwegian political establishment, not the Norwegian nation, and sometimes even as a foreign element inside the national body politic.

When the anti-marketeers narrowly carried the day in the referendum of 1972, the MFA was widely seen as one of the major culprits. The impact on MFA self-esteem was tangible; one of its major goals had always been to maintain the basic trust needed to pass itself off not only as the representative of the Norwegian state, but also of the Norwegian nation. The EC issue had revealed that this was not necessarily so, and also that the MFA personnel could just as well be presented as the 'unfaithful servants' of the people, to quote the title of a pamphlet which summed up the opinion of the anti-marketeers.[18] The loss of prestige had immediate and lasting effects at all levels.

Prodded by frightened politicians, the MFA more or less gave up informing the public about EC matters, and the question became something of a taboo subject in Norwegian public life for the next 15 years. When it surfaced once again, it was due to the external pressure exerted by the new co-operation between the EC and EFTA as well as the prospect of the end of the Cold War. Still, due to the lingering memories of how it had been compromised by its role in the 1972 referendum, even in the period leading up to the new referendum in 1994 information material produced by the MFA could not be presented as such to the nation for which it was meant, but had to be packaged with material produced outside the MFA and presented as somehow emanating from the state at large.

To sum up, from the very beginning the Norwegian MFA had to fight for domestic recognition. The business community came around to seeing the need for diplomacy by the 1930s. As it gained power at this time and became the state-bearing party after World War II, the leadership of the Labour Party also warmed to the idea of diplomacy, as it was now their own prerogative to conduct it. If that meant that all important elites in Norway came to acknowledge its importance, however, the lack of rapport between most elite groups and a majority of the people uncovered by the 1972 referendum showed among other things that large swathes of the people put no faith either in the words of diplomats or possibly in the institution of diplomacy itself. In other words, domestic recognition was still not a given for the Norwegian MFA.

THREE ROUNDS OF REORGANIZATIONS

Round One

If these historical memories make up an important part of the horizon of MFA personnel, so do the long series of reorganizations which followed in the wake of the 1972 trauma. In the first round a Division of Planning and Policy Analysis was established in 1973 and the division of labour between the MFA and the Ministry of Commerce changed. Sweden had already proceeded to outsource international trade functions from the MFA and into the Ministry of Commerce in 1963. If the finesses of manning the border between these two areas was something of an evergreen in the history of the Norwegian central administration, the issues to be delineated were certainly new. The major bones of contention were tasks related to GATT, UNCTAD, and business with so-called state-trading (that is, Communist) countries. Of course, these were important areas, although the number of personnel was relatively small (the Ministry of Commerce and Shipping initially wanted 14 of the MFA's positions (hjemler), while the Foreign Ministry offered eight; in the end, the tally came to nine). Nonetheless, neither of these factors can account for the intensity with which the infighting was conducted.[19] To add to the puzzle, when the Ministry of Oil and Energy was established at around the same time (in 1978), the MFA was not particularly interested, despite the obvious, vital and wide-ranging social, economic and political importance of this issue area for a major energy-exporting country like Norway.[20]

The MFA consistently insisted on maintaining overall, direct and preferably exclusive right of command vis-à-vis Norway's foreign missions, as well as the right to man them. This was done by citing that part of the general instruction to the MFA where it is laid down that the MFA has overall responsibility for foreign policy, and to insist on keeping as high a measure of control over overseas postings as possible.

It is notable, furthermore, that it was not the political leadership of the MFA which was the driving force here, but the MFA personnel, through their unions. In Norway, the question of which tasks should belong to which ministry is in principle the prerogative of the Cabinet. Practical aspects of reorganization, on the other hand, are itemised in general agreements between the state as the employer and the civil servant's unions as being a matter for negotiation. In practice, it is also a matter of negotiation where the allocation of tasks ends and the concretization of practical aspects begins, and so the MFA unions are key players in these matters. One also notes that MFA unions quite often elect high-ranking civil servants as key negotiators. Hammering out the MFA position on reorganizations was an in-house matter.

The MFA personnel first used their clout to sideline the basis for negotiations passed by their own political leadership.[21] Once the two ministries had been able to reach a mutual proposal to put before the Cabinet, the MFA unions engaged in intense and successful lobbying in parliament, and succeeded in exploding parts of the concessions which the MFA had given to the Ministry of Commerce and Shipping in the previous negotiations.[22] And then, the MFA unions blackballed personnel from the Ministry of Commerce and Shipping who applied for what they saw as traditional MFA sinecures.[23] The author of the only study made of this renegotiation game does not explicitly try to explain why MFA personnel expended all this time and energy. Working inside a traditional rationalistic framework, she betrays a certain puzzlement about MFA priorities, and writes it off as porkbarreling:

> Discussions about the possibility for Ministry of Commerce personnel to serve at missions abroad do not really seem to be informed by an ends-and-means approach. This goes for MFA arguments in particular. A lot of personnel resistance was justified with reference to which positions that would have to be made available for Ministry of Commerce personnel. These were located at so-called 'creampuff stations' like London, Rome, Paris, Geneva and Washington.[24]

Porkbarreling as such is not an explanation, however, since the MFA unions did not decide to fight over a number of other material goods. And the possibility that this was a fluke is ruled out by the recurrence of the same pattern during the second round of negotiations.

Round Two

Once again, the example of Sweden looms large when it comes to explaining why the reorganizations got underway. In 1983, the Swedish MFA had gathered general diplomatic matters, matters of foreign economic policy and matters of foreign aid in a tripartite MFA umbrella structure with three ministers, but with the Foreign Minister as administratively responsible and hence first among equals. The Norwegian committee of state secretaries, which was given the task of drawing up suggestions for how to go about a reorganization, decided to follow the Swedish experience.

When the Foreign Minister, Knut Frydenlund, opened what was to become the second round of reorganization by going public with his intentions in 1986, he stressed the need for 'intense preparations, also vis-à-vis MFA personnel and their unions'.[25] Bearing in mind the intense efforts made by the MFA personnel in the first round of renegotiations, and also that the Foreign Minister himself was both a career diplomat and a social democrat, and thus well versed in the strengths of the MFA unions, this was hardly an unexpected move on his part. Still, in November 1987 there were open clashes between the political leadership of the MFA and the unions over this issue. The state secretary told a leading newspaper that MFA personnel had problems with tolerating her since she did not come from their own ranks, and that she wanted to reorganize the MFA in a more 'modern and efficient' direction. Specifically, she wanted to do away with special MFA arrangements such as recruiting by means of a specifically formed committee on a yearly basis and putting recruits through a specially designed one-year in-house academy (aspirantkurs), the legal obligation to accept posts abroad (flytteplikt) and the use of a specific legal code to regulate MFA operations. In effect, she intended to streamline the MFA to fall into the same mould as the rest of the Norwegian central administration.

The response from the MFA unions was swift and fierce, with one of their heads telling the same newspaper the next day that 'State secretary Kari Gjesteby cannot be very familiar with the MFA and those working there. I want to distance myself from her account.'[26] This was an extremely strong public statement by a bureaucrat about his or her political superior. In the upshot, the state secretary was circumvented in the reorganization negotiations, and a few months afterwards was relieved of her position.

The absence of the state secretary notwithstanding, the opposing party in the negotiations was still the Ministry of Trade, and negotiations quickly heated up. Once again, the contested issues concerned positions and personnel, with the Cabinet and the Ministry of Commerce and Shipping wanting two secretaries general, and the MFA unions wanting only one. In December 1987, the Cabinet duly voted to have only one secretary general.[27] In a rearguard action, the unions of the Ministry of Commerce and Shipping attempted to have two directors general with administrative responsibility, one for the trade section of the expanded MFA (which, instructively, immediately became known by the rubric MFA-MT) and one for the general section (which in regular everyday speech came to be known as MFA-MFA). The MFA unions were also able to stop this move.[28] In a coup de grâce, the MFA unions were able to have this position filled by a ranking diplomat.

Once again, the interesting thing is the kind of rhetoric MFA personnel used to score these victories. And once again, the tactic used was to appeal to the need for having a tightly organized corps of diplomats who would be legally obliged to accept positions abroad (flyttepliktige), who would have undergone similar training in the Ministry's own academy and who would see foreign policy in a general perspective. Thus, when the state secretary challenged these institutions, she also challenged the very platform on which the MFA personnel saw themselves standing. In short, she questioned key elements of the Norwegian MFA's esprit de corps. The MFA responded by insisting that administrative responsibility should rest with people who had first-hand field experience – that is the diplomats. This principle was kept intact, but a dent was made in the principle that diplomats with a legal obligation to accept positions abroad could be recruited only after having attended the MFA's in-house academy. Thus no position in the reorganized MFA was barred from personnel within the Ministry of Commerce, and those officers who had served more than four years had one year to apply for the status of being under a legal obligation to move abroad.

Round Three

The Ministry of Commerce and Shipping became part of the reorganized MFA on 1 January 1988, and was joined by the Ministry of Development Cooperation two years later. In July 1996, however, Sweden once again reorganized its MFA by establishing a separate Ministry of Commerce and Industry which was supposed to handle all matters of bilateral trade. Norway followed suit on 1 January 1997, as some 60 positions out of a total of around 1200 were allocated to a newly constituted Ministry of Commerce and Industry.[29]

If one compares the relatively mild reaction of MFA personnel to losing these positions with the state of affairs in the area of security politics, one sees a clear tension. Ever since Minister of Defence Johan Jørgen Holst expanded the MoD's analytical capacity in the mid-1980s and formed a separate Department for Security Policy headed by a director general, competition between personnel from the two ministries has grown. At present, the Department consists of 22 personnel, including a director general, a deputy director general and three secretarial staff, as well as three sections each headed by an assistant director. This far outstrips MFA capacity. MFA personnel routinely complain that the MoD nurses a typical sectoral and 'military' approach to foreign policy, with no understanding of how security policy relates to Norwegian positions overall. MoD personnel, on the other hand, routinely counter by pointing out that MFA personnel have no domestic equivalent to the military behind it, that they have little or no formal training in security policy, do not know the issues well and tend to decamp for other positions once they begin to learn. All this is less than surprising, dovetailing as it does with the literature's standard expectations of how specialist and generalist personnel located in different ministries inside the same central administration relate to one another. There is a puzzle nonetheless, and it is to do with why the issue area of security policy seems to activate these tensions to a higher degree than do others.

The puzzle is reinforced by the fact that there exists yet another case which did not spark outright protest from MFA personnel, in the shape of the upgrading of the Office of the Prime Minister as a focal point for foreign policy coordination. Although MFA personnel do tend to grumble about this privately, they are quick to point out that these positions are often manned by MFA personnel, and there has been little or no organized controversy about the matter.

CONCLUSION

I noted at the outset that, in order to improve on the explanations of MFA behaviour put forward by East and associates, one would have to explain:

a) why MFA personnel insist on representing politics in terms of 'high' and 'low' categories;
b) why they are not particularly interested in inter-ministerial coordination;
c) the lack of correlation between rational factors determining the seeming importance of a task on the one hand, and the attention actually given to it by MFA personnel on the other;
d) the continued involvement of MFA personnel in tugs-of-war with both the political leadership and the Ministry of Commerce and Industry over questions which from a rational perspective seem to be in the administrative realm;
e) the lack of overt and prolonged resistance of the kind repeatedly shown vis-à-vis the Ministry of Commerce and Shipping when the Prime Minister's Office took over vital chunks of the coordination of EU matters in the early 1990s;
f) why the 'no' in the 1972 referendum on Norwegian membership of the EC came as such a shock to the MFA.

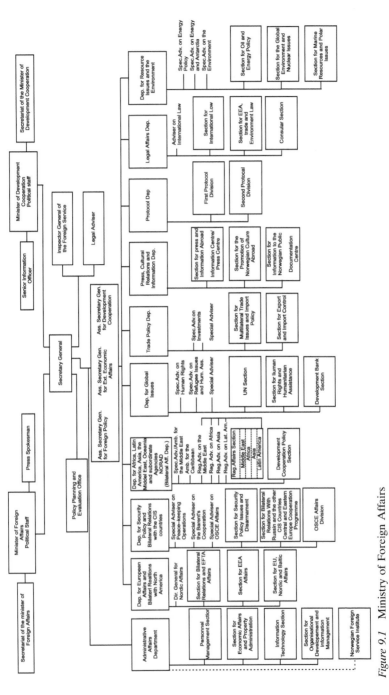

Figure 9.1 Ministry of Foreign Affairs

Source: Norwegian Ministry of Foreign Affairs

An explanation has to start with the one factor which seems to be essential to their esprit de corps, dominates their horizon and upholds their identity vis-à-vis other entities. The MFA refuses to ascribe overwhelming importance to interdependence as a process which blurs the difference between the kingdom of Norway and the outside world because the manning of the border between the two is seen as the prerogative of the MFA. More specifically, the MFA consistently sees itself as the mediator not between the inside and outside in general, but between what it holds to be the vital interests of the nation state of Norway on the one hand and the outside world on the other. Since 'vital interests' are moveable goalposts relative to 'interdependence', the latter phenomenon can easily be bracketed within them.

Inasmuch as diplomacy since its very inception has been about mediation, and MFAs are the major historical institutions which mediate between modern states, in one way this amounts to pointing out the obvious.[30] The historical setting out of which MFAs emerge confers upon those institutions an identity as mediators or, if one prefers, MFAs are 'path-dependent' on being mediators. What seems to have been overlooked in the study of MFAs, however, is how this question of identity may be linked to the question of action in general,[31] and foreign policy in particular.[32] In conclusion, I will put forward my alternative explanation of MFA behaviour by trying to outline how this may be done.

The tasks in which MFAs are interested will be the tasks which go with their identity as mediators. Inasmuch as MFAs by dint of their very identity will be state-centric, which will be for as long as 'foreign' is defined as 'other states', the tasks to be mediated will be those that the MFA and those groups on whose behalf it mediates see as the vital tasks of state. Which tasks these are will of course vary across time and space, but this means that to MFA personnel there will be a difference between 'high' politics (tasks which are seen as vital) and 'low' politics (the leftovers). The difference between high and low politics will remain then, if not in the analyses of interdependence theorists, then in the stories which MFAs tell about themselves and the tasks they perform. That should explain point (a) above.

Where point (b) – the lack of interest in coordination – is concerned, this becomes moot, since East and his associates as well as other students of the Norwegian MFA concede that the MFA very much maintains the ability to veto efforts at mediating tasks they have come to see as vital. Given our explanation, this is all that is needed, and the rest of the question of coordination falls away. Of course, East is right to point out that there may be a certain hollowness about such a strategy, inasmuch as it will indeed erode the MFA's standing in the arenas where it decides not to fight.

As to point (c) – how MFA personnel go about their task preferences – MFA personnel will fight to keep what is seen as vital tasks and those on whose behalf it mediates. One notices an extremely interesting trend here. It is to do with the relative attention which should be given to new issues such as facilitating mediation between third parties (in the Middle East, Guatemala and so on), relief in cases of manmade disasters, peace-enforcing operations and ecological work on the one hand, and more traditional MFA work on the other. This issue, which has been intensely debated inside and outside the Norwegian MFA, is a tangible example of how what should be mediated is always an issue of continuous negotiation. One may of course interpret Norway's interest in this kind of diplomatic work as belonging to an idealist tradition of world politics, or, alternatively, as a good Realpolitik marketing investment for a small country afraid of being forgotten by the rest of the world.[33] An alternative interpretation, however, would stress how this kind of diplomacy mediates between the nation-state of Norway on the one hand, and world society on the other. As demonstrated perhaps best by James Der Derian,[34] it is in no way new that diplomacy, in addition to being about maintaining a dialogue of states, is also about mediating between other entities. Indeed, in a situation where the international society of states is being enveloped in a wider world society of sundry actors, one would expect the state to use diplomacy as one of the strategies by which it can sustain itself inside that world society. Seen in this light, the forays of Norwegian diplomacy into these previously sparsely chartered waters may not be exceptional. On the contrary, they may be harbingers of how the institution of diplomacy will react to the ongoing strengthening of world society.

If the issue of mediation may explain selection processes inside the MFA which have proved puzzling to earlier observers, it may also explain why MFA personnel expend so much time and effort on seemingly irrational pursuits during times of reorganizations, that is, point (d). A diplomat (or, a civil servant working in the foreign ministry) is a diplomat because he or she is a specialist in and an expert on mediation. What constitutes this expertise will vary across time and space. In the Norwegian case, this expertise is not first and foremost seen as emanating from a specific social background (aristocratic, civil servant), a specific education (although into the 1930s it was a much debated question whether a training in law should be a prerequisite),[35] or indeed any other dimension of what rationalist social scientists refer to as 'background variables'. Rather, it is acquired through the in-house academy as well as the subsequent hardship which goes with being a field diplomat. This is how you become a type of civil servant different from other civil servants, and how you become a member of the guild. Hence the enormous effort exerted by MFA personnel in order to keep the institutions of the flytteplikt and the in-house academy.

What remains to be discussed is exactly which institutions the MFA mediates between at the present juncture. The ongoing discussion of the relative weight of 'new' tasks is relevant here, inasmuch as it has the potential to change the emphasis when it comes to which institution is being mediated on the outside. Traditionally, this has been other states, but there has also been 'world society'. Most of the new tasks have 'world society' as one (if not necessarily the only) referent to be mediated. On the inside, it is very clear that the kingdom of Norway is what should be mediated, but what exactly is the kingdom of Norway? It is definitely the state understood as the political apparatus, and here we may have an explanation why the build-up of mediating expertise at the Prime Minister (PM)'s office has not been met with more resistance. If the PM's office is obviously a key institution to be mediated, a strengthening of ties which leaves MFA organizational structure intact and tends only to move MFA personnel on a tour to the PM's office for home service is not a serious threat. The concentration of security policy expertise at the MoD, on the other hand, is a serious threat for two reasons. First, it would be an enormously time-consuming and at the present juncture possibly a hopeless undertaking to represent security policy as not being a vital task for the kingdom of Norway. Secondly, the MoD is an alternative mediating institution which cannot be represented as an acknowledged superior institution on whose behalf the MFA should mediate, as can the Prime Minister's Office. This should address point (e).

Point (f) – the shock of 1972 – may be explained in the same manner. If the PM's office is among the inside institutions to be mediated at the present juncture, so is the nation. Among many other things, however, given the previous MFA involvement as sketched above, the 'no' in the referendum could easily be represented by MFA personnel as an act whereby the nation denied the MFA the right to represent it and to mediate on its behalf. An alternative representation, which would point out that the nation was indeed split inasmuch as the majorities were tiny, would break with the constitutive rules of referenda and would therefore be hard to sustain. If the 'nation state' is the hegemonic form to be mediated at the present juncture, then the threat of losing the nation as a mediated institution also threatens the entire identity of the MFA as a mediator. The shock, then, was as basic as a shock can be, namely casting into doubt the MFA's representation of its own identity. Identity, then, and not instrumental rationality, is the factor which is mostly lacking from previous studies of the Norwegian MFA, and which must be added in order to explain its behaviour at home as well as abroad.

NOTES

1   I should like to thank Maurice East, Brian Hocking, Olav F. Knudsen and also Einar Ansteensen, Eva Bugge, Jan Wilhelm Grythe, Sverre Jervell, Henrik Ofstad, Kjetil Skogrand, Olav Stokke, Johan Vibe and Geir Westgaard for their comments.

2   Maurice A. East 'The organizational impact of interdependence on foreign policy-making: the case of Norway', p. 138, in C. W. Kegley Jr and Patrick McGowan, eds, *The Political Economy of Foreign Policy Behavior* (London: Sage Publications, 1981).

3   East, 'The organizational impact of interdependence on foreign policy-making', p. 138 and pp. 142–3.

4   M. East and Leif-Helge Salomonsen 'Adapting foreign policy-making to interdependence: a proposal and some evidence from Norway,' *Cooperation and Conflict* 16:3, 1981, pp. 171–2.

5   East, 'The organizational impact of interdependence on foreign policy-making', p. 148.

6   M. East, 'Coordinating foreign policy: the changing role of the Norwegian Foreign Ministry', *Cooperation and Conflict* 19:2, 1984, p. 121–34.

7   East, 'Coordinating foreign policy', pp. 127, 130–1 (added emphasis).

8   East, 'Coordinating foreign policy', p. 132.

9   Svein Efjestad, *Utenriksdepartementets rolle i samordningen av fagdepartementenes internasjonale saker. En studie av beslutningsprosessen i utenriksadministrasjonen på områdene internasjonal samferdsel og miljøvern* (Master's thesis presented to Oslo University, Department of Political Science, 1980).

10 F. H. Hinsley, *Power and the Pursuit of Peace. Theory and Practice in the History of International Relations*, (Cambridge: Cambridge University Press, 1963), p. 250n.

11 M. S. Anderson, *The Rise of Modern Diplomacy 1450–1919* (London: Longman, 1993), p. 110.

12 Roald Berg, *Norge på egen hånd 1905–1920. Norsk utenrikspolitikks historie. vol. 3.* (Oslo: Universitetsforlaget, 1995), p. 56.

13 East & Salomonsen, 'Adapting foreign policy-making to interdependence', p. 174.

14 Olav Stokke, *Norge og den tredje verden. Program, oppfølging og perspektiver for en ny økonomisk verdensordning* (Oslo: Universitetsforlaget, 1979), pp. 50–3.

15 East & Salomonsen, 'Adapting foreign policy-making to interdependence', p. 173.

16 *Norges diplomatiske og konsulære representasjon i utlandet* (Oslo: Royal MFA, 1996). As of 1997, the MFA budget is Nk 11.7 billion and a total of around 1050 plus 600 people are to be found on the payroll. *Analyse av ressursbruken i Utenriksdepartementet* (Oslo: Statskonsult, Rapport 7, 1996), pp. 16, 41–2.

17 R. N. Torgersen and T. Dyrstad, *Saksbehandlerboka* (Oslo: Gyldendal, 1991), p. 25, quoted in J. Trondal, *Tilknytningsformer til EU og nasjonale samordningsprosesser. En studie av norske og danske departementer* (Oslo: University of Oslo, Arena Working Paper no. 15, 1996), p. 60.

18 Nils Petter Gleditsch, Oyvind Osterud and Jon Elster, *De utro tjenere. Embetsverket i EF-kampen* (Oslo: Pax, 1974).

19 See account in Liv S. Bøe, *Utenrikshandelens politiske organisering: En analyse av en reorganiseringsprosess* (Master's thesis presented to the University of Oslo, Institute of Political Science, 1987), pp. 27–89.

20 Bente Egjar Engesland, *Norges forhold til OPEC: Fra konflikt til samarbeid? Analyse av en beslutningsprosess* (Oslo: The Fridtjof Nansen Institute, Report No. 1, 1989), p. 153; Dag Harald Claes, *The Politics of Oil Producer Cooperation* (Doctoral thesis to be presented to the University of Oslo, Institute of Political Science, 1997), ch. 7. Both authors express puzzlement where the priorities of the MFA are concerned. I will attempt to solve this puzzle below.

21 Bøe, *Utenrikshandelens politiske organisering*, p. 66.

22 Bøe, *Utenrikshandelens politiske organisering*, p. 80.

23 Bøe, *Utenrikshandelens politiske organisering*, p. 97.

24 Bøe, *Utenrikshandelens politiske organisering*, p. 75.

25 Quoted in Dag Nystrøm, *Sammenslåingen av Utenriksdepartementet og Handelsdepartementet: En politisk styrt prosess?* (Master's thesis presented to the University of Oslo, Institute of Political Science, 1991), p. 52.

26 Quotes from Nystrøm, *Sammenslåingen av Utenriksdepartementet og Handelsdepartementet*, p. 84.

27 Nystrøm, *Sammenslåingen av Utenriksdepartementet og Handelsdepartementet*, p. 90.

28 Nystrøm, *Sammenslåingen av Utenriksdepartementet og Handelsdepartementet*, p. 75.

29 During the summer of 1997, after more than ten years of debate, there was yet another reorganization. It is particularly interesting that the resistance by key senior personnel to employing the desk system as the general organizational principle was overcome. Since the reorganization is taking place at the time of writing, however, it is still not possible to say whether the desk system will remain, although it seems clear that the changes will be big enough to make this a 'fourth round of reorganizations'.

30 James Der Derian, *On Diplomacy. A Genealogy of Western Estrangement* (Oxford: Blackwell, 1987).

31 See Erik Ringmar, *Identity, Interest and Action. A Cultural Explanation of Sweden's Intervention in the Thirty Year's War* (Cambridge: Cambridge University Press, 1996) and Iver B. Neumann, 'Ringmar on War and Identity', *Cooperation and Conflict* 32:3, 1997, pp. 309–30.

32 Ole Wæver, 'Resisting the Temptations of Post Policy Analysis', in Walter Carlsnaes and Steve Smith, eds, *The European Community and Changing Foreign Policy Perspectives in Europe* (London: Sage Publications, 1994).

33 I. B. Neumann and Ståle Ulriksen, 'Norsk forsvars- og sikkerhetspolitikk', in Torbjørn L. Knutsen, Gunnar M. Sørbø and Svein Gjerdåker, eds, *Norsk Utenrikspolitikk* (Oslo: Cappelen Akademisk, 1995).

34 Der Derian, *On Diplomacy*; see also I. B. Neumann, 'John Vincent and the English School of International Relations', in I. B. Neumann and O. Wæver, eds, *The Future of International Relations: Masters in the Making?* (London: Routledge, 1997).

35 Jens A. Christophersen, 'Avgjørelsesprosessen i norsk utenrikspolitikk', in Gunnar Jervas, ed., *Utrikespolitik i norr* (Lund: Studentliteratur, 1973).

10 Russia
The Ministry of Foreign Affairs: Through Decline towards Renewal
Ivan G. Tiouline

In the course of many decades the Soviet and Russian diplomatic services developed a close symbiosis. Although the Ministry of Foreign Affairs (MFA) of the Russian Soviet Federative Socialist Republic (RSFSR) was established in 1944, it performed only formal and decorative functions. Moreover, the Russian Ministry was largely considered a dumping ground for incompetent or dishonoured diplomats. The Russian declaration of sovereign status in June 1990 and the subsequent appointment of Andrei Kozyrev as Minister did not change much in the traditional relationship between the Union and the Republican MFAs. However along with the dissolution of the Union and as the inter-republican talks transformed into negotiations between sovereign states, the Russian MFA's role increased dramatically. Moreover, the Soviet MFA was disgraced by the supportive attitude of its leaders towards the coup leaders during and after the August 1991 putsch.

However, a new page in the Russian MFA's history was turned when the Commonwealth of Independent States (CIS) was established in December 1991. By President Yeltsin's Decree of 16 December 1991 titled: 'On the Diplomatic Service of the Russian Soviet Federal Socialist Republic (RSFSR)', the following missions were assigned to the MFA:

- to assume effective control over the dissolving Soviet MFA, together with its buildings, property, educational institutions, as well as embassies, consulates and other representations abroad;
- to prepare a new organizational and personnel chart for the Russian MFA within a month, as well as proposals for the future employment of the staff of the Soviet MFA;
- to conduct within one month negotiations with the CIS members as well as with other ex-Soviet sovereign states in order to establish joint coordination and consultative mechanisms in the field of foreign policy;
- to produce a Provisional Act for the Russian diplomatic service before 1 January 1992;

- to establish a Government Protocol Service in order to create a common practice for protocol in the RSFSR.[1]

At the same time this created a number of pressing problems for the Russian MFA. It seems a paradox that reform of the Ministry was interconnected with its decline.

It should be kept in mind that Mr Kozyrev inherited a staff that was dwarfed by the behemoth Union MFA. While initially the Russian MFA comprised 70, later 240 persons, the Soviet MFA possessed 3500 in the central office plus thousands overseas. That provided a special reason for Mr Kozyrev to compare the two ministries with David and Goliath when addressing the problem of integration of the two during his speech to top executives of both the MFAs on 23 December 1991. While paying credit to the high professional standards of the Union MFA and praising revolutionary accomplishments of the Russian MFA, Mr Kozyrev set forward the goal of creating an integrated structure comprising both to serve Russian democracy. He specified the following tasks:

- first, to trim both personnel and expenditure in a way that no damage was done to the diplomatic service;
- second, to incorporate junior and intermediate diplomats of both MFAs in such a manner that the staff of the Russian MFA would not monopolize the 'revolutionary' viewpoint, while the old school would not be considered the sole proprietors of professionalism;
- third, to select and appoint the appropriate persons for the top positions, namely Deputies to the Minister and Department Heads;
- fourth, to reform the Ministerial organizational structure, bearing in mind that retaining the Committee for Foreign Trade and Economy, which was established during the last months of the Union MFA, seemed rather inappropriate.[2]

Some of the tasks outlined by Mr Kozyrev were soon accomplished. It was stated during his address that practical responsibility for governing the Russian MFA was vested in his own deputies, but none of the former Union MFA's Deputies to the Minister were included in this group. However other problems were much more difficult to solve.

It should be noted that throughout its history the Soviet diplomatic service imitated the British-American organizational pattern. That implied a major organizational centre focused on a very active Minister, working in collaboration with a substantial number of his deputies. All of them were career diplomats possessing extensive experience and are structured on 'the tree-branch principle'. Such an organizational scheme remained unaltered in the contemporary Russian MFA with every Deputy Minister supervizing a 'branch'. At the same time the structural composition of the central HQ was reformed substantially.

Adopted before the war and retained in later years, this structure was built, as in most other countries, on the territorial and functional principle. But while this principle remains, the recent period, especially the years since the start of Perestroika, has seen the pattern change visibly in favour of smaller structural units. This trend has marred the entire post-war period.

Until the mid-to-late 1950s, the Foreign Ministry's territorial units comprised four or six European divisions, the American division, the Near and Middle East division, three African divisions, two Far East divisions (there were three at one time). The French colonies and overseas territories as well as the Spanish, Portuguese, Dutch and Belgian colonies were under the charge of the First European division together with the mother countries while the British colonies and dominions were under the charge of the Second European division together with Britain. The disintegration of the colonial system and changes in the global political structure led to changes in the pattern of the Foreign Ministry's territorial subdivisions. By the start of Perestroika it included six European divisions, the USA division, two Latin American divisions, three African divisions, the Near and Middle East divisions, two far Eastern divisions, the Southern and Southeast Asia divisions while the former British dominions remained under the charge of the British division.

With the start of Perestroika and the appointment of a new minister, the Soviet Foreign Ministry embarked on a radical reconstruction which it badly needed. But long-awaited changes were accompanied by the totally unwarranted abolition of established structures and patterns that had proved their worth. The reformers who came to the ministry quickly changed the face of the service.

The new pattern of territorial subdivisions was brought into being by merging them and regrouping regions. Some solutions were logical: for instance, Canada was transferred from the British sphere to the North American region, Australia to the Far East, Malta to Mediterranean Europe.

Some of the changes, however, could not be accounted for even by referring to 'new thinking'. Regions were designated on ideological principles: Europe was placed under the charge of a new Directorate of the Socialist Countries of Europe, and Asia under that of a new Directorate of the Socialist Countries of Asia. In other words, an obviously absurd change was made by dividing the German and Korean problems and separating Vietnam from the rest of Indochina, not to mention the fact that Switzerland, which has always gravitated towards the Franco–Italian region, was incorporated into the German sphere, the Maghreb placed in the Arab East, and so forth. And while the breakup of the socialist camp resulted in revised geopolitical concepts, restructuring went on until the Soviet Foreign Ministry ceased to exist.

As for the functional subdivisions of the Ministry, the total number amounts to no more than ten, excluding purely administrative departments.

They include the secretariats, policy planning and analysis, the press and information, protocol and the consular service, treaty law, history and archives as well as the subdivisions concerned with numerous general and global problems, including the UN, disarmament, and regional conflicts.

As far back as the 1960s, these subdivisions began to expand slowly: first the decision was made to set up the Directorate for the Planning of Foreign Policy Measures mentioned earlier, then the ministry got part of the disbanded Committee for Cultural Relations with Foreign Countries under the USSR Council of Ministers (it became a division bearing the same name but having considerably reduced powers); further new divisions were set up with the transfer of the Executive Secretariat of the Commission for UNESCO and the abolition of the Information Department of the CPSU Central Committee (foreign political propaganda). No changes whatever occurred in the next two decades but from 1985 at least 15 functional subdivisions were added, many of which are still there.

It is worthy of note that whereas territorial subdivisions grew in number under the impact of external, objective developments (the rise of new states), the increased number of functional subdivisions may be seen as evidence of hegemonist trends that bred further functions. Indeed, the Soviet Foreign Ministry at its final stage included even the former Ministry of Foreign Trade plus other agencies involving foreign economic ties.

Incidentally, it was due to this trend that by the end of the Soviet period the USSR Foreign Ministry Collegium did not include a single territorial subdivision head – there were only heads of functional directorates. This may also be interpreted as reflecting the new foreign policy orientation, which prefers general, global arenas to bilateral relations.

It should be noted that some of the functional subdivisions were established slowly. For instance, when talks on various nuclear missile systems and chemical, bacteriological and conventional weapons were drawing to a close, a subdivision was set up concerned with problems of arms limitation and disarmament. At that time the ministry also came to include a subdivision for security and co-operation in Europe and a subdivision for humanitarian co-operation in the context of the Belgrade, Madrid, Budapest, Vienna, and Stockholm meetings held within the framework of the all-Europe process.[3]

The first reform of the Russian MFA in 1992, did not rectify the distortions and deficiencies mentioned above, but rather enhanced the importance of a number of existing subdivisions. Some artificial structures were disbanded, like the Foreign Economic Relations Committee, while new departments were established, such as those in charge of CIS affairs and liaison with the Parliament, political parties and public organizations. Departments became the basic structural unit. This step resulted in the creation of an extended hierarchical ladder: deputy director of department, head of directorate, deputy head of directorate, head of desk, reinforcing the 'partition' between leader and executor. A departmental director is, in principle, vested with the same functions and is as responsible as a former head of division; the officials listed above used to serve as heads of section.

Some unwise decisions were also taken regarding the territorial subdivisions. At one time, the CIS republics fell under the jurisdiction of the adjacent territorial department in charge of the 'far abroad'. Whilst the Caucasian republics went to the department covering Turkey, the Central Asian states were transferred to the department monitoring China. This constituted a division of the former Soviet territory into spheres of external influence, though Mr Kozyrev never lost a chance of describing all the 'near abroad' republics as units within the Russian sphere of 'vital interests'.

At the end of 1993 another reorganization occurred, which aimed at a better balance between territorial and functional departments. At the same time due to some unknown factors, the organizational structure did not retain the Analysis and Foreign Policy Planning Division (AFPPD), established in the 1960s. This was especially remarkable given sharp press criticism of the MFA for its 'unreasoned, improvized and unstable' policies. The AFPPD was reestablished only in the first half of 1995. The resultant organizational chart of the MFA is given below.

LIST OF DEPARTMENTS OF MINISTRY OF FOREIGN AFFAIRS OF RUSSIAN FEDERATION (1 OCTOBER 1996)

I Regional Subdivisions

1. First Department in Charge of CIS Affairs
2. Second Department in Charge of CIS Affairs
3. Third Department in Charge of CIS Affairs
4. Fourth Department in Charge of CIS Affairs
5. First European Department
6. Second European Department
7. Third European Department
8. Fourth European Department
9. Department for Cooperation in Europe
10. Department for North America
11. Department for Latin America
12. Department for Middle East and North Africa
13. Department for Africa
14. First Asian Department
15. Second Asian Department
16. Third Asian Department

II Functional Subdivisions

1. Department for International Organizations
2. Division for Foreign Policy Planning
3. Department for Security and Disarmament
4. Division for Liaison with the Members of the Federation, Parliament and Political and Public organizations
5. Division for International Humanitarian Co-operation and Human Rights
6. Division for Cultural Co-operation
7. Secretarial Division of Commission for Co-operation with UNESCO
8. Department for Information and Press
9. Department for Economic Cooperation
10. Legal Department
11. Personnel Department
12. Consular Service Department
13. State Protocol Department
14. Department for History and Documentation

As a result of these reforms of the MFA, the personnel crisis became deeper. As was mentioned above, the Russian MFA had inherited large and uneven diplomatic cadres from the Union MFA. Partly this was a legacy of the Soviet system of recruiting and training diplomatic personnel. For decades its primary sources were two institutions, namely the Higher Diplomatic School (HDS), which was established in 1939 and renamed the Diplomatic Academy (DA) in 1974, and the Moscow State Institute of International Relations (MGIMO is the recognized acronym), which was established on the foundations of the Faculty of International Relations of Moscow State University. The DA enrolled for a term of two years the specialists who had already received a higher education in social, political and other sciences and were mobilized by the Party for diplomatic work. The MGIMO adopted students fresh from high school for a five year course resulting in a university-type diploma. MGIMO was the *alma mater* for the majority of the Soviet diplomatic corps, government elite, academicians and international journalists.

Along with this, the HDS continued training diplomats from people of an entirely different type. It had to admit so-called party recruits, that is, people who had held various jobs as Comsomol (Young Communist League) functionaries, civil servants or economic executives and were 'recruited by the party' to 'reinforce' the diplomatic service. Whereas before the war and in the early post-war years HDS graduates were appointed as a rule to major diplomatic posts, in Khrushchev's and particularly Brezhnev's time people selected by the party became the main reservoir of senior and leading

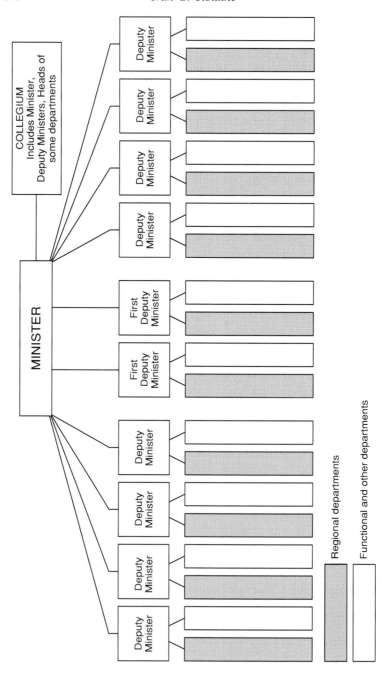

Figure 10.1 The Foreign Ministry Administrative Division

diplomatic staff. These people entered the diplomatic service without any formal training. They included some people who had received a sound education and met high cultural standards and who quickly mastered the diplomatic profession. But most of them remained outsiders. They had no knowledge of either diplomatic problems or foreign languages, and so all that they could do was to sermonize and set 'guidelines'. They were unfit for creative work and found themselves at sea in subdivisions concerned with global affairs and delicate problems of relations with the Western world. At best, they found a niche for themselves in developing countries and above all in socialist community countries, where they implemented party diplomacy with 'fraternal' familiarity. In the Soviet embassies in Western countries they occupied the position of secretary of Party organizations, having the rank of councillors and ministers (ambassadorial status is not employed here), labour organization chairs, or administrative and management heads within the embassies.

When serving in the central headquarters, they were employed in functional subdivisions by the simple method of inflating the existing organizational structure using reserved extra positions. The main areas in which they operated were those involving work on party committees and in personnel departments, spheres in which they felt confident but in which they acted in an overbearing manner, raising all sorts of barriers to the careers of young people and professional diplomats.

This account of Party personnel policy in the Soviet MFA is essential to the recognition of the fact, that although the Soviet MFA ranks were entirely filled with party members having party cards of the same colour, the status of these cards was different. This fact was always present in the minds of the professional diplomats, creating 'caste' feelings of separation from these 'aliens'. The leaders of party organizations in foreign missions have felt this particularly acutely since the first years of Perestroika, especially from the time when the notion of 'de-ideologization' was introduced.

In the middle of 1990 the CPSU Central Committee adopted a decision to disband unified party committees with diplomatic representation abroad. By the same decision the organizational structure was inflated to include 150 extra positions for the ex-secretaries who now became personnel managers for the embassies, while in large consulates new consular positions were introduced for the same purpose. The so-called 'party draft' into the Diplomatic Academy was terminated, though it was superseded by the 'people's deputy draft' for the same party functionaries so that they could assume positions as ambassadors and consuls.

The Perestroika years in the Soviet MFA were accompanied by cadre reshuffling as well as by the emergence of new operational directorates. By a special decision Economic Minister positions were introduced. In 22 major embassies they were occupied by former party, state and managerial officials who had lost their previous jobs. They were assigned with a serious task, namely to define the strategies for trade, economic and technological co-operation with the home countries. These people, however, were hard to accommodate and often created conflicts with embassy economic task forces and trade representations. Though these facts were hardly a secret, the last Cabinet just prior to the August 1991 coup made a decision to establish such positions for an additional 25 countries.

All these posts were created irrespective of the fact that a large number of diplomats had already been given the task of covering a variety of economic areas. In the Soviet embassy in Washington DC there were the following positions: a counsellor for sea transportation for the fishing industry, a counsellor for agriculture, for land improvement, culture (two posts), information services, a counsellor responsible for a magazine with no readers entitled 'The Soviet Land', and a counsellor responsible for construction of a new embassy building – a total of more than 20 counsellors. A similar situation of diplomats doing next to nothing could be observed in other embassies too; few of these people engaged in useful activities. For example a counsellor for agriculture in the Soviet embassy in London once complained that each year he was asked by the Soviet Ministry of Agriculture to collect statistics on the output of broiler chickens.

Some more serious matters should be mentioned here. In many embassies there were counsellors for liaison with Communist parties of the host countries. In 1955 the State Committee for Cultural Ties was established, and counsellors for culture were dispatched to several dozen countries. Their work duplicated that of the representatives of the Union of the Soviet Societies for Friendship and Culture (SSFC), who were mere third or second secretaries. Naturally, the SSFC objected and achieved promotion of its representatives to similar rank. After the CPSU Central Committee established its Department of Information, a number of counsellors were sent to the embassies overseas. They started intruding into the business of counsellors for culture and duplicated the responsibilities of press attaches and counsellors in charge of the Agency for Press News (APN) activities. For example in the Soviet embassy to Mongolia, 22 Party or Comsomol functionaries were included in the list of the diplomatic corps having the ranks of either counsellors, secretaries or consuls, with the sole responsibility of managing the affairs of the Soviet settlement there. This situation continued to 1991. A similar situation obtained in the Soviet embassies in Cuba, Vietnam, the GDR, Poland, Angola, India, Egypt, Iraq, Algiers, Nigeria, Syria and other countries.

Between 1955 and 1989 the number of Soviet MFA's embassies and institutions abroad grew by 250 per cent, while personnel increased by 360 per cent. While the first figure represents the real dynamics of development in both international relations as well as bilateral ties of the USSR in the post-war period, the second figure reflects the games that the party and the cadre bureaucracy played with the foreign ministry.[5]

All these distortions demanded surgery as reflected in the reorganization plans declared by the new management of the Russian MFA. At the same time, some basic skills had to be retained and employed for the service of the new state, namely the collective and individual experience of the diplomats. A balanced approach was required to adopt a rational trimming of personnel numbers. As was pointed out by a number of experts, personnel reorganization should be preceded by an elaboration of the future strategy for Russian foreign policy in order to substitute the deideologization formula of the Perestroika era with Russian patriotic interests.

Such an approach seemed rational in the light of the spirit prevailing both within the MFA and its foreign missions. Many will agree that in the case of the Union Foreign Ministry, Perestroika resulted in continual change throughout those years. There is no denying that surgery was needed to rid the Ministry of the evils of the earlier personnel policy steeped in nepotism, favouritism and paternalism. But that was not all, for staff, especially leading officials, began to be moved about like balls on a billiard table; unnecessary restructuring began with existing subdivisions being merged or broken up into smaller units as new subdivisions. At the same time, the Ministry started claiming that some of its new functions were unsuitable.

The psychological condition of the Soviet MFA of the time may be characterized as pessimistic, permeated by a wait-and-see attitude. With the Union institutions agonizing and with delays in introducing reform, staff were uncertain as to their future. This resulted in increasing apathy and indecision. While in the central office, given its size, it was easier to deal with these concerns, it was more difficult to do so in the embassies. Separation from home and confinement amongst a small group of individuals resulted in a general decline in morale and increasing professional incompetence, indifference to the state interest and loss of a sense of duty; cases of defection multiplied. Organizational change clearly needed to be accelerated in order to check these developments.

It was only at the beginning of 1993 that the Russian MFA managed to produce a strategy for foreign policy, which was judged as inadequate by most experts. This further inhibited the creative potential of diplomats. While senior Russian MFA officials repeatedly declared that no officer was to lose his job on the grounds of former affiliation with the Union MFA, this increasingly occurred and produced much depression and discontent. Usually, some pretext was invented and the experienced diplomats had to resign. This personnel drain was accompanied by uncertainty and instability in the conduct of foreign policy and mounting public criticism. Whilst in 1988 only 40 diplomats left their jobs in the Union MFA, in the Russian MFA the loss totalled 400 in 1992, increasing to 750 in the subsequent two years.

The real catalyst in this painful process was inadequate financing against the background of the overall economic crisis in Russia. The state cut the MFA budget dramatically. Only 60 per cent of the minimum requirements were provided for both the central HQ and the foreign offices. A similar situation existed in diplomatic missions. In some areas, only 25 per cent of required expenditure was met and in the worst case only 15 per cent. Due to the financial shortages some of the distant embassies and consulates were closed, so that Russia had fewer missions than the UK or France at the time.

Excessive budget deficits left the MFA with a few options, one of them being mobilization of resources from sources other than state financing. One of them was payments for consular services. However, these could not solve the whole problem. According to 1994 data they covered about ten per cent of expenditure on the MFA's headquarters and eight per cent of that spent on overseas operations. Non-state generated income was chiefly spent on the establishment of the all-Russian system of passports.

It turned out that one-sixth of the MFA's staff was in urgent need of living quarters. During three years of the Russian MFA's functioning not one square metre of living space was provided for its staff nor any money for that purpose. According to current trends in real estate prices, a junior diplomat has to work for 70 years to earn enough money to buy a one-room apartment. Pensions for retired diplomats were also meagre. Such wellknown former ambassadors as Dobrynin or Troyanovsky, who devoted all their lives to the diplomatic service, received around 100 thousand rubles per month, while a retired colonel receives 350 thousand.

In one third of Russian diplomatic offices abroad the wages were fixed at the level of 1975. In 12 countries Russian ambassadors were entitled to less than a thousand dollars monthly. This, together with the changing mentality produced by the new market conditions resulted in a deterioration of the social value of a diplomatic career. The overall personnel numbers shrank by one thousand, to as low as three thousand in total. The number of diplomats serving abroad diminished from 9500 to 7500.[6] Those who left the MFA were mostly young men with promising careers. At the same time the number of new personnel also decreased because the majority of MGIMO graduates, who used to comprise the bulk, preferred the business sector to the diplomatic service.

A personnel crisis was not the only manifestation of the decline of the Russian MFA during its first five years of existence. Another was uncertainty regarding foreign policy goals, priorities and strategy. During the first five years of the existence of a truly independent Russian MFA there were multiple goals, not all of which were achieved.

While the Russian MFA inherited the personnel, the real estate and the equipment from the disbanded Union Ministry, the character of foreign policy had to be changed drastically. Instead of messianic globalism, Russia had to adjust itself to the level that it could afford. This reality was understood, although the specifics of foreign policy remained obscure.

Initially, it was declared that Russia had no enemies and no threats. At the same time the working premises were built upon global co-operation with the United States and Western democracies in general in order to establish the New World Order prescribed by President Bush. After a couple of years had elapsed, a new notion came into being, that of equidistant co-operation and reserved partnership with the West. According to the foreign policy doctrine adopted in 1993, the term 'highest priority' was used to describe attitudes and relations both in the West and in the East. That resulted in much chaotic action and a state of indecision.

Subsequently the territory of the former Soviet Union was declared the 'sphere of vital national interests' to Russia. That was contrary to expectations cherished both in the West as well as in some of the newly independent states. At the same time no significant policy integration was achieved between Russia and CIS member countries, such as Kazakhstan or Belorussia. It was in the wake of the Presidential elections of 1996 that Russian foreign policy was redirected towards institutionalized integrationism.

Another manifestation of MFA decline was its inability to act as a coordinator of Russian foreign policy. Many political leaders and a number of state ministries and establishments participated in the process of making foreign policy, with the MFA being sometimes the last to learn about developments in its domain. Much depended on the personalities heading the institutions which are the foreign ministry's natural partners in its conduct of Russian foreign policy. For example, at the time when the Ministry for Foreign Economic Relations was headed by Peter Aven, the process of reorientating Russian foreign economic policy was well coordinated. At this time Russia tried to accomplish a major thrust into Western markets whilst trade with traditional partners was a low key priority. But when Sergei Glazyev superseded Mr Aven, a shift from the West to the CIS and China occurred. Such an adjustment was not supported by appropriate action in the Foreign Ministry.

Depending on who headed the Finance Ministry, the Ministry of Economics and the Central Bank, Russian foreign loans strategy changed several times. After a period of anticipation of massive currency loans from international institutions there was a reappraisal of priorities and greater reliance on foreign government loans rather than those from the World Bank and other multilateral institutions. Again, such a shift was poorly coordinated within the Foreign Ministry. The impact of World Bank recommendations on the domestic situation in Russia, which had the twin effects of fighting inflation and inducing higher unemployment, were not anticipated within the Ministry.

During the period under consideration, the economic establishment had the potential key role of influencing Russian partners within the CIS. While

Russian economic institutions were subsidising directly or indirectly the economies of the less viable newly independent states, the amount, direction and forms of support were rarely coordinated by the foreign minister. When Russia was discussing the restructuring of Kazakhstan debt and at the same time was negotiating military and space bases agreements, the debt was restructured as a separate issue, while Almaty managed to get Moscow to pay for the rental of the Russian military facilities on its territory.

One of the recent examples in this field was provided by the former first vice-premier, Oleg Soskovets, during his talks with his Ukrainian counterparts in Spring 1996. While the Russian military and foreign policymakers were pressing Kiev for a favourable solution on the division of the Black Sea Fleet, the major concern for Kiev was the massive debt owed to Moscow due to the trade imbalance. While the Foreign Ministry was planning to use Ukrainian debt as a major bargaining tool for gaining agreement on the fleet issue, Mr Soskovets simply granted his Ukrainian counterparts a strategic debt restructuring scheme. As a result, the Fleet agreement was postponed, as well as a framework political agreement between Russia and the Ukraine, and President Yeltsin could not accomplish his long sought trip to Kiev, which had been planned as a prominent feature of his Presidential campaign.

Another example of poor coordination with other institutions was the handling of the conflicts in Eurasia. In Russia's management of the Chechen war, the role of the Foreign Ministry was defined as the agency dealing with the Organisation for Security and Co-operation in Europe (OSCE), the UN and the West in general. When the Foreign Ministry was stating Russian intentions concerning the cease-fire agreements, the problems of status and the humanitarian issues that were relevant to OSCE concerns, these declarations were rarely supported by the military negotiators on the Russian side. Thus the Foreign Ministry was considered by foreign negotiators to lack credibility. Russian intervention in the civil war in Tadzhikistan was largely planned and accomplished by the defense ministry and the border guards acting upon orders from the Kremlin. The Foreign Ministry had to justify and explain the operation after the event.

One of the goals of the Foreign Ministry was to establish UN and OSCE approval for the Russian peacemaking mandate. To that end, special efforts were made to turn Russian-dominated peacekeeping missions into joint actions by the CIS states in order to give them an umbrella of international recognition. Alas, the Foreign Ministry failed here too. For example, in the case of Abkhasia, where Russian peacekeepers were sent by the Presidential decree in June 1994, the relevant CIS document calling for 'the joint CIS operation' was signed after six months of talks with other Commonwealth members. It was not a surprise that no CIS detachment other than the Russian was ever sent to join the mission. Neither was it insignificant that the international umbrella was not provided.

While unable to coordinate the foreign policy activities of the Russian Federation, the MFA also failed to achieve a working relationship with the emerging business elite, despite attempts such as the creation in 1992 of the Foreign Policy Fund with the backing of some businessmen. The aims were to further co-operation between the diplomatic establishment and Russian business community in order to foster the interests of the latter abroad. Unfortunately this initiative was still born, and was quickly forgotten.

It should also be mentioned that the extensive co-operation between academics and the MFA when Mr Shevardnadze was Foreign Minister virtually disappeared. A special agency within the MFA known as the Scientific Co-ordination Centre, had the responsibility of providing links with the academic community. The practice of joint seminars between diplomats and researchers, and exchange of expertise became a regular feature. The work of the academic partners of the MFA was adequately funded, but the deep financial crisis in Russia undermined this activity. This was reinforced by a perceived indifference on the part of the MFA towards co-operation with the academic community. The MFA established the Scientific Council, which grew into a formal institution which met occasionally for discussions on isolated issues, without any tangible impact on the operation of the MFA. When the Council was disbanded, many foreign policy scholars became even more convinced that it was an indicator of the MFA's lack of interest in co-operation with the academic community.

The decline of the MFA was so evident to the public that a highly critical reaction in the press developed. Naturally, some political interests used this for their own ends, increasing the level of the attacks on the MFA as well as on the Minister personally. An indirect indicator of the decline of the MFA was the reaction of the President, as reflected in his Address to the State Duma in February 1995. Mr Yeltsin was very specific: '. . . effective conduct of foreign policy requires establishment of an effective mechanism for inter-ministerial coordination reporting to the President'. Observers considered such a statement as a recognition of the failure of the MFA to create such a mechanism. However, if a coordinating body was to be established within the President's office, then the MFA would be stripped of some of its prerogatives.[7]

After the President made this declaration, a number of contradictory decisions in the form of Presidential Decrees ensued. Some were aimed at improving conditions for diplomats, others at developing MFA resources and strengthening the status of the MFA in general.[8]

According to these decrees, the salaries of diplomats stationed in countries with harsher climates and in countries where their income was relatively low, were to be increased. For those diplomats who were serving in countries with unstable political and military situations, bonuses were introduced. US$ 30 million was allocated for repairing and reconstruction of the MFA buildings abroad. Welfare for MFA staff was to be supported by a special fund for social and material development, which acquired its resources from ten per cent of the MFA's non-budget income collected from consular service and Diplomatic Corps Service Division (UPDK) activities. However many analysts observed that despite these changes Russian diplomats' salaries were not to be increased. Therefore the threat to the Russian diplomatic service which has developed in recent years is still a real one.

The main criticism was aimed at the Decree which formulated the status of the MFA and its role in the process of foreign policy decisionmaking. This new Presidential Decree appeared as Mr Kozyrev succeeded in halting the formation of a foreign policy inter-ministerial coordinating and supervising body within the President's office. According to some observers, a similar body was formed by the minister himself within the framework of the MFA statute. In support of this view, some analysts referred to the declared intention of re-establishing a Department for Analysis and Foreign Policy Planning. Moreover, a number of observers considered the Presidential Decree as a substantial augmentation of the Foreign Minister's authority, the greatest since the end of World War II. In pursuit of strengthening the powers of the 'dual President-Minister', the Decree takes an unprecedented step in focusing more authority within the MFA and its Minister than ever before. According to the Decree, the MFA is to 'determine general foreign policy strategy of the Russian Federation' and to conduct Russian foreign policy; coordinate and supervize activities of other federal institutions 'in order to guarantee uniformity in Russian foreign policy in the relationship with foreign states and organisations', and to 'issue legal acts when qualified which are binding for other executive branches of the Federation'.

There is no procedure for either appointing or endorsing the Minister by the legislature, because the Minister as well as his deputies are appointed by the President. As for the department and other subdivision heads, the Minister is responsible for appointing them. The Minister also submits proposals to appoint and to dismiss ambassadors, as well as the heads of official delegations. Since the power to appoint ambassadors and the heads of official delegations is vested in the President, there is no need for any approval here either. Russian journalists noted that this represented 'the return of nomenclature', about which Mr Kozyrev had warned in the past.[9]

The Presidential Decrees stimulated a new wave of criticism directed at the MFA and its Minister. It was met with a specific response from the Prime Minister who established a special commission headed by Mr Shahrai, later replaced by Mr Ignatenko. This Commission was to inspect and scrutinize the performance of the MFA with the goal of preparing relevant recommendations. Though the findings of that Commission were not reported to the public, some results were evident in October 1995. According to press reports, the President declared his dissatisfaction with the performance of the MFA during a meeting with his advisers at the beginning of October.

Some days later at a press conference, the President openly stated that he was going to press Mr Kozyrev to resign. Mr Kozyrev was blamed for his ineptitude in coordinating foreign policy and in developing a dialogue with government bodies also responsible for the formulation of foreign policy. But on the following day the President announced that Kozyrev needed a first deputy due to his frequent travels abroad. This deputy would, among other duties, monitor the activities of the Foreign Ministry central body, and oversee personnel policy. The presidential reversal concerning the position of the Foreign Minister resulted in greater ambiguity within the Ministry and triggered renewed criticism in the press.[10]

A new symptom of the instability of the Russian MFA and its head was the establishment of the President's Council on Foreign Policy announced at the end of December 1995 which was to perform coordinating functions in the foreign policy of the Russian Federation.[11] This, together with the fact that Mr Kozyrev was elected a deputy of the State Duma and had to choose between the minister's and the deputy's post, was not only considered a sign of the weak role of the MFA, but also gave support to the rumours about the imminence of Kozyrev's retirement. The increasing speculation in the press was halted by the unexpected President's Decree of 5 January 1996, declaring the retirement of Mr Kozyrev. After three days the post was occupied by Evgeni Primakov following another President's Decree.

In the aftermath of the uncertainties during the five formative years of the Russian Federation, the MFA can be seen to have started to reverse this period of decline. However, it should be noted that the process is gradual and by no means irreversible. The major problems haunting the Russian MFA can be classified as personality problems, institutional issues and budgetary obstacles.

Much of the failure and setbacks for the MFA discussed above resulted from the choice of Foreign Minister. Personality crises were omnipresent in the period of Kozyrev's ministership. The problems started with the parliamentary opposition to the Cabinet, although this was only one indicator of Kozyrev's poor communication and coordination skills. Eventually he lost support even within the Cabinet. Both the Defense Minister and the Foreign Intelligence Chief (Mr Primakov at that time) repeatedly criticized, directly or indirectly, Kozyrevian policy options.

While Mr Kozyrev tried to hide behind the President, it became obvious that he was a political liability rather than an asset in the context of national elections. Finally Mr Kozyrev produced an all-round shift in MFA strategy concerning rejection of NATO enlargement, favouring Russian interventionism within the CIS and advocating closer co-operation with China and Iran.

His new policy with a distinct anti-Western orientation produced displeasure in the West, indignation among his fellow democrats and suspicion within the government. The Communist opposition simply dismissed what it regarded as careful manoeuvering. In the end, this shift failed to produce a national consensus on foreign policy.

Mr Primakov seems to satisfy almost everyone both in Moscow and abroad. He is the first Foreign Minister in Russia/Soviet Union since 1917 with the unique qualifications of an orientalist, an Academician and a former Intelligence Head. Additionally, he has the skills of an able communicator and an honest broker between the warring factions inside the Kremlin. During his first year at the helm of Russian foreign policy his achievements were not dramatic. However, he passed the tests of administrator, communicator and policymaker reasonably well. This is important given the fact that the role of the MFA depends very much on the personal characteristics of its head.

By 1996, policy and administrative issues were in better shape than was the case a year before. The fear within the MFA of overlapping commissions and institutions monitoring and judging its performance, were avoided by the Presidential Decree of 1996 which stated that the MFA was to be 'the primary coordinator of foreign policy'.

The structure of the MFA once again shifted towards relationships with the CIS, and four new departments were established. While the first department deals with general CIS issues, the rest address the Commonwealth countries on a regional basis: the Western, the Caucasian and the Central Asian republics respectively. However, some of the institutional problems remain unresolved. It is not clear in what circumstances the Security Council is to co-operate with the MFA as a partner and when it will override the MFA. The daring and sometimes reckless performance of General Lebed as the Secretary of the Security Council in the second half of 1996 seemed likely to reinforce this problem.

The budgetary situation remains a strong factor demoralizing MFA personnel. With an unbalanced budget, the MFA is far from acquiring even the minimum funds necessary for its operations. Support for overseas missions was a headache for the Minister during 1996, and it will remain so for some years to come.

In the autumn of 1996, with Mr Yeltsin partially inactive due to his heart attacks, the role of personalities and power play again overshadowed the importance of institutions and orderly procedures. As was observed in the weekly news magazine *Itogi*: 'Russian foreign policy again lost its attribute of being Presidential'.[12] At the same time some observers argue that this is a favourable development, that Russian foreign policy under Mr Primakov is going to assume the characteristic of being 'national rather than presidential'.[13] A significant indicator is that the Council for Foreign Policy practically vanished as soon as it had been established on paper. It looks as if under current political trends in Russia, the activities and performance of the MFA will be determined far more by personalities than institutional mechanisms. But for the MFA finally to overcome its decline and to assume an enhanced status demands, above all, political and economic stability within the Russian Federation.

NOTES

1   *Diplomaticheskii vestnik* 1, 1992, p. 6.
2   *Diplomaticheskii vestnik* 1, 1992, pp. 27–8.
3   V. Kariagin, 'Diplomaticheskaia slujba: vchera, segodnia, zavtra', *Mejdunarodnaia jizn* 10, 1994.
4   A. Migranian, 'Vneshniaia politika Rossii: Katastroficheskie itogi trioh let'. 'Pora sdelat pauzu, pomaeniat i politiku, i ministra', *Nezavisimaia gazeta*, 10 December 1994. S. Karaganov, 'Bez rulia i bez vetril', *Moskovskie novosti* 66, 25 December 1994.
5   *Diplomaticheskii vestnik* 2/3, 1992, pp. 28–35.
6   *Diplomaticheskii vestnik* 11/12, 1993, pp. 39–41. *Segodnia*, 25 November 1994.
7   *Segodnia*, 12 February 1995.
8   *Izvestiia*, 17 March 1995, p. 3.
9   *Segodnia*, 24 March 1995. N. Petrova, 'Vneshniaia politika doljna stat prezidentskoi', *Nezavisimaia gazeta*, 17–18 May 1995.
10 M. Pavlova-Silvanskaia, 'Zaranee obiavlennaia otstavka', *Novoe vremia* 43, 1995, pp. 8–9.
11 *Nezavisimaya gazeta*, 149, 27 December 1995, p. 1.
12 *Itogi*, 24 September 1996.
13 *Moscow News*, 8–15 September 1996

11 South Africa
The Ministry of Foreign Affairs: From Isolation to Integration to Coherency
Marie Muller

South Africa's Foreign Ministry was first established in 1927, shortly after the Balfour Declaration confirmed the Union's status as independent and equal within the British Commonwealth.[1] After the National Party took power in 1948 and with the changed situation internationally after World War II, there was renewed impetus for reform within the Ministry. In 1951 the first general review was conducted and a separate Africa Division created within the Department. With the exception of this new creation, a functional organization structure was retained (Political, Economic and Consular Divisions; Protocol Division; Administrative and Accounts Divisions; Divisions with 'specific assignments') until the next major reorganization in 1969.[2] By this time South Africa had become a republic, left the British Commonwealth and was increasingly under pressure from a decolonizing international community which regarded South Africa's internal policies as discriminatory and unacceptable. With the 1969 review the Foreign Ministry was reorganized primarily along geographical lines, though a distinction was still made (within the Political Branch) between bilateral and multilateral relations. Over the years the information service had been added to, separated from and once again added to the Foreign Ministry. In 1983 the internal and external information services were separated, the Foreign Ministry retaining the latter.[3]

By the late 1980s, when South Africa's isolation from the international community was at its most complete, the multilateral dimension had virtually disappeared from the organizational structure of the Ministry and the geographical organizing principle was very much to the fore. Diplomatic ties were mainly with Western Europe and North America, with some use of sub-diplomatic representation elsewhere. This was reflected in the structure of head office. Some functional elements had, however, been reintroduced due to the unique needs of the time and providing, amongst others, for 'strategic' and 'economic' planning to deal with sanctions and other isolating measures against the country. The structure of the Ministry also provided for liaison and control with regard to the 'independent TBVC states' (Transkei, Bophuthatswana, Venda and Ciskei). Overall this reflected not only South Africa's unique position in the world and the perception of the relevant decisionmakers of this position, but also the agendas, strategies and responses of the Ministry to these realities. The approach was broadly 'realist' and 'state-centric' rather than issue-oriented and emphasized bilateral rather than multilateral relations.

In apartheid South Africa the main task of the Ministry of Foreign Affairs was to defend the domestic racial policies of the government and attempt to stem the tide of isolation and foreign pressure on the country to change its ways. Its recruitment and socialization patterns were attuned to this and as a bureaucracy it was imbedded in a system dominated by white males, many of whom accepted the paradigm of 'total onslaught'. Nevertheless, under the leadership of Minister Pik (R. F.) Botha, one of the most senior foreign ministers of his time, the Ministry was often regarded as a more progressive ('*verligte*') branch of government. Possibly at least partly due to this reputation, the influence of the Ministry in foreign policy decisionmaking was somewhat diluted in favour of more hawkish elements, such as the military, when the State Security Council, the principal Cabinet committee, was elevated to a key foreign policy organ under P. W. Botha. However, it still formed part of an inner bureaucratic elite within the government of the old South Africa and as such was not very susceptible at all to outside influences such as parliament or society generally.[4] Even if some diplomats found it increasingly difficult to defend the internal and regional policies of the government (such as those associated with the destabilization of neighbouring countries), they were subject to very little direct input from South African society as a whole, and they were in more ways than one a highly select group. Aspiring diplomats had to have at least a basic university degree and were carefully vetted, amongst other things, for their political beliefs; until at least the middle 1980s only whites were eligible and the career possibilities of women were rather limited.[5]

By the time De Klerk made his historic speech on 2 February 1990, heralding a new political era in South Africa, Central and Eastern Europe had been changed by the end of the Cold War. Important changes relating to this would soon be underway in the South African Foreign Ministry. Though it took a little longer for South Africa to fully regain its position in international organizations, the Ministry was already preparing for this by some meaningful organizational changes which were being effected from 1991 onwards. In fact, with hindsight it is clear that much of the groundwork for changing the old, apartheid and Cold War Foreign Ministry to a new, post-apartheid and post-Cold War Foreign Ministry was done in the interim period between the De Klerk speech and the establishment of a democratically elected Government of National Unity in May 1994. This is not to say

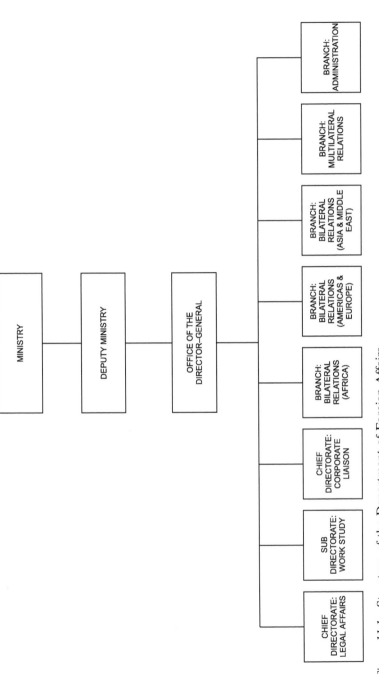

Figure 11.1 Structure of the Department of Foreign Affairs

that South Africa's reintegration into the international community and the restructuring of the Foreign Ministry in order to deal with this was complete by 1994. South Africa's external relations after 1994 continue to change. In tandem with this, but also as a by-product of internal political change in South Africa, the Foreign Ministry is continuously changing.

This chapter will trace the challenges facing the South African Foreign Ministry since 1990 and the changes effected in response to these. Changes between 1990 and 1994 will be reviewed, but special emphasis will be placed on developments since 1994. The story of the South African Foreign Ministry after 1990 was one, first, of integration and, subsequently and increasingly, of a search for coherency. The new South Africa is engaged in a quest for a new identity, and this quest is manifest in the deployment of its foreign policy and the development of its external relations. The tale of the Foreign Ministry is an essential part of this quest.

ORGANIZATION AND AGENDAS

After 1990, but especially since 1994, the South African Ministry of Foreign Affairs has been faced by an altogether new set of issues determining its operational environment. These may be grouped under two broad headings, according to the source or location of such issues: *domestic issues or aspects of the domestic operational environment*, and *external and foreign policy issues or aspects of the international operational environment*. It should be borne in mind that both these environments underwent radical change from the late 1980s, as South Africa negotiated a political transition to majority rule and the international arena saw the end of the Cold War which had dominated it since World War II. Moreover, as has been noted above, changes are still taking place in both areas.

Domestic Issues

The new, post-apartheid South Africa was immediately faced by a different domestic operational environment. In the Ministry this was anticipated even before 1994 and some proactive changes were effected. In essence the changed domestic environment turned on processes of democratization, which implied broader participation and democratic control not only over internal policies but also with regard to foreign affairs. In a comparative context this is, at least in some of its aspects, unique and only time will tell how far the pendulum will swing. The changes required have centred on some specific issues:

- making the Foreign Ministry more representative of South African society, including incorporating former TBVC and ANC 'diplomats' and, coupled to this, making it less elitist;
- giving a greater voice in foreign affairs to parliament, NGOs and civil society generally or, differently put, making it less secretive and authoritarian.

The first issue as well as that of the role of parliament, will be dealt with in this section. Linkages with NGOs and civil society generally, will be dealt with under the next main heading – strategies and responses. Also to be dealt with under the present heading – and by way of an extension of the issue relating to the relationship with parliament – is the matter of where the Foreign Ministry of the new South Africa fits into the broader bureaucratic structures. This implies a look at some constitutional stipulations pertaining to the conduct of foreign affairs, including the issue of the role of subnational governments in foreign relations. The important issue of the role of the President is, of course, also dealt with.

Not so much related to the processes of democratization, but nevertheless of great importance in making the new democracy a success, has been the issue of making the Ministry more effective and less ad hoc and reactive in its functioning. This relates to the desire for greater coherency in South African foreign policy, a new coherency which will finally put both the past and the transition behind it and will herald a truly new identity for South Africa internationally. The theme will be picked up both in this main section and in the next, as it has relevance for formulating, implementing and communicating a consistent foreign policy.

External and Foreign Policy Issues

The external operational environment of the Foreign Ministry of the new South Africa is far more diversified and in a sense, therefore, much more complex than that of the pre-1990 period. In a sense all options are now open to South Africa, which necessitates, to a far greater degree, that choices be made. Life as a pariah, unpleasant as it may be, is fairly simple. This is not true for a country reborn on the moral high ground and comprising a highly pluralistic and politically still divided 'rainbow nation'. Superimposing this on an international arena in transition due to the demise of the old bipolar system and the uncertainties still pertaining in the absence of new fixed power relationships, further adds to the complexity of the situation and the multiplicity of issues confronting the Ministry.

In essence what is now needed, much more so than ever was the case in the old South Africa, is prioritizing with regard to foreign affairs.[6] When, during the transitionary phase, the issue arose regarding affirmative action and how this would affect the careers of existing (white, male) diplomats, the

Director-General of Foreign Affairs declared that the continued expansion of the service would largely solve the problem. However, it would soon turn out that severe budgetary constraints would obviate such a simple solution to the problem.

Apart from financial constraints, putting abstract policy principles into actual policies also implies prioritizing. During the transition period before 1994, the Working Group on International Affairs of the African National Congress (ANC) had drafted a foreign policy document outlining its aims vis-à-vis the outside world. This indicated quite clearly the future directions of foreign policy, namely its emphasis on relations with Africa and Southern Africa in particular; its emphasis on human rights, the environment, arms control and disarmament, on multilateralism, and on good neighbourliness generally; and, its determination to seek a more equitable global economic dispensation.[7] Similar aims were echoed after 1994: at a gathering of South African Heads of Missions in September 1995, the Minister of Foreign Affairs, Mr Alfred Nzo, put forward six guiding principles which underline South Africa's foreign policy approach to the new situation. These reflect a commitment to the promotion of human rights; the promotion of democracy; justice and international law in the conduct of relations between nations; international peace, and to internationally agreed-upon mechanisms for the resolution of conflicts; the interests of Africa in world affairs; and economic development through regional and international co-operation in an interdependent world.[8] In addition to these aims and principles, emphasis has also been placed on the principle of universality – 'essentially the opening of diplomatic doors to any state that would care to forge ties'[9] – and on seeking to 'actively serve and promote the interests of South Africa'.[10] However, the imperatives of actual practise would soon show that the translation of (fairly) abstract principles into real policy was not an easy matter. What is more, a prioritizing of the various principles or aims would have to take place.

In this regard a number of specific problems have already come to the fore, including:

- how is an emphasis on relations with Africa and Southern Africa in particular and on good neighbourliness generally, as well as a firm commitment to the promotion of the interests of Africa in world affairs and to economic development through regional and international co-operation in an interdependent world to be put into practice?
- how can an emphasis on and commitment to the promotion of human rights and of democracy be weighed against other considerations such as old friendships and support given during the liberation struggle?
- how is an emphasis on arms control and disarmament to be weighed against the material benefits to be gained from continued arms manufacture and trade as well as the goodwill of the nuclear powers?

- how is the principle of universality to be implemented when ties with one country may exclude ties with another, such as in the case of the two Chinas?
- how is South Africa to deal with a globalizing world whilst itself situated on a marginalized continent?
- more generally: what exactly are the interests of South Africa and how are they best attained?
- how are South Africa's controversial relations with the pariahs of the world such as Libya, Cuba, Iran to be dealt with?

There is no room here to deal with the interesting debates which surround these specific problems. Mention can only be made of some direct impacts which prioritizing has had on the organizational structure of the Ministry.

Making the Ministry more Representative and Incorporating Former TBVC and ANC Diplomats

With the new South Africa on the horizon, most of the previous require-ments for recruitment to the Ministry of Foreign Affairs came to be either disregarded or overruled. It was clear that a complete revamping would have to take place as soon as the Transitional Executive Council (TEC) was in place in 1993, in other words well before the 1994 elections. However, the real changes would come thereafter, as at least some of the former TBVC and ANC 'diplomats' had to be integrated into the Ministry. It also had to be made generally more representative of South African society as a whole, which necessitated the recruitment of many more 'non-white' (Black, Coloured and Asian) South Africans, and many more women. In many cases those returned from exile outside South Africa had to regain their South African citizenship and the requirement of a basic university degree had sometimes to be waived in order to make a sufficient number of candidates available. Naturally, a new political orientation was also required from aspiring diplomats. In spite of many difficulties and various accusations to the contrary, important changes have occurred in the composition of Ministry personnel over the past few years. Certainly it will take more time to make it fully representative of South African society – if that is literally to be the criterion. In the meantime 'integration' difficulties within the Ministry have been cited by some as contributing to its limited ('minimal', even) role.

Giving a Greater Voice to Parliament

In the words of Raymond Suttner, MP and Chairperson of the Portfolio Committee on Foreign Affairs of the South African National Assembly, '[t]he evolution of the relationship between legislature and executive in the new dispensation is still being worked out. Nothing is final. This is a transition period.'[11] Suttner is also of the opinion that the process of decisionmaking on foreign affairs has not changed substantially after April 1994 even though he says that 'the new parliamentarians elected on 27 April 1994 were not prepared to follow in the steps of their predecessors and explicitly rejected the idea of being mere rubber stamps of the cabinet.' According to him foreign policy is made by the President, Deputy President, Minister and Deputy Minister of Foreign Affairs and various other Ministries in particular Trade and Industry, Defence, Home Affairs and Health. Of these he regards the Presidency and the Ministry of Foreign Affairs as the main actors and argues that there remains little room for input from the public or parliament. 'The idea of such an interaction is welcomed in public statements by the Ministry, but major decisions in fact take place without an opportunity for such an input.' However, he does concede that new rules have provided some opportunities for certain modifications of the old situation. He refers to the following in this regard: the new parliament has taken steps to ensure greater accountability of the Ministry, and the process to review the budget is particularly important in this regard; some briefings of the Portfolio Committee by the Ministry relating to significant international controversies or crises have occurred, but there is no record of briefing of the Committee by the Ministry at the behest of the Ministry, prior to an important decision or visit; and, whereas the previous constitution left the power both to negotiate and ratify treaties in the hands of the President, the interim constitution and the 1996 constitution leaves the power to ratify in the hands of parliament. Suttner argues that this may provide an opportunity for inducing greater public awareness of South Africa's international obligations as well as popularizing some of the important treaties.

However, he concedes that involvement in the process of decisionmaking is entirely absent. The Committee does not want to have a part in the actual implementation of policy and does not deny the need for speedy action by the executive. It does not want to stand in the way of flexibility that may be needed in day-to-day diplomacy, but it does insist on an opportunity to make a contribution towards an overall pattern, an input within the decisionmaking process, to contribute to the framework of foreign policy decision. If Suttner is to be believed, therefore, there has been a greater role for parliament under the new government. However, this 'reform' still has a long way to go and is not yet applicable to substantive policy issues.

Others have argued that the final constitution implies a watering down of the influence of parliament on foreign policy issues.[12] It has also been pointed out that there seems to have been a waning of interest both by parliament in general and the Portfolio Committee in particular. According to this point of view the Committee now seems less interested in actual foreign policy issues and concentrates more on internal and administrative issues concerning the Ministry (budgetary concerns and affirmative action) in its annual report of June 1996. What is clear is that there has been a bit of irritation between the Ministry and the Chair of the Portfolio Committee[13] although of course, such a relationship is not necessarily an unhealthy thing!

In order to fully comprehend the position of the Ministry of Foreign Affairs within the structures of government generally, it is necessary to look at another political development, the withdrawal of the National Party from the Government of National Unity (GNU). It has been argued that the withdrawal, on 30 June 1996, afforded the ANC the opportunity to decide on policy matters with much less restraint than previously because it removed the constitutional requirement that forced the President to consult with the Executive Deputy Presidents on all substantive matters of foreign policy.[14] This could, of course, have some bearing on the processes of democracy. However, whether it actually affects the position of the Ministry of Foreign Affairs vis-à-vis other government structures is to be doubted. The real question is whether the Ministry is decisive in foreign policymaking, for obviously it is involved in implementation on a daily basis.

Much has been said and written about the role of the President and the (lack of a) role of the Foreign Minister, Alfred Nzo; Nzo has repeatedly been criticized for not playing the role he should be playing and leaving too much to the Deputy Minister, Aziz Pahad.[15] Whether this would explain the role of the President is, of course, another matter, though it could have a bearing on coordination in the management of external relations.

The person of President Mandela is an invaluable national asset to South Africa. He enjoys great personal status as a statesman, is charismatic and obviously quite successful in many instances of personal diplomacy. He has, however, come in for some sharp criticism for overplaying this role. One commentator described South African foreign policy since 1994 as: '(f)or the most part . . . based on what President Mandela desires at a given moment'.[16] The same commentator also ascribed some of the ambiguity in South African foreign policy to 'a lack of likemindedness between Mandela and the Department of Foreign Affairs. . . Mandela as head of state says one thing and the structures of the Department of Foreign Affairs advocate something completely different.'

Certainly, the problems which could emanate from a situation where the expertise and slow and careful processes typical of the Foreign Ministry are bypassed, came to the fore in the so-called Nigerian crisis of November 1995. According to reports, the initiative to isolate Nigeria (taken during the Commonwealth conference) was launched 'on the spur of the moment by President Nelson Mandela, who announced his intentions to Mr Nzo at a predawn meeting in New Zealand after he heard of the executions.'[17] Not only did nothing come from this presidential initiative, taken in support of human rights and democray, but the diplomatic price paid for it was dear:

South Africa was clearly sidelined thereafter as a key player in resolving the Nigerian crisis and the message conveyed to South Africa was that it cannot act unilaterally. This was later openly acknowledged by Deputy Minister Pahad: '. . . SA is now isolated from the rest of the continent on the Nigerian issue. It is incumbent upon us not to believe that we have the capacity to go it alone', he declared. 'In future, we must act in the multilateral context.'[18] And it may, of course, be argued that such diplomacy will involve careful preparation in which many different officials in the Ministry will be involved.

The more recent case (December 1996) of the Presidential announcement of South Africa's intention to establish formal diplomatic ties with the People's Republic of China and downscale relations with the Republic of China at the end of 1997 – an apparent attempt to prioritize with regard to a long standing and intensely debated matter – is particularly interesting. It also smacks of some bypassing of the Ministry. This is not to say that those manning the relevant desks in the Ministry were against such a policy move, but it would seem as though they cautioned repeatedly that *how* such a move was made would be crucial; apparently their advice was largely ignored and the announcement not discussed with them beforehand.[19] However, the policy move as such was regarded by many as a victory for the 'democratic forces', notably the Chair of the Portfolio Committee who had been pressing for the 'switch' all along. He had, however, also cautioned that 'any decision to end diplomatic relations with Taiwan will have to be accompanied by very strenuous negotiations to continue relations on other levels.'[20]

The influence in foreign affairs of Deputy President, Thabo Mbeki, a likely successor to Nelson Mandela, should also not be discounted. As has been observed: '(t)he influence and role of the office of the deputy executive president also needs to be studied more closely. Thabo Mbeki, a well trained diplomat who is intellectually and conceptually well-tuned to the shifting dynamics of global affairs, plays a decisive role in setting the government's foreign policy agenda.'[21] The same commentator continues:

> As a result of the uncertainty as to how government departments and agencies interact, both horizontally and vertically, and given the style of the current foreign minister, other departmental voices are increasingly heard, including those dealing with trade, defence, finance and home affairs. Provinces are also beginning to tread on foreign policy turf . . . .

The final aspect to be discussed here, namely the involvement of subnational units in foreign affairs in South Africa, is a particularly interesting and, for South Africa, new development.[22] The 1996 Constitution follows the international pattern of centralizing foreign relations. However, it is instructive that some international agreements become binding on the Republic only after approval by both the National Assembly and the proposed National Council of Provinces. This represents the nine provinces 'to ensure that provincial interests are taken into account in the national sphere of government'. The Council accordingly serves as 'a national forum for public consideration of issues affecting the provinces', and offer the latter an opportunity to participate in the legislative process. The schedule of concurrent legislative competence contains several so-called functional areas that may have implications for international relations, especially for relations between a province and a neighbouring independent state. It is, however, not easy to identify matters in the schedule of exclusive provincial legislative competence which may affect relations with a neighbouring country. Also, the provinces' indirect legislative role in matters relevant to South Africa's foreign relations is qualified by the Constitution's provisions on conflicts between national and provincial legislation.

However, other provisions leave some scope for the establishment of coordinative structures in the field of foreign relations. A number of extra-constitutional factors can be identified that may encourage or have already persuaded South Africa's provinces to establish an international presence. There are, however, also factors militating against provinces' foreign relations. In practice, the factors making for provincial participation in international relations have outweighed those working in the opposite direction. Several South African provinces are known to have engaged in foreign relations of various kinds, including the signing of development assistance agreements with foreign (overseas) governments, visits to and from provincial leaders involving foreign (overseas) counterparts, and the establishment of economic, educational and friendship links with foreign (in many cases overseas) countries. Apart from these activities, it is entirely conceivable that there has been extensive informal 'interelite' contact between several provinces and neighbouring countries, as well as 'direct-dial diplomacy' between provinces and adjacent countries – both forms of 'transregional microdiplomacy'.

Where does all this leave the Foreign Ministry? By its own account, the Ministry 'recognises the fact that provinces need to spread their wings into the international arena to investigate and gain international support for their desperate developmental needs' and 'welcomes the participation by provinces in our foreign policy formulating process'. However, the Ministry also had cause for concern over the provinces' international activities, as most of these took place without its prior knowledge or input. This created 'a perception of a lack of coordination and communication' between various South African actors and ultimately implies a severe lack of professionalism.[23]

In an effort to bring some centrally directed order to the provinces' activities abroad, the Foreign Minister appealed to provincial Premiers to see to it that all activities conducted with the international community regardless of states, provinces and organizations, be so done through and/ or in consultation with the Ministry of Foreign Affairs. To assist in this, the

Ministry created, in 1995, a new Directorate of Provincial Liaison within the Chief Directorate Inter-governmental Relations and Public Affairs. (In late 1996, the Directorate was incorporated in a newly-established Chief Directorate Regional Development – see below.) It was designed to act as liaison between provincial governments and the various branches of the Department of Foreign Affairs 'in order to coordinate activities of mutual concern outside the borders of our country'. Other instruments such as meetings of an Intergovernmental Forum and of a Technical Intergovernmental Committee, each representing the central government and the provinces, have also been created; and more proposals made, both by the Ministry and others, in the area of coordination mechanisms. It is very likely that further innovation will follow.

Prioritizing

As early as 1991 a new shift in emphasis on multilateral affairs was already clearly evident in the organizational structure of the Foreign Ministry, and this was to become one of the main features of the reformed Ministry. The Directorate International Organisations (housed within the Chief Directorate Strategic Planning and International Organisations, which in turn was part of Branch Overseas Countries) was replaced by a Chief Directorate Multilateral Relations, and by 1992 the latter had been replaced by a complete Multilateral Affairs division, separate from Branch Overseas Countries. Numerous subdivisions were in time created in order to deal with a variety of issues relevant to multilateral relations. Whereas the pre-1991 Directorate International Organisations had comprised a total number of eight people, by 1995 the division, now called Multilateral Affairs Branch, had about 90 people working on the full spectrum of issues relevant to the multilateral level.[24] These include, amongst others, international and regional economic affairs; environmental affairs; narcotics and crime prevention; arms control and nuclear matters; human rights, humanitarian and social matters (including women's and children's rights, humanitarian assistance and disaster relief). By the beginning of 1996 the Ministry had permanent representatives at the UN (New York, Geneva and Vienna), the European Union (Brussels), the International Atomic Energy Agency (Vienna), the Organisation of African Unity (Addis Ababa) and the Southern African Development Community (SADC) (Gaborone). A number of international organizations were represented in South Africa by this time, including the Commonwealth, the International Finance Corporation (IFC), the International Labour Organisation (ILO), the International Organisation for Migration, the United Nations High Commissioner for Refugees (UNHCR), the United Nations International Children's Emergency Fund (UNICEF), the United Nations Development Programme (UNDP), the United Nations

Educational, Scientific and Cultural Organisation (UNESCO), the World
Bank Group, and the World Health Organisation (WHO). South Africa
was not only important in its own right, but also as a gateway to Africa.

On the bilateral front the Ministry had, by early 1992, developed the small
Eastern Europe section into a fully-fledged Directorate Central Europe and
Commonwealth of Independent States and Georgia. By then relations had
been established with most of these states, with economic expectations playing an important role. This contrasted very sharply with the situation prior to
the changes in Eastern Europe, when there were no formal ties between
vehemently anti-communist South Africa and the communist countries of
that region. The relevant Directorate of the Ministry was subsequently
further restructured to respond to the changing political map in that part
of the world. However, interestingly, relations with these countries were
more cordial in the interim (1990–4), than after the establishment of the
Government of National Unity.[25]

During the interim period, South Africa had also been responding to
opportunities opening up in the Middle East and Latin America. Economic
expectations also played an important role here. In addition, the perceptions
at the Ministry were changing and the Middle East was 'moved' from Asia to
the African continent. Provision for relations with Africa generally within the
Ministry had shown considerable growth, even during the transition period.
By February 1996 South Africa had official relations with 50 African countries and offices had been opened in 25 of these. (The theme of prioritizing
in favour of the continent and the region, will be studied in more detail
below.)

Growth in relations with Asia and the Far East was a little slower than in
some other cases, but by 1995 these ties were quite unrecognizable: in 1990
South Africa had only four missions in Asia and Oceania (Australia, Republic of China, Hong Kong, and Japan), but by the end of 1995 there were
many more: Australia, Republic of China, India (both in New Delhi and
Bombay), Hong Kong, Indonesia, Japan (both in Tokyo and Kyoto), Republic of Korea, Malaysia, Pakistan (both in Karachi and Islamabad), Singapore
and Thailand. South Africa also had an 'interest section' in Beijing and ties
with Vietnam, though the representative stationed in Thailand had to service
Hanoi as well. Ties with Nepal were also 'awaited'. In addition South
Africa had established diplomatic relations with some other countries
in Asia, though permanent missions had not yet been exchanged: Cambodia,
Laos, Myanmar (Burma), the Philippines, Afghanistan, Sri Lanka, and
Mongolia.[26] This, of course, necessitated better provision for Asia at headquarters. The considerable extension of relations with Asia has, without a
doubt, a lot to do with trade and other economic considerations, though
there are also cultural ties with a newly powerful section of South
African society.[27]

The Protocol section of the Ministry, responsible, *inter alia*, for handling state visits, the accreditation of South African representatives to foreign governments and vice versa, and generally regulating and administering the presence of foreign representatives in South Africa, has also expanded considerably since 1990.

It is quite clear, therefore, that although there still is some scope for further growth and some of this has been occurring during the course of 1996, the Ministry had expanded quite phenomenally by late 1995, due mainly to the changed political situation within South Africa but also to some initial prioritizing of foreign policy goals. At the same time, however, there was criticism of some aspects and perhaps more need for restructuring on the basis of priorities. The fact that there was no diminishing of missions in the West and that limited resources were, therefore, not available for a more emphatic shift to the African continent, was subject to much criticism. However, as has been mentioned, many new missions were opened and Branch Africa, which was now listed before Branch Overseas Countries in the Ministry's official List, was completely restructured. It also came to incorporate some interesting new sections, such as the Directorate Provincial Liaison, already discussed above.

Another important innovation within Branch Africa came about as a direct result of intensified involvement in the continent and specifically in Southern Africa, and the commitment to regional co-operation. South Africa's policies with regard to the Southern African region is set out in a framework document issued by the Ministry in August 1996. This document recognizes the need for co-operation with other line-function departments in South Africa. However, the Ministry has been organizing itself thoroughly for its task and created a Chief Directorate of Regional Development in late 1996.[28] This is responsible for the design and development of South Africa's multilateral economic and political objectives within the Southern African region, and had a lot to do with the country's election to the presidency of SADC during 1996. The Chief Directorate comprised three Directorates: Provincial Liaison Regional Co-ordination and National Contact Point. The Directorate Provincial Liaison will be responsible for all provincial affairs issues, apart from the province–SADC interface.

The Directorate Regional Co-ordination is to plan and coordinate South Africa's position as Chair of SADC, in co-operation with the Vice-Chairman, Mozambique. It is envisaged that this Directorate will liaise closely with the Offices of the President and Deputy President, Chair of the Council of Ministers, the Mozambican government, the SADC Executive Secretary and all South African Missions abroad with regard to their regional responsibility. Apart from its involvement in the Organ on Politics, Defence and Security created during 1996,[29] the Directorate is also responsible for political initiatives, for example the Berlin initiative, the Protocol on Illicit Drug Trafficking, and so on.

The Directorate National Contact Point is to be responsible for the coordination and evaluation of South Africa's participation in SADC, with three levels of responsibility:

- the national level, where it coordinates contact with SADC as a whole, involving the South African government and all its departments;
- the departmental level, where, within the Ministry, it coordinates all SADC related activities;
- the sectoral level, where it maintains close contact with the Department of Finance, the Sector Co-ordinating Unit for the Sector on Finance and Investment.

In addition to the above the Directorate is also responsible for the Southern African Customs Union (SACU), the coordination of South African Technical Assistance in the region, and the coordination of South African participation in other SADC activities.[30]

STRATEGIES AND RESPONSES

Even though the South African Foreign Ministry has been hampered by financial constraints and the difficulties of rapid transformation, it has on the whole responded to its changing environment, both domestic and international, in some interesting ways. How effective this response has been, is perhaps a question to which answers will only come in time. It is, in other words, as yet too early to properly evaluate the success or otherwise of the adaptive strategies adopted.

One area in which the Ministry under the post-1994 government has been much more active than under any previous government, has been in developing links with sections of civil society in South Africa. Certainly the respectability of the new government has contributed much to the ease with which it has been able to involve many academics and NGOs across a broad spectrum. However, had it not been for a firm resolve (at least for the moment) in the new South Africa to do away with secretiveness and authoritarianism and move towards transparency and inclusiveness, it is doubtful whether the Ministry would have attempted such extensive links in the first place.

One of the most noticeable manifestations of this new type of linkage has been the drafting and distribution of the Ministry's *Foreign Policy Discussion Document* during 1996. To aid debate, the Ministry held a conference in September. The process of dealing with the Discussion Document was two-way: the Ministry solicited inputs into the foreign policymaking process, while at the same time using the opportunity to explain itself to civil society. In addition to the conference itself, the Ministry also stimulated a lively debate in the media regarding foreign policy issues, and a number of written submissions were made to the Ministry. Although there was considerable criticism of the conference, it did create a valuable opportunity for debating foreign policy issues.[31] It was not the first occasion of its kind – about a month earlier a workshop was held at the Ministry on Reform of the United Nations. It was resolved that the process would continue, and more workshops are planned. The Ministry has also been issuing occasional papers on important policy issues.[32]

The Ministry has had its problems with the media and at one stage it was reported that Deputy Minister Pahad was contemplating bringing in outside help to improve its image.[33] However, it has made some provision for media liaison in its organizational structure. The Deputy Minister has also been critical of the media in stating that '(t)he media . . . will have to become more informative and analytical about the world, otherwise the demand for greater participation (by ordinary citizens) in policy formulation will just become a slogan.'[34]

Finally, some reference should be made to relations with the Ministry or Department of Trade and Industry. According to one commentator, relations between this Ministry and the Ministry of Foreign Affairs will 'probably be the most crucial issue in the near future' for the South African political leadership to resolve.[35] Consideration will have to be given to the existence of two separate departments: Foreign Affairs and Trade and Industry. This would certainly facilitate policy homogeneity and would enhance the Ministry of Foreign Affairs' expertise in foreign trade and multilateral economic issues. Despite the fact that the Ministry would feel threatened by such a move, the two ministries have come to a partial solution by 'synchronised political and economic approaches towards particular countries'.[36]

CONCLUSION

In the light of the impressive expansion of the activities and international reach of the Foreign Ministry since 1990 and its serious attempts, in many areas, at adapting to changed circumstances, it would hardly be appropriate to apply the image of 'decline' to this case. The Ministry rose to the challenges presented by an entirely new operational environment to an impressive degree given financial, time and capacity constraints. However, much remains to be done and it is seriously hampered in this by the lack of commonly accepted values and of a precise definition of South Africa's national interests. It will, without a doubt, be involved in some difficult choices regarding both policy and its own structure. In all of this its success should be measured in terms of how well it stands up for itself as an institution as well as promoting South African interests.

NOTES

1   For a more detailed discussion of the constitutional development of South Africa and how this related to the establishment of the South African Foreign Ministry (or Department of External Affairs, as it was originally called), see Marie Muller, 'The Department of Foreign Affairs', in Albert Venter, ed., *South African Government and Politics* (Johannesburg: Southern Book Publishers, 1989), pp. 242–3.

2   Marie Muller, 'The institutional dimension: The Department of Foreign Affairs and Overseas Missions', in Walter Carlsnaes and Marie Muller, eds, *Change and South African External Relations* (Halfway House: International Thomson Publishing Southern Africa, 1997), p. 53.

3   Muller, 'The Department of Foreign Affairs', pp. 250–1.

4   Deon Geldenhuys, *The Diplomacy of Isolation. South African Foreign Policy Making* (Johannesburg: Macmillan, 1984), pp. 138–9. This source is extremely valuable in analyzing the political/bureaucratic status of the Foreign Ministry during the era of isolation and even before.

5   Muller, 'The Department of Foreign Affairs', pp. 265–6. After the entry into force of the 1983 Tri-cameral Constitution, 'Indians' and 'Coloureds' were also recruited, and much made of the few who made it to fairly senior positions. Muller, *South Africa and the Diplomacy of Reintegration*, (University of Leicester, Centre for the Study of Diplomacy, Discussion Papers in Diplomacy, No. 16, April 1996), p. 7.

6   This has been stressed by various commentators, including Ministry spokesman. See, for example, the following: Joseph Diescho, *South Africa and the Diplomacy of Reintegration*, (Pretoria: Unisa Press, 1996); Mervyn Frost, 'Pitfalls on the moral high ground: Ethics and South African foreign policy', in W. Carlsnaes and M. Muller, *Change and South African External Relations*; Chris Landsberg and Zondi Masiza, *Strategic ambiguity or ambiguous strategy? Foreign policy since the 1994 election* (Johannesburg: Centre for Policy Studies, Policy Review Series, 8:11, October 1995; Greg Mills, 'South African Foreign Policy: The Year in Review', in *South African Yearbook of International Affairs 1996* (Johannesburg: SAIIA, 1996), pp. 1–8; Greg Mills, *South Africa's foreign policy in a 'globalised' world* (talk given at the South African Institute of International Affairs Pretoria Branch, 21 November 1996).

7   See Greg Mills, ed., *From Pariah to Participant. South Africa's evolving foreign relations* (Johannesburg: SAIIA, 1994), pp. 220–40.

8   As reported in *South Africa Yearbook 1996* (Pretoria: South African Communications Service, 1996), p. 179.

9   Mills, *South Africa's foreign policy in a 'globalised' world*.

10   *Yearbook 1996*, p. 179.

11   Raymond Suttner, 'Parliament and foreign policy', in *Yearbook of International Affairs 1996*, p. 137.

12   Roland Henwood, 'South African foreign policy and practice 1995/96 – an analysis', in *South African Yearbook of International Law* (Pretoria: Unisa

VerLoren van Themaat Centre for International and Comparative Law, 1996), pp. 247–9. Henwood analyzes the constitutional and actual involvement of parliament and especially the Portfolio Committee with foreign affairs, in some detail. For a slightly older contribution on the role of parliament, see *Parliament & Foreign Policy: The International & South African Experience. A Conference Report* (Bellville: Centre for Southern African Studies, University of the Western Cape, 1995).

13   See for example *The New Nation*, No. 110, 28 June 1996, p. 34. This is also confirmed by comments by Ministry officials and Suttner himself.

14   See Henwood, 'South African foreign policy and practice 1995/96 – an analysis', pp. 245–6 for a fuller discussion of the withdrawal and the effect on foreign policy formulation.

15   Muller, *South Africa and the Diplomacy of Reintegration*, p. 13. Also see for example: *Die Burger*, 23 May 1996, p. 15; *Sunday Times*, 2 June 1996, p. 17; *Sunday Tribune*, 30 June 1996, p. 9. It is true, however, that the Minister has been spending much more time on overseas visits than the Deputy Minister: in 1995 Nzo spent a total of 139 days out of South Africa, and Pahad, 42 days.

16   Diescho, *South Africa and the Diplomacy of Reintegration*, p. 2.

17   *Sunday Times*, 2 June 1996, p. 17.

18   *Enterprise*, No. 96, March 1996, p. 106.

19   This was gathered from various remarks made by Ministry officials in the few days following the announcement.

20   Raymond Suttner, 'Dilemmas of South African foreign policy: the question of China', in *South Africa and the Two Chinas Dilemma* (Johannesburg: SAIIA and Foundation for Global Dialogue, 1995), p. 9.

21   Van Nieuwkerk, 'Unpacking the foreign policy black box', p. 3.

22   This discussion is taken from Geldenhuys, *Subnational governments and foreign relations* (paper presented at an HSRC conference on 'Institutional development in divided societies', Mount Amanzi, 14–16 August 1996).

23   The Director General of Foreign Affairs and the Minister of Foreign Affairs, as quoted in Geldenhuys, *Subnational governments and foreign relations*, p. 24.

24   Compare *Department of Foreign Affairs List August 1990* and *Department of Foreign Affairs List July 1995* (Pretoria: Department of Foreign Affairs).

25   See Sara Pienaar, 'Relations with Central and Eastern Europe', in Muller and Carlsnaes, *Change and South African External Relations*, pp. 121–30 for an analysis of this. Provision for this part of the world in the structure of the Ministry, had actually been decreased slightly by 1995.

26   Greg Mills, 'South Africa and Asia: new opportunities, lessons and dilemmas', in M. Carlsnaes and M. Muller, *Change and South African External Relations*, p. 192.

27   See Mills, 'South Africa and Asia: new opportunities, lessons and dilemmas'; Themba Sono, *A Scenario for the New South Africa: Where are we heading?* (Universiteit van Pretoria, Instituut vir Strategiese Studies (ISSUP) Bulletin, No. 4, 1996).

28   Information supplied to the author by the Ministry.

29   For a full discussion see: Jakkie Cilliers, *The SADC Organ for Defence, Politics and Security* (Institute for Defence Policy Papers, No. 10, October 1996).

30   Such as the annual Heads of State Summit, Consultative Conference and Council of Ministers Meetings.

31   Jean-Jacques Cornish, 'Foreign policy needs local spark', *The Star*, 12 September 1996, p. 2.

32   For example the *Draft discussion document on a Framework for Co-operation with the countries in the Southern African region* and the *National External Security Strategy: draft input to chapter six of the National Growth and Development Strategy*, both contained in Occasional Paper No. 1 of 1996.

33   *Sunday Times*, 2 June 1996, p. 20. Also see: *Die Burger*, 3 May 1996, p. 12.

34   Aziz Pahad, 'Bearing the burden of success', in *Enterprise* (No. 96, March 1996), p. 106.

35   Mills, 'South African Foreign Policy: The Year in Review', p. 5.

36   Martin Creamer, 'Rustomjee outlines trade mission strategy', *Engineering News*, 3 May 1996, p. 13.

12 United Kingdom
The Foreign and Commonwealth Office: 'Flexible, responsive and proactive'?[1]

David Allen

The international system and the place of Britain within it has been in a constant state of flux for most of the twentieth century. This has required the Foreign Office, strategically placed at the centre of the management of Britain's external relations but (as the introduction to this volume suggests) challenged on occasions by other departments, to adapt itself constantly in order to maintain its position. The current structure and role of the Foreign and Commonwealth Office (FCO) reflects this cumulative adjustment to change over a considerable period of time, although the pace of that change can be seen to have 'quickened' in the past 30 years. In the last decade alone, the FCO has been faced with major changes in the international environment – the collapse of communism in Europe, the end of the Cold War international system and the disintegration of the Soviet Union and Yugoslavia – as well as a major domestic change – the election of a Labour government in May of 1997, after an 18 year period of successive Conservative administrations.

The history and role of the Foreign Office in the making and implementation of British foreign policy has been told in a number of places[2] and needs only a brief rehearsal here. The Foreign Service can be traced back to 1479 and the Foreign Office to 1782. Until the mid-1960s the UK chose to handle its imperial and post imperial relationships separately from its dealings with the rest of the world. The Colonial Office, the India Office, the Dominions Office and the Commonwealth Relations Office merged over time to form the Commonwealth Office and, in 1968, the Foreign Office and the Commonwealth Office themselves merged to form the present FCO. The present Diplomatic Service was established in 1965 amalgamating the Foreign Service, the Commonwealth Service and the Trade Commission Service.[3]

The administration of British aid has a complex history of semi-detachment from the FCO. Overseas aid was traditionally administered by the

Foreign Office but in 1964 the Labour Government created a separate Ministry of Overseas Development headed by a Cabinet minister. Since then Conservative governments (1970–4 and 1979–97) have chosen to handle aid through an Overseas Development Administration (ODA) under the overall control of the FCO while Labour governments (1964–9 and 1974–9) preferred a separate Ministry. In 1997 the incoming Labour government maintained this pattern by establishing a Department for International Development headed by Clare Short with a seat in the Cabinet.

The Foreign Office and now the FCO have always had a central role in the management of Britain's external policies. This role has been challenged by the relative decline of Britain's position and role in the international system throughout the twentieth century (most spectacularly since 1945) and by the changing nature of international relations: the shifting agenda, the changing basis of power and influence, and the growth of interdependence and of multilateral attempts to manage that interdependence. The central contention of this chapter is that the decline of Britain's relative position in the international system has been in no way matched by a similar decline in the influence and importance of the FCO within the British system. The continued strength of the FCO has, in recent years, played a major part in enabling Britain to 'punch above its weight' in the international system. Faced with the contradictory pressures of changing demands and diminishing resources, the FCO has firmly resisted 'external' attempts to reform it, whilst demonstrating an effective willingness and ability to make the necessary internal adaptations. It is a measure of the FCO's adaptive ability that the Diplomatic Service has successfully retained its separate and unique status within the British administration and that successive Foreign Secretaries have preserved their senior position within the British Cabinet hierarchy. The position of Foreign Secretary remains one of the most important posts in the British government although the particular importance of the relationship between Prime Minister and Foreign Secretary may well have been modified in recent years by the growing power of the Chancellor of the Exchequer and the significance of the position of Deputy Prime Minister under both Major and Blair.

ORGANIZATION AND AGENDAS

In recent years the FCO has faced a number of specific issues in addition to the general problem of managing the consequences of Britain's general decline in the international pecking order. The biggest external challenge has arisen from the need to adjust both the procedures and substance of British foreign policy to the growing importance of the European Union (EU). Participation in the EU has given particular emphasis to the blurring of the boundaries between domestic and foreign policy. A considerable amount of EU business is conducted by officials from the Home Civil Service working in domestic ministries such as the Department of Trade and Industry (DTI) and the Ministry of Agriculture, Fisheries and Food (MAFF). Where once all dealings with foreign governments were conducted through the FCO and Britain's embassies abroad, now there are direct dealings between domestic ministries and their opposite numbers in the other EU member states. This has raised a number of issues of both coordination and control that have challenged the FCO's dominant role in the identification and pursuit of British interests overseas.

The general expansion in the number of states in the international system has challenged the FCO's determination to preserve Britain's global power status by retaining a global representation. The FCO just about managed to do this in response to the proliferation of states as a result of decolonization in the 1960s and 1970s; the new challenges posed by the emergence of new states following the break-up of the Soviet Union and of Yugoslavia in the 1990s have proved more testing and the FCO has struggled to keep up with its major European rivals. In 1995 Britain maintained 221 posts in 188 countries (compared with just 136 countries in 1968), while Germany maintained 229 posts, France 253 posts and Italy 265 posts.[4] While Britain had 2472 UK-based staff serving overseas, Italy had 2833, Germany had 3551 and France had 4851,[5] although these figures partly reflect a continuing British tradition of, and preference for, employing quite high numbers of local staff. The rapid expansion of tourism and travel along with an increase in the number of states has increased certain of the demands on overseas posts whilst the increased ease and speed of both travel and communications has raised contradictory doubts about the purpose of, and need for, overseas posts.

These and other issues relating to both change and Britain's declining resources have meant that the FCO has been the subject of a number of formal inquiries and reviews in recent years. The Plowden,[6] Duncan[7] and Berrill[8] Reports in 1964, 1969 and 1977 respectively all made recommendations which the FCO was inclined to resist, whilst more recently the 1992 Structural Review, the 1995 Fundamental Expenditure Review and the 1996 Senior Management Review were all conducted 'in house', albeit with the participation of outside consultants, and produced recommendations that the FCO was more inclined to accept. The latter reviews were partly occasioned by a self-perceived need to rethink certain aspects of the FCO's work. These aspects were its staffing policies in the face of demands for racial and sexual equality of opportunity and for more rapid career advancement in a Diplomatic Service that had become 'top-heavy' as a result of various administrative reorganizations; its postings policies as more FCO spouses were reluctant to sacrifice their own careers in order to accompany FCO staff abroad; and its staff training and development policies as the demands for functional expertise increased. The reviews were also partly occasioned by the need to find further financial savings and partly by the general trend of governmental reform (market testing, financial devolution, delayering, performance targeting and analysis and so on) which has developed in recent years.

During Mrs Thatcher's period in office, the FCO was subjected to continuous criticism by a dominant prime minister who became increasingly interested, as all long-serving prime ministers tend to, in playing a major role in foreign affairs.[9] Mrs Thatcher's frustration and problems with the EU, which she associated with the pro-European leanings of the FCO, led her to contemplate, but in fact never to implement seriously, the possibility of building up Downing Street's foreign policy capabilities as a counter to the central role of the FCO. In Charles Powell, an ex-FCO official, Mrs Thatcher had an ambitious and effective Private Secretary for Overseas Affairs who was more than capable of assisting her in her occasional forays against the FCO – his part in the drafting of her attack on the EU and its President, Jacques Delors, in a speech made at the College of Europe in 1988 is a case in point.[10] Mrs Thatcher also appointed a succession of ex-ambassadors to advise her but, by and large, they were always careful not to undermine their previous employers when briefing her. Under Mrs Thatcher, plans for the establishment of a Foreign Affairs Unit along similar lines to the American National Security Council[11] were overtaken by the events that led to her eventual resignation. Neither John Major nor Tony Blair so far have shown any similar inclination to side-step either the Foreign Secretary or the FCO.

The FCO is staffed by members of the Diplomatic Service and of the Home Civil Service. Before the 1997 Labour government established the Ministry for International Development, the FCO had a Diplomatic Wing and an Aid Wing (Overseas Development Administration). The Diplomatic Wing is staffed by around 6000 UK-based personnel (around 4000 in the Diplomatic Service and 2000 Home Civil Servants mainly in support roles in London) who serve both at home and abroad. In 1995 there were around 2500 UK-based staff serving abroad and they were assisted in posts by 7500 locally engaged staff. Recruitment to the Diplomatic Service remains extremely competitive with the Diplomatic Wing offering jobs to just 1 in 120 applicants to the fast stream and 1 in 86 applicants to the main stream. In the Diplomatic Wing, there are twice as many men as there are women but in the senior grades there are still very few women indeed. In its publicity the FCO makes much of the fact that in 1995, for the first time ever, female fast stream entrants outnumbered male entrants.

The Aid Wing is staffed by members of the Home Civil Service. The FCO have been forced to accept considerable reductions in budgets and overall staffing levels (21 per cent since 1980). The FCO vote (minus the variable costs of peacekeeping operations) is around £1 billion at 1995 prices whilst the ODA receives around £2.2 billion (the fifth largest aid budget in the world). The FCO thus has a relatively small budget in contrast to the £20+ billion allocated to the MOD or the nearly £100 billion expenditure of the Department of Social Security. The FCO has hardly any programme expenditure (unlike the ODA) and so budget cuts can be directly translated into staff slots or overseas posts. As a consequence FCO morale has been quite badly affected in recent years by the constant budgetary pressures. Staff who have become disillusioned, either by budget reductions, seemingly inconsiderate postings policies or the lack of opportunity for career advancement have been able to find better paid and often less demanding employment in the private sector.

The FCO is headed by the Foreign Secretary who is always a senior member of the Government. There are usually at least three junior ministers (four when ODA is situated within the FCO) one of whom, in recent years has been designated Minister for Europe. In the past a separate European Ministry has been proposed and, under Edward Heath in the 1970–4 administration, a Cabinet minister with EC responsibilities was appointed. The FCO has always resisted attempts to separate EU business from the overall responsibilities of the FCO and successive Foreign Secretaries have shown little enthusiasm for suggestions that the present Minister of State for Europe be elevated to Cabinet rank. A Foreign Secretary stripped of his EU responsibilities would suffer an enormous loss of stature so central is the EU to many internal and external policy issues.

The FCO and the Diplomatic Service is headed by a Permanent Under-Secretary (PUS) who is responsible both for the administration of the FCO and the work of overseas posts through a Board of Management and for strategic policy advice to ministers through a Policy Advisory Board. In recent years the work of the PUS has become increasingly focused on the management of the FCO in London. The post of Political Director, which was initially created so that Britain could play its part in the EU's system of European Political Cooperation – now the Common Foreign and Security Policy (CFSP) – is now effectively the top policy advisory post. Whereas 20 years ago the PUS would always accompany the Foreign Secretary or Prime Minister on his travels overseas now it is usually the Political Director who clocks up the air miles whilst the PUS stays at home to look after the shop.

The FCO carries out its six core functions (foreign policy advice and implementation, management of Britain's remaining Dependant Territories, public diplomacy including the British Council and the BBC World Service, commercial work, consular work and entry–clearance work) via 13 Commands (reduced from 16 after the Senior Management Review), each under the direction of an Assistant Under-Secretary. Between the AUSs and the PUS there is a further management layer of Deputy Under-Secretaries (DUS). It is this layer that has been most criticized in recent years and the trend has been to reduce the number of DUS posts thereby pushing policy responsibility down as far as possible and making the heads of the various Commands directly responsible both to ministers and the top level of FCO policy management.

The Commands are further sub-divided into Departments, Units and Divisions leaving just a scattering of Departments and Units outside the Command structure (Economic Advisers, Legal Advisers, Overseas Estate Department, PUSs Department, the Policy Planning Staff and the Aid Policy and Resources Department). The Commands fall into three broad categories: *Geographical* (there were seven, there are now five following the recent decision to create unified Europe and Asia Commands), *Functional* (including three multilateral Commands dealing with the European Union, International Organisations and International Security, and two Commands dealing with Public Services and Trade and Investment Promotion) and *Administrative* Commands dealing with Finance, General Services and Protocol.

The basic FCO unit remains therefore, the geographical desk within a geographical Department and Command. Although there has been a considerable growth in functional departments in response to the 'internationalization' of a number of traditional domestic issues and to the growth of multilateral forums, the FCO has resisted suggestions that, as a multi-functional organization, it should reorganize itself around its functions. The Fundamental Expenditure Review of 1995 argued for the preservation of a structure based on regional and multilateral organization partly because of the high estimated cost of restructuring the FCO and partly because of the continuing logic of geographical specialism. The FCO believes that its knowledge of specific countries and its development of bilateral relationships that span a number of specific functions, adds significant value to the advancement and coordination of British interests. If the FCO were to be reorganized along functional lines then the fear would be that a number of functions could then be 'hived off' to domestic ministries along the lines suggested by the CPRS Report (see below)

The FCO faces two types of coordination problem in its management of Britain's external relations. Firstly it has to ensure effective internal communication and coordination both within the FCO in London and between London and the network of overseas posts. Secondly, as the agenda expands to directly involve many Home Departments in both the shaping and execution of external policy, the FCO has a major responsibility to ensure coherence and consistency across Whitehall. In pursuing this second objective, the FCO also has a clear interest in retaining as much overall control over British foreign policymaking and implementation as is possible.

Within the FCO, the problems raised by the proliferation of functional and multilateral commands cutting across the geographical divisions is best illustrated by reference to arrangements for dealing with the countries of Western Europe and the EU. Until very recently, relations with individual West European countries (the utility of distinguishing between West and East European countries was of course challenged by the developments after 1989) and the management of posts in these countries were handled by several geographical departments grouped together in a Western Europe Command. However bilateral relations with most EU member states are dominated by EU and NATO issues which are handled by the separate EU and International Security Commands respectively. To further complicate matters, dealings within the EU and NATO frameworks are characterized by the heavy involvement of other Government departments, especially the DTI, MAFF and the MOD. In Brussels, Britain has no less than three posts, accredited to Belgium, the EU and NATO respectively, and the potential coordination problems are obvious. At one time, this coordination problem extended right to the very top of the FCO with no less than four DUSs having responsibility for Western Europe and it was thus one of the major issues addressed by the 1995 Senior Management Review.

Across Whitehall the coordination of British foreign policy is not in the exclusive control of the FCO; long gone are the days when all contacts with the outside world were handled by the FCO. Nowadays just as the FCO has sprouted a number of functional departments that in many ways 'shadow' the work of Home Departments so, in turn, most Home Departments have developed their own international and European sections. The FCO continues to play a major role in the coordination of all these different aspects of Britain's external policy but the British system also recognises that, with reference to a number of cross-cutting issues, the FCO is not the unchallenged sole determinant of the overall British interest but merely an 'interested' department amongs many others. In these cases, the Cabinet system and the work of the Cabinet Office provide consistency and coherence. At the very top of the decisionmaking process, the British Cabinet is meant to be collegial and the doctrine of collective responsibility pertains. In practice many decisions are delegated to Cabinet Committees of which the Committee on Defence and Overseas Policy and the Committee on the Intelligence Services both chaired by the Prime Minister and the Sub-committee on European Questions, chaired by the Foreign Secretary, are the most important in relation to foreign policy.

The work of these ministerial committees and of their official counterparts is supported by the Cabinet Office, headed by the Secretary of the Cabinet who is also the head of the Home Civil Service. There are five separate Secretariats within the Cabinet Office of which three (the Overseas and Defence Secretariat, the Joint Intelligence Secretariat and the European Secretariat) have external relations coordination responsibilities.[12] The Secretariats are quite small, staffed mainly by home civil servants but also

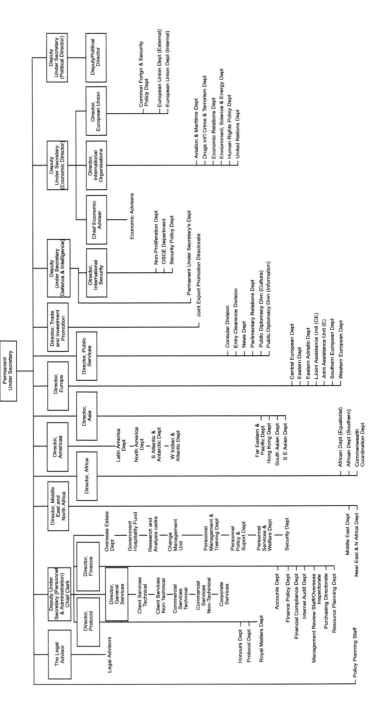

Figure 12.1 FCO Senior Management Structure

by members of the diplomatic service. The relationship between the FCO and the staff of the Cabinet Office is a close one; in no sense are they rivals although on issues where the FCO is in dispute with other government departments it is the Cabinet Office staff who record the minutes of the meetings at which government policy is thrashed out.

It might be expected that the FCO would fit uneasily into the broader Whitehall picture because of the separate recruitment, training and career structure of the Diplomatic Service, and because so many members of the Diplomatic Service spend so much of their careers in posts overseas. However, while there is undoubtedly some rivalry and while some members of both the Diplomatic Service and the Home Civil Service clearly retain prejudiced and stereotyped views of each other, it is hard to find examples of external policy being adversely affected by internal bureaucratic conflict involving the FCO as one of the warring parties. On the contrary, the most spectacular interdepartmental dispute of recent times, which had major external overtones, was the Westland crisis,[13] which centred on a dispute between the DTI and the MOD. As we shall see below, the FCO is in almost permanent conflict with the Treasury over the allocation of government resources, but no more so than any other government department in recent years.

The FCO has been the subject of a number of formal enquiries in recent years. The Plowden Report delivered in 1964 'provoked the most radical changes and the least controversy'.[14] It was responsible both for the creation of the unified Diplomatic Service and for the eventual amalgamations that led to the establishment of the FCO. Despite the obvious decline in British global influence that was apparent by the mid 1960s the Plowden Report was 'friendly' towards the FCO in its assumption that Britain should nevertheless maintain the foreign policy capability of a global power. To this end, Plowden recommended improved conditions of employment for the Diplomatic Service which it felt should be maintained at a level approximately ten per cent above basic requirements so as to allow for enhanced training, leave and travel. These proposals were never implemented and subsequent enquiries were never so generous in their recommendations.

In 1969, after the traumas of devaluation and the military withdrawal from east of Suez, the Duncan Report[15] was much tougher on the FCO. It set out to achieve savings of between five and ten per cent by distinguishing between two distinct areas of British attention. Duncan recommended that the countries of Western Europe plus North America should be grouped together in an *Area of Concentration* while the rest of the world (including Japan and the whole of the Middle East!) would form an *Outer Area*. Countries within the *Area of Concentration* and one or two other 'special cases' would be served by Comprehensive Posts, which would be staffed in the traditional way, but most of the countries that fell within the *Outer Area* would be served by much reduced Selective Posts from which there would be virtually no political reporting. The main emphasis of diplomacy was to be on commercial work and the Duncan Report made it clear that it did not consider a foreign policy apparatus suitable for a global power with comprehensive political and commercial interests any longer appropriate for Britain. This view of the role of the FCO and the Diplomatic Service was of course strongly contested by the FCO, whose delaying tactics were all that were required as the change of government that occurred in June 1970 led to the shelving of the Duncan Report.

Even more radical however was the report produced by the Central Policy Review Staff (CPRS) under Kenneth Berrill. Charged with recommending 'the most suitable, effective and economic means of representing and promoting British interests both at home and overseas' the CPRS team came up with a proposal that the Diplomatic Service and the Home Civil Service be merged effectively creating a Foreign Policy Group. This suggestion was based on the assumption that the necessary specialisms required to advance British interests were to be found in the Home Civil Service and that the essentially political advice, expensively provided by the Diplomatic Service, was no longer relevant to British needs. In addition, the CPRS Report called for the closing of 55 posts on top of the 30 that had been closed since Duncan reported. The CPRS Report was nothing more than a direct attack on the FCO and all that it stood for, and it provoked an enormously hostile response. Typical was the reaction of one of Britain's senior Ambassadors whose Paris embassy was singled out for particular attack for the 'lavishness' of its hospitality. In his diaries, Nicholas Henderson records 'This is the third such enquiry in the past fifteen years. True, Plowden and Val Duncan did the service no harm but the setting up of yet another and outwardly more hostile enquiry has not been good for morale'.[16] The FCO produced a line by line rebuttal of the entire Report and they were supported in their endeavors by Jim Callaghan, the Prime Minister, who had fond memories of his time as Foreign Secretary. The CPRS Report provoked such a hostile reaction, with hundreds of servings diplomats threatening to resign rather than face incorporation into the Home Civil Service, that it probably never stood much chance of being implemented. Despite its spirited and successful defence, the FCO showed in later years that it recognised some of the problems highlighted by the CPRS Report, even if it rejected the proposed solutions.

More recently, the FCO has been given a searching examination by the Foreign Affairs Committee of the House of Commons, particularly over its response to new commercial challenges in the Far East and over its management of public diplomacy via the BBC World Service and the British Council (both of whom are FCO responsibilities and paid for under the FCO vote). In the 1990s the FCO has responded to the general climate of government reform by holding its own internal Structural Review in 1992, a Fundamental

Expenditure Review (FER) in 1995 and a Senior Management Review (SMR) in 1996. The acceptance and implementation of these more recent reports are part of the FCO's response to a changing environment to be considered in the next section.

STRATEGIES AND RESPONSES

The FCO has responded well to change. As we noted above, its basic tactic has been to resist strongly all attempts to impose reform from outside, whilst internally making some quite radical adjustments to the way that it organizes itself and carries out its work. The changes in the substance of foreign policy and the blurring of boundaries between foreign and domestic policy have forced the FCO to work much more closely with other government departments, both within Britain and abroad, and to organize itself for the demands of multilateral as well as bilateral diplomacy and negotiation. The FCO has sought to manage the interface with other government departments as smoothly as possible.[17] It has considered and sensibly rejected the idea of charging them for the work that its overseas posts carry out for them; it has instructed those of its departments, such as European Union Department (Internal), who 'face' domestic ministries to consult with them about their requirements vis-à-vis FCO posts overseas and it has sought to maintain its position, if not of supremacy, then at least of 'primus inter pares' in the overall direction of British foreign policy. Foreign policy is increasingly about coordination and the FCO is clearly the most important of the coordinating departments and has made considerable efforts to maintain this position, while continuing to argue the case for its separate identity. This has not been seriously challenged since the CPRS Report of 1977; instead the FCO position was endorsed by the 1994 White Paper on the Civil Service which stated that 'The Diplomatic Service is a separate branch of the public service with its own particular needs and structure.'[18]

The growing complexity of the foreign policy agenda has forced the FCO to develop more and more functional competencies but it has responded to this challenge by firmly sticking to an organizational structure that subsumes functional expertise to geographical and multilateral Commands and therefore emphasizes the importance of the FCO's coordination role in relation to other government departments. Similarly the FCO, by preserving the pivotal role of the ambassador in overseas posts, has resisted the argument that domestic specialists who are posted overseas should report directly to their 'home' departments. Thus, in the name of coherence and consistency, the FCO has successfully defended its role as 'gatekeeper' both at home and abroad, even though the participants in the foreign policy process are increasingly drawn from a number of non-FCO sources.[19] This is most clearly seen in the key roles that the FCO and the UK Permanent Representation to the EU (UKREP) play in the overall management of British policy towards the EU.[20] The FCO's EU Command is responsible for coordinating instructions to UKREP (even though policy may have been thrashed out in the Cabinet Office) and Britain's Permanent Representative, the head of UKREP, is always appointed from the Diplomatic Service even though more than 50 per cent of UKREP's staff are drawn from outside the Diplomatic Service. It is the Permanent Representative who is responsible for the overall presentation and negotiation of British interests in Brussels and who returns to London each Friday to participate in EU policy meetings both within the FCO and the Cabinet Office.

Changes in British society and in the approach to work and working conditions have forced the FCO to reconsider the way that it recruits staff and carries out its business. Attempts to open up the recruitment process have had mixed results; whilst the FCO can point to figures that suggest a steady increase in the employment of women[21] and in the decline of candidates from private schools, its record on the employment of representatives of ethnic minorities is not impressive and it attracted highly unfavourable publicity in January 1996 when its most senior woman, Pauline Neville-Jones, resigned 'noisily' after being denied the position of ambassador to Paris, on the face of it because she was both female and unmarried. On a variety of staff matters the FCO is increasingly in competition with a number of other employers for the talents of the young high flyers that it used to recruit with ease. Relatively poor pay, poor conditions of service, long working hours, slim chances of rapid promotion in a service where a number of senior posts have been cut on efficiency and economy grounds, have all taken their toll and the FCO has been relatively slow to respond, leading to reports of growing dissatisfaction and low morale.[22] Whether the arrival of a Labour Government intent on 'opening up' the FCO to a wider recruitment base and more open and modern working practices are likely to restore the once high morale of the Diplomatic Service remains to be seen. Many of the most unpopular changes to the nature of the work, and thus to the prospects of a satisfactory career, have been driven by the constant need to find financial savings. It does not seem very likely that this pressure will be significantly eased in the foreseeable future and so the FCO will continue to be handicapped in its efforts to create a modern service capable of attracting and retaining high quality staff.

Recent reports have recognized the fact that, in a number of areas the FCO has been relatively slow to move with the times and efforts have been made to catch up. In its use of information technology the FCO has been slow, in comparison to other government departments and other foreign ministries (see a number of the other chapters in this volume), to adopt advanced methods of electronic communication. However, while it has taken a long time to introduce a secure e-mail system, the FCO was one of the first British government departments to provide a public service on the Internet. The FCO web site (*www.fco.gov.uk*) was first established in 1995 and is generally regarded as first rate – a new site was added in December 1997 to serve the UK Presidency of the EU during the first half of 1998. The FCO web site serves both to enhance the public diplomacy side of the FCO's work and to provide instant access to nonclassified information for overseas posts. The aim is to get everything online as soon as its embargo is lifted and most speeches or reports delivered to Parliament are now available before they are released to the media through traditional channels.[23]

As well as seeking to preserve its central role in Whitehall by improving its links with other government departments, the FCO has also had to develop strategies for reforming its own internal structure and management practices, partly in response to changes in the foreign policy environment and partly in response to the general pressures for governmental reform that have developed in the last decade. The FCO strategy has been to be seen to participate in this process of change and reform with as much enthusiasm as possible, while preserving its separate status and warding off any attempts to downgrade its overall significance by placing organizational emphasis on functional rather than geographical and multilateral coordination tasks.

To this end, as well as reemphasizing, reinforcing and, where appropriate in Europe and South Asia, reorganizing, its geographic Commands, the FCO has also sought to implement a policy of devolving both financial and management responsibility down through Commands to departments and to overseas posts in line with similar developments elsewhere in the government service. The FCO has sought over time to remove a complete layer of senior management (DUS level) by making geographic Commands directly answerable to the PUS and to give more responsibility at departmental level to officials, by encouraging them to brief ministers directly rather than moving documents through several layers of authorization and control. Attempts have also been made to improve the role of policy planning in the FCO (partly in association with other EU foreign ministries), to better associate the work of the Research Department with its customer departments and to reorganize the management structure so that those responsible for policy planning and advice and those responsible for the management of resources are more closely associated with each others work. This latter objective has been partly achieved by devolution and partly by unifying the Policy Advisory Board and the Board of Management and strengthening their links with the Commands as well as their 'visibility' to the rest of the FCO.

The FCO has revised its mission statement twice in recent years so as to relate its corporate objectives more clearly to its core functions and also to facilitate better monitoring of those objectives and their attainment. The

FCO Annual Departmental Report is now replete with lists of objectives and targets with regard to political and economic work as well as commercial, consular, entry clearance and information work, and with records of their achievement.

Another area where the FCO has been forced to respond to change in recent years concerns the growing interest of the wider public, both at home and abroad, in foreign policy. Domestic publics, particularly in the developed world, are now less trusting of governments and more aware of what they are up to in the foreign policy area. Britain is no exception to this general post-war trend which has, if anything, accelerated since the end of the Cold War. The FCO must now pay more attention to both Parliament and the wider public in Britain whilst the state of public opinion in those countries which Britain seeks to influence is now also a factor that needs to be given far more attention than in the past. The FCO can be criticized for being slow to react to this phenomenon. Commentators have noted the persistent refusal of the FCO to either acknowledge or seek to reach a consensus with the significant 'Falklands lobby'[24] which nevertheless exerted influence on British attempts to change its policy on the ownership of the Falkland Islands, and the FCO and the British government in general can be faulted for their failure to seek a broad domestic consensus on a whole host of EU issues.

Similarly the FCO was heavily criticized for its recent attempts to cut the budget and restrict the activities of both the BBC World Service and the British Council at a time when the importance of this type of public diplomacy was becoming more rather than less significant. However, this issue has now been addressed by the FCO. The FER devoted a whole section to the growing importance of public diplomacy and to the need for the FCO to develop a public diplomacy strategy statement as well as individual country strategies. The BBC World Service and the British Council are to have their objectives reevaluated with a view to aligning them more closely to the FCO's aims and objectives. The FCO Information and Cultural Relations Departments are to be restructured. David Howell, the then chairman of the House of Commons Foreign Affairs Committee, underlined the need for the FCO to focus on better public diplomacy when he wrote that 'the emphasis needs to be on building up British-friendly attitudes'[25] in those countries that the FCO wishes to influence. He went on to criticize the spending priorities of a Government that continued to spend £29 billion on defence at a time when the major military threat had evaporated, whilst cutting spending on British overseas diplomacy to half the French level and one third the German level.[26] There is some evidence of the FCO seeking to build new domestic constituencies or linkages with NGOs, and the new Labour government has given considerable emphasis to its attempts to build a closer relationship with British business. Although Mr Richard Branson was not appointed, as some newspapers predicted, to the post of British Ambassador to Washington, Mr Derek Fatchett, Minister of State at the FCO, did announce recently, in a speech to the Institute of Export's partnership 2000 Conference[27] that 'New Labour is determined to bring a more business-like approach to Government and to the Foreign Office'. He went on to say 'The Foreign Office has got the message. Gone are the days when it might be said to stand aloof from trade promotion. Today trade promotion is our largest single activity accounting for 25 per cent of our resources and 34 per cent of our staff overseas.' Nowadays FCO commercial officers work closely with the DTI and with Business Link staff. The FCO runs, jointly with the DTI, an Invest in Britain Bureau and an Export Forum. There are now a few more opportunities for interchange with non-diplomats than there were before although, aside from the commercial sector, the FCO remains reluctant to involve outsiders in its policy work. Nevertheless, the FCO has recently introduced a series of short term attachments to overseas posts for business people to work on specific projects or promotions and it has extended its interchange programme with industry, through which it has opened up a number of longer term positions in Commercial Sections in embassies for private sector candidates on secondment.

The growing interest of the wider public in foreign policy has given foreign policymaking and implementation an additional dimension which the FCO and its political masters have yet to fully understand. The pressures from the public often seem irrational: over Somalia, the Falklands invasion, atrocities in Bosnia, the question of European integration or the sale of arms to undesirable regimes, the British public seemed and seem to be calling for action and intervention by the British Government but they also have made it clear that additional costs, whether human or financial will not be tolerated. In the face of these contradictions the Government has been inclined to vacillate and to allow public opinion to gain the upper hand. It is by and large a failure of leadership and of will by government that has left the FCO exposed to the whims of public opinion and the media. The problems that it has faced in pursuing a consistent policy towards the EU in recent years is a case in point. The FCO alone cannot be expected to master this new foreign policy environment but, given a clear lead by government, it can be expected to provide the necessary support.

CONCLUSIONS

In most of the areas discussed above, the FCO has developed strategies for responding to change in recent years. These responses tend to resemble 'fine tuning' rather than radical reform but they have enabled the FCO and the Diplomatic Service to retain their central position in the making and implementation of British foreign policy. It is certainly the case that British influence in the world has continued to decline although participation in the European Union has halted that absolute decline somewhat, by enabling Britain to benefit from its collective power. In many ways Britain still aspires to maintain the foreign policy of a world power; little attempt has been made in recent years to significantly cut back Britain's global responsibilities or ambitions. Indeed in 1995 the British government went to considerable lengths at its 'Britain in the World Conference'[28] to emphasize the fact that Britain retained its global role and should not be thought of as 'merely' a European power. It is probably not that surprising, therefore, that Britain should continue to attempt to maintain a foreign ministry and diplomatic apparatus appropriate to a power with global pretensions, albeit at reduced cost. The interim answer to the question about the decline of foreign ministries posed by this volume, has to be therefore, that, in the British case, no such decline is immediately apparent.

However, this situation may not continue in the immediate future and this chapter will conclude with some thoughts on the likely impact of the Labour administration, which took office in May 1997. In many ways the new Foreign Secretary, Robin Cook, seemed determined to introduce significant changes into both the substance and procedures of British foreign policy. His commitment to make British foreign policy 'greener'[29] and to give the British public a bigger say in British defence and diplomacy, his determination to pursue an 'ethical' foreign policy[30] and his recognition that domestic and foreign policy are indivisible,[31] all suggest further change for the FCO to respond to. His establishment, with the support of the Prime Minister, of an independent institute (The Foreign Policy Centre) to generate foreign policy ideas was seen as a direct challenge to traditionalists in the FCO despite the reported support[32] it received from Sir John Kerr, the head of the Diplomatic Service. On the other hand, Mr Cook has moved to strengthen the FCO's control over Britain's remaining colonies (British Overseas Territories), following the problems that arose between the Ministry for International Development and the volcano-stricken island of Montserrat; he resisted calls to review the position of senior FCO officials involved in European policymaking[33] (in particular that of Sir Stephen Wall, Britain's Permanent Representative in Brussels) who were regarded in some Labour quarters as being too close to the previous administration; and both he and the Prime Minister have made no secret of the fact that they were advised in opposition by a number of distinguished ex-FCO mandarins (Robin Renwick, David Hannay, Rodric Braithwaite, David Gilmore and Michael Butler) who might have been expected to have kept the interests of their old department in mind when proposing further strategies for change.

One area of possible change which previous governments have resisted concerns developments in the EU and the institutional consequences of pursuing a Common Foreign and Security Policy. The British government, despite finding it increasingly difficult to devote the necessary resources to its foreign policy machine, has not been tempted by the European option of pooling resources, particularly overseas. Proposals to establish joint EU embassies and eventually to establish a full-blown European diplomatic service have been stoutly resisted by Britain in favour of retaining a national foreign ministry and diplomatic service, even though, recently, Britain has gone along with an increasing concentration of CFSP activity in Brussels.[34] Since Labour came to power there have been reports that the Treasury would like the FCO to consider merging its consular work with that of other EU countries.[35] However even if this were to be taken seriously, the FCO has made it clear that commercial work, immigration control and some aspects of political work would have to remain under separate national control. The FCO is more likely to counter the Treasury proposals about consular work by giving further consideration to plans, that already exist, to shut down certain consulates and replace them with a telephone hotline to officials based in London. It would take a bigger swing towards further EU integration than the Labour government has so far been willing to consider for the FCO to come under any serious threat from a Brussels-based alternative.

The title of this chapter posed an implicit question about the ability of the FCO to be flexible, responsive and proactive in the face of change. The conclusion would seem be that, while the FCO has undoubtedly proved itself to be a foreign ministry capable of both responsiveness and flexibility, it has yet to be tested by, or called upon to serve, a government willing to adopt a more proactive foreign policy. If the new Labour administration were to actively pursue the objectives, laid out in Robin Cook's mission statement,[36] of 'exercising leadership in the European Union, protecting the world's environment, countering the menace of drugs, terrorism and crime, spreading the values of human rights, civil liberties and democracy and using its status at the UN to secure more effective international action to keep the peace of the world and to combat poverty', then the FCO just might find its organization and working practices more fundamentally tested than it has to date.

NOTES

1   'The FCO has permanent aims which remain valid: to enhance the security of the UK and that of the Dependent Territories, to promote their prosperity, to promote and protect British interests and influence abroad and to protect British nationals abroad. But in this competitive environment, both international and domestic (with continuing downward pressure on public expenditure), the FCO must be flexible, responsive and proactive, at all levels, to help Britain take full advantage of the new opportunities overseas.' *Fundamental*

Expenditure Review, Foreign and Commonwealth Office (Diplomatic Wing), September 1995, p. 1.

2   See in particular; William Wallace (ed.) *The Foreign Policy Process in Britain*, (London: Royal Institute of International Affairs, 1975); John Dickie, *Inside the Foreign Office*, (London: Chapmans, 1992); Michael Clarke, *British External Policy-Making in the 1990s*, (London: Macmillan for the Royal Institute of International Affairs, 1992), Simon Jenkins and Anne Sloman, *With Respect, Ambassador: An Inquiry into the Foreign Office*, (London: BBC, 1985), Ruth Dudley Edwards, *True Brits: Inside the British Foreign Office*, (London: BBC Books, 1994); Laurence Martin and John Garnett, *British Foreign Policy; Challenges and Choices for the 21st Century*, (London: Royal Institute for International Affairs/Pinter, 1997)

3   Clarke, *British External Policy-Making*, p. 77

4   Foreign and Commonwealth Office including the Overseas Development Administration, *1996 Departmental Report: The Government's Expenditure Plan 1996–97 to 1998–99, Command 3203* (London: HMSO, 1996) p. 19.

5   Foreign and Commonwealth Office, *1996 Departmental Report*, p. 14.

6   *Report on the Committee on Representational Services Overseas*. (1962–64), (Plowden Report) (London: HMSO, 1964).

7   *Report of the Review Committee on Overseas Representation* (1968–69) (Duncan Report), Command 4107 (London: HMSO, 1969).

8   Central Policy Review Staff, *Review of Overseas Representation* (London: HMSO, 1977).

9   For an analysis of Mrs Thatcher's role in foreign policymaking see in particular Christopher Hill, 'United Kingdom: Sharpening contradictions' in Christopher Hill (ed.) *The Actors in Europe's Foreign Policy*, (London: Routledge, 1996) pp. 71–7.

10 Dickie, *Inside the Foreign Office*, pp. 280–3.

11 Dickie, *Inside the Foreign Office* p. 283.

12 Peter Hennessy, *The Hidden Wiring: Unearthing the British Constitution*, (London: Victor Gollancz, 1995) p. 251.

13 Lawrence Freedman, 'The case of Westland and the bias to Europe', *International Affairs*. 63:1, Winter 1986–7, pp. 1–19.

14 Dickie, *Inside the Foreign Office*, p. 62.

15 Andrew Schonfield, 'The Duncan Report and its Critics', *International Affairs*, 46:2, April 1970, pp. 247–68.

16 Nicholas Henderson, *Mandarin: The Diaries of an Ambassador, 1969–1982*, (London: Weidenfeld and Nicholson, 1994) p. 126.

17 See for instance the role played by the FCO in the current Defence Review being conducted by the Ministry of Defences, *The Guardian*, 4 July 1997 and the recent joint publication with the DTI of a White Paper: Foreign and Commonwealth Office and Department of Trade and Industry '*Free Trade and Foreign Policy: A Global Vision*' Command 3437, (London; HMSO, 1996).

18 *The Civil Service: Continuity and Change*, Command 2627 (London: HMSO, 1994).

19 For an example of the sort of challenge that the FCO has had to rebuff see Tessa Blackstone, 'Too many Britons abroad', *The Guardian*, 21 May 1993.

20 Clarke, *British External Policy-Making in the 1990s*, pp. 102–4.

21 Bruce Clark, 'Women fill more than half the top diplomatic posts' *Financial Times*, 25 March 1996. See also Ruth Dudley Edwards, *True Brits*, ch 6, pp. 97–108.

22 Robert Mauthner. 'Diplomatic Disquiet', *Financial Times*, 24 January 1994.

23 See Dan Jellinek, 'Civil Surfers', *The Guardian*, 30 October 1997.

24 See Charles Carstairs and Richard Ware (eds) *Parliament and International Relations*, (Milton Keynes: Open University Press, 1991) pp. 86–8.

25 David Howell, 'Britannia's business' *Prospect*, 15 January 1997, pp. 6–9.

26 Howell, 'Britannia's business', p. 29.

27 Source is the *FCO web site: http://193.114.50/texts/1997/nov/13/export.txt*

28 See Philip Stephens, 'Wrapped in a bigger map', *Financial Times*, 24 March 1995; Martin Woolacott, 'Jilted Britain looks for a new special relationship', *The Guardian*, 22 March 1995; Hugo Young, 'There is a role elsewhere – but not without Europe', *The Guardian*, 30 March 1995; Ian Davidson, 'A place in the world', *Financial Times*, 29 March 1995.

29 Leyla Boulton, 'Cook pledges move to 'green' Foreign Office', *Financial Times*, 27 February 1996.

30 John Kamfner, 'Government to pledge 'moral' foreign policy', *Financial Times*, 12 May 1997.

31 'If you want to deliver a progressive domestic agenda, you need to have a European and international component to it', *The Guardian*, 18 December 1997.

32 Stephen Castle, 'Cook opens up a rival to Foreign Office', *Independent on Sunday*, 1 March 1998.

33 John Kampfner, 'Mandarins face scrutiny from Labour on Europe', *Financial Times*, 31 January 1997.

34 See David Allen, 'Who Speaks for Europe: The search for an effective and coherent external policy' in John Peterson and Helene Sjursen (eds), *The Common Foreign and Security Policy of the European Union*. (London: Routledge, forthcoming).

35 John Kampfner, 'Call to share consular tasks', *Financial Times*, 2 February 1998.

36 See John Kampfner and Bernard Gray, 'Cook makes pledge on human rights', *Financial Times*, 13 May 1997.

13 The United States
The State Department's
Post-Cold War Status
Maurice A. East and C. Edward Dillery

Foreign ministries throughout the world are faced with a variety of challenges and proposals for change and adaptation. The challenges include changes taking place in both international and internal factors that affect foreign policymaking in general. However, only a brief overview of the dynamic of international systemic and relational factors will be noted here. Rather, the emphasis is more on the internal and domestic factors that contribute to change in foreign policymaking.

CHARACTERISTICS OF THE POST-COLD WAR WORLD[1]

At the international level, there have been major changes in the characteristics of the international system, and these changes are providing the impetus for changes in foreign policymaking in countries around the world. Three characteristics of change in the post-Cold War international system are likely to affect foreign policymaking. The first is greater uncertainty. The Cold War provided a relatively high degree of structure in international affairs. The cumulative conflict of that era provided much predictability. When the US and the Soviet Union were arrayed against one another on issues, then the position of allies of these two superpowers could be predicted with considerable certainty. Similarly, the polarized nature of conflict during the era gave it a degree of structure and predictability that was not confined to the bipolar East–West world. For example, the rise of the Third World was, in its various institutional manifestations, a direct consequence of, and contributor to, the structure and predictability of the Cold War world.

A second post-Cold War change is of greater complexity. This dimension is related to the previous one. As the Cold War structure began to disintegrate, new dimensions of complexity began to emerge. As alliance systems collapsed, issues of inclusion and exclusion took on new importance. Coalitions and organizations that were based on the Cold War structure began to search for new missions and new raison d'être as that structure began to dissipate. To name just two, Swedish concepts of neutrality between East and West and the main Third World international organization, the Non-Aligned Movement, were both profoundly affected by the end of the Cold War. New international political actors emerged, including new nations, regional entities, and NGOs. New conflicts and long-dormant issues, such as ethnic nationalism, transnational environmental degradation, migrations of peoples, are prominent on the post-Cold War international agenda.

The third change in the international system is a greater diffuseness of power and control. The post-Cold War world saw the disappearance of one of the super-powers, which set in motion in the other superpower an ongoing re-examination of its international orientation.[2] This coincided with the growing significance of other power centers, for example, in the Asia–Pacific and the European Union. Thus it was no longer the case that international power and control were vested primarily, if not solely, in one or two nations. More nations were beginning to play significant roles in international affairs. At the same time, regional issues were taking on greater salience for many more nations as the all pervasive East–West global conflict receded. Nations large and small were faced with the fact that they had to take more responsibility for dealing with issues and managing conflicts in their near abroad.

INTERNAL AND DOMESTIC FACTORS

Generally, there are three classes of internal factors that can affect the dynamic underlying efforts at changing foreign policymaking. First, there are the motivations driving the desire for change. Second, there is the general perceptual context surrounding foreign policymaking and particularly the foreign ministry. Third, there are the specific actions (or inactions) taken by the foreign policymaking system in response to the change dynamic.

With regard to the first of these internal factors – motivations for change – there are three distinguishable forces. One is a general perception of changed priorities in foreign policy leading to a desire to re-examine a foreign policymaking system reflecting the Cold War situation. A second motivation is resource constraint and a sense that resources need to be reallocated between foreign policy and other competing demands. A third factor is a more general ideological or philosophical perception of a need for a restructuring of government relations. As is often the case, all of these factors are likely to be at work to a greater or lesser degree in most if not all nations. But having distinguished between them, it should be possible to analyze each separately and make judgments as to their relative saliency for various nations.

The second set of factors comprises the perceptual context of foreign policymaking. What are the predominant perceptions of the foreign policy sector held by the public? Within the governmental sector, what is the perception of foreign policymaking and particularly of the foreign ministry, which is the predominant institutional manifestation of the foreign policy system? Finally, one must assess the specific actions relating to the efforts to change the foreign policymaking system. Judgments must be made about the significance, seriousness, and effectiveness of actions taken by the various actors involved in the change process.

Factors Affecting the US Foreign Policy System

Before looking more closely at the domestic dynamic at work in the US, it is necessary to note briefly several aspects of the US Department of State that impinge on any analysis of the US foreign policy system. It must be noted, however, that the degree to which these factors are truly unique to the US can only be established by more comparative study of foreign ministries around the world.

First, there is the historical pre-eminence of the State Department among executive branch departments. Foreign ministers throughout the world are traditionally considered to be high ranking members of their governments, often considered the second ranking ministers in the Cabinet; but this is frequently determined by the governing political party or parties. In the case of the US, this pre-eminence is based at the outset on constitutional age and the prominence of the early secretaries, including former presidents Jefferson, Madison, Monroe and John Quincy Adams, as well as John Marshall, who went on to become Chief Justice of the US Supreme Court. The State Department derives its importance within the Cabinet as 'first among equals' (the term derives from the fact that the State Department was the first executive agency established under the Constitution in 1789).[3] Furthermore, in the legal line of succession, the Secretary of State is the first Cabinet Officer in line to succeed to the presidency.[4] It is this historical pre-eminence that is contrasted to today's status within the US government of the State Department and the Secretary of State.

Second, the US State Department may be faced with stronger, larger and more powerful 'competitors' in the foreign policy system. Specifically, the Defense Department, the National Security Council staff, and Congress are all very well developed and aggressive players in US foreign policy. In resource terms, and in the words of Kegley and Wittkopf, '. . . the [State] Department is a bureaucratic pygmy among giants.'[5] Even more notable is that the resources received by the State Department recently have been declining at a time when the post-Cold War missions of the Defense Department have involved it even more in foreign policy matters and when the White House is asserting itself even more forcefully in the making and coordinating of foreign policy. Third, there is the Foreign Service culture that is often mentioned as a negative factor affecting the State Department and the foreign policy system. Foreign services around the world have been described as too elitist, too generalist and unable to adapt to the domestic political requirement of the government. But there are several aspects of this culture that seem unique to the US Foreign Service:

– the traditionally more homogeneous and elitist image of the Foreign Service grates against a national culture that is more populist and pluralist than most. This has given it an unfortunate popular image that has diminished its ability to generate public support for its mission;
– the generalist orientation in the Foreign Service is particularly unfortunate because of the rapid and aggressive expansion of international activity on behalf of other 'specialized' government agencies and departments. The Foreign Service has been slow to acquire sufficient specialized skills within the service to compete with these other agencies for influence;
– the focus on traditional 'high politics' issues in the Foreign Service and in US foreign policy has been made it more difficult to adapt to the increasing importance of economic and other 'non-traditional' transnational foreign policy issues;
– the Foreign Service personnel system is totally separate from the rest of the federal civil service. This has caused the State Department problems in dealing with its own civil service employees, and it has made it difficult for the Foreign Service to work with other federal employees in the face of the strong pressures to downsize and reduce the federal government across the board;
– finally, the Foreign Service is still affected by the attacks by Senator Joseph McCarthy in the 1950s who falsely accused officers of being Communists. McCarthyism's impact on the Foreign Service was long term and devastating. Extraordinary security consciousness and an elaborate system of horizontal clearances resulted. The result is 'a most cautious way of doing business. It reflects an institutionalized desire to diffuse responsibility... rather than to accept responsibility oneself.'[6]

A fourth factor is the perception within the US polity that the role of the US in a post-Cold War world is changing and in a state of flux. This is reflected in the strong expectations of a 'peace dividend' that will permit funds to be reallocated from foreign and defence policy to meeting domestic needs. It is reflected in the reduced concern for things international in public opinion polls and in the virtual absence of foreign policy in Clinton's second inaugural address. It also underpins the sense of lack of direction in foreign policy seen in the writings of foreign policy opinion elites at the outset of the second Clinton administration. Finally, the US public and government are going through a period of questioning and re-examining the role of the government generally in achieving our national goals and objectives. How much government can we afford? What functions can government perform best? What functions can best be performed by other entities? To what extent can government functions be performed more effectively by adopting techniques from the private and business sectors? Again, this thinking is by no means unique to the US, and it is not nearly as well developed as one finds, for example, in New Zealand today (see below). But it is definitely part of the domestic milieu of foreign policy and will be discussed in more detail.

The US Case: Motivations for Change[7]

As noted above, there are three general motives for driving change and adaptation in foreign ministries: (1) perceived changing foreign policy priorities; (2) resource constraints and needs to reallocate; and (3) a philosophic desire to restructure government. Each of these is likely to be relevant to every case. But having some idea of the relative importance of these factors in a particular instance can be helpful in understanding the responses (or lack of them!) of foreign ministries. By way of comparison, a recent study concluded that, in the case of New Zealand, the strongest motivation for foreign ministry change and adaptation was the strong philosophical or ideological commitment to bring about major public sector management reform throughout the government and that it was now the Foreign Ministry's turn.[8] Recognizing the overriding importance of this motivation was important to the Foreign Ministry as it planned to implement the changes.

Turning to the US case, there was no single clear overriding motivation to reform the State Department. At least, no one such single force was perceived within the State Department. There were several factors. One was the 'Reinventing Government' effort established by President Clinton and headed by Vice President Gore, called the National Performance Review (NPR). In May 1993, the Vice President visited the State Department to solicit ideas for reinventing foreign policymaking. Reporting on this visit, a State Department publication noted:

> A theme frequently sounded by the Vice President was the need for a devolution of authority and responsibility from the upper reaches of the bureaucracy to the action officers down below . . . . only some weeks earlier . . . that same theme was heralded by [Secretary] Christopher, who then followed it up with a reorganisational directive that calls for abolishing many deputy assistant secretary and Seventh Floor job slots. . . .[9]

However, former Secretary of State Eagleburger, writing in 1996, seemed to indicate that this reorganizational directive had not been implemented:

> Reinventing diplomacy should begin with the lead U.S. foreign affairs agency, the Department of State. Its chief problem is Balkanization at

the upper levels, and a critical initial step is a radical reduction in the number of assistant secretaries.[10]

Another force was pressure to reduce the budget deficit. This factor is noted by many recent articles on the State Department as the first and primary force behind current efforts to reform the Department, including Mr Eagleburger's article cited immediately above. Quoting the first sentence of one such article: 'Demands to balance the federal budget are having a greater impact than international events on many changing aspects of U.S. foreign policy and the machinery through which it operates.'[11] Yet a third force for change are the shifting priorities of foreign policy in a post-Cold War world. This was the starting point for two recent major studies of the US foreign service of the future.[12] Suffice it to say that, in contrast to the New Zealand case, there is nothing approaching a consensus on the motivations underlying the calls for change in the US foreign policymaking system. This has had the unfortunate consequence of making it more difficult to focus organizational attention on dealing with the challenge.

The Perceptual Context for the US

Along a number of dimensions, the public perception of foreign policymaking and the foreign policy community in the US is relatively negative. First, there is a generalized perception that now that the Cold War is over, there should be a shift in priorities and resources away from things international and into things domestic. There should be a peace dividend to be realized. In addition, there is still a wide-spread image of the foreign service as being elitist and privileged – diplomats at cocktail parties drinking wine and snacking on canapes, living in luxurious housing with servants, gardeners and chauffeurs. Calls to reduce spending on foreign affairs tend to fall on receptive ears.

Foreign assistance programmes also contribute to the negative perceptual context. There is a widespread belief that foreign aid is wasteful, going to ungrateful nations with widespread corruption, for schemes that never seem to succeed. Recent surveys have also shown that the public thinks the US spends about 18 per cent of the federal budget on foreign aid, more than on Medicare. In fact, we spend well under one per cent of our wealth on foreign aid, the lowest level among developed nations.[13]

Another oft-mentioned negative is the State Department's lack of a strong, well organized special interest group or clientele capable of being mobilized on behalf of the foreign affairs budget. This is a problem that foreign ministries around the world are faced with; yet some have managed to build a more supportive public base than others. Finally, from the perspective of the opinion elite, there has been some significant controversy raised over the general priorities (or lack thereof) in the Clinton Administration's foreign policy. The most well known article argues that current foreign policy priorities are misplaced, with too much emphasis being put on lesser or peripheral issues and too little on the major issues and actors likely to impact on the US over the long haul.[14]

When examining the perceptual context of the foreign affairs community from the Congressional perspective, one finds many of the public sector factors mentioned above. In addition and more recently, the tug of war between Senator Helms, the chair of the Senate Foreign Relations Committee, and the community has made it appear as if the State Department and the White House are 'stonewalling' and are unwilling to accept their share of the discretionary cuts necessary to meet balanced budget goals and guidelines. The arguments on the other side stress the magnitude of the budget cuts already taken – a 50 per cent reduction in real dollars since 1984, according to Ambassador Craig Johnstone.

Another unfortunate dimension of the Congressional perception arises out of the conflict over the merging of the US Information Agency (USIA), the Arms Control and Disarmament Agency (ACDA), and the US Agency for International Development (USAID) into the State Department.[15] In response to Vice President Gore's call for reinventing government through the NPR, 'Secretary Christopher proposed, among other things, the consolidation of three foreign policy agencies – USIA, ACDA and USAID – into the Department of State...'. However, by February 1995 the White House announced that the three agencies would remain independent. Senator Helms almost immediately proposed that there be a major consolidation and the three agencies be eliminated, and he incorporated this into SR 908, called the Foreign Relations Revitalization Act of 1995. As of spring 1997, it appeared that USIA and ACDA will be fully integrated into the State Department as part of the Financial Year 1997 authorization Bill. USAID will remain a distinct agency but will share and integrate certain administrative and support functions with those of the State Department.

Finally, within the US government more broadly, there are large numbers of departments and agencies that continue to be heavily involved in various international activities. To the extent that cuts in State Department resources lead to reduced activities by these other agencies, this creates inherent conflicts and turf-battles over a variety of issues, pitting the State Department against other agencies. The latter often possess more specialized resources, more immediate interest, and a greater sense of ownership in the issue than does the State Department.

Specific Actions Taken
With a diverse set of motivations for change facing the State Department and with a generally unfavourable perceptual context for foreign affairs funding it

is difficult to discern a coherent strategy for change currently being pursued by the Department. In an article appearing in the *Foreign Service Journal*,[16] there is a discussion of some of the reasons for the lack of a coherent strategy, and the following comments appear:

- '...lack of White House and State Department leadership...'
- '...perceived attitude of denial of the State Department toward Congress' continued reduction of U.S. influence in the world...
- ...'Christopher seemed much more involved in short term [sic!] problems such as the Middle East peace process than with the long-term health of the diplomatic corps....'
- '...defense of the foreign affairs budgets and agencies has been delegated to others in senior management, but in the reality of Washington ...only Christopher or President Clinton can speak with authority. Both have been tardy to do so....'
- '...erratic management of the [budget] cuts...refusing to identify which part of the foreign affairs community he is prepared to sacrifice, meaning that all parts – even the most critical – are equally vulnerable to congressional budget axes.'

Although there have been some notable organizational changes in the State Department in the post-Cold War era (to be discussed below), the sense is that these changes have not been enough. One 1996 article summarizes recent changes as follows:

> ...neither the Bush nor the Clinton administration launched a broad bipartisan review to design a new foreign policy concept and policy machinery... . The foreign policy agencies established during the Cold War continued with changes only at the margins.[17]

As the State Department began to focus on pressures deriving from its relations with other parts of the US Government, several questions emerged to guide deliberations. Firstly, how should the Department interact with Congress? Much like the Executive Branch, the Congress is examining its views on the proper role of the US in the post-Cold War world. With the 1996 re-election of domestically oriented more conservative majorities in both chambers, tension between the branches can be expected to continue. One far-reaching Congressional act, The 1993 Government Performance and Results Act (GPRA) merits comment. This legislation requires all US government agencies to move to a programme budgeting process by the end of the century. By requiring five year strategic plans (the first due in 1997), it is a key aspect of what has elsewhere been referred to as new public management and will have a significant impact on the Department's planning process, discussed below.

A second broad set of issues related to the Department's role within the US government's foreign policy system. More specifically:

– How should the Department interact with the National Security Counsellor and the NSC Staff? This issue became even more important as the gulf between the courtiers (White House) and the baron (the Secretary of State) widened.[18]

– How should it deal with a Department of Defense (DOD) that has increased its emphasis on non-conventional warfare and peacekeeping activities? The great resources of DOD give it great weight in responding to foreign policy crises.

– What should be the relationship to the Central Intelligence Agency (CIA) as it gives more attention to economic intelligence, to terrorism and other global threats, trying to compensate for the diminished stature of its principal Cold War target? How should the Department react as the CIA moves more openly into diplomatic reporting?

– What is the status of the old debate about aid for pure development versus aid for influence now that the Agency for International Development (AID) has lost the anti-Soviet raison d'être perceived by many outside the agency for many of its programmes? Should AID be made part of the Department at a time when it is clear that the resources for aid are likely to diminish steadily?

– How should US public diplomacy be conducted in the new era? The USIA was hit harder by budget cuts than other foreign affairs agencies.

– The Arms Control and Disarmament Agency (ACDA) appears to carry out activities duplicated in the Department. Should this continue? Can the Department adequately negotiate and monitor disarmament treaties; do bilateral relations cause the Department to be 'too soft' on treaty violators?

– What should be the Department's role in promoting US exports, now that this has become a principal goal of US foreign policy? The Commerce Department has this as its primary mission through its own branch of the Foreign Service, the Foreign Commercial Service.

– How does the Department avoid duplication of the efforts of the Treasury, which maintains its own overseas presence and plays a prominent role in reporting on financial issues.

– What role should the department play in the increasing activities of law enforcement agencies? The FBI, Secret Service and DEA are all increasing their overseas presence to deal with international crime; much of this involves direct liaison with local law enforcement officials.

– A myriad of other agencies have also developed foreign affairs interests and have personnel stationed in US embassies, usually at some cost to the Department. How should these activities be coordinated and paid for?

Main 'internal' organizational issues
Within the Department itself, a number of issues emerged as central in thinking about how to respond to the pressures for change:

– In organizing for the challenges of the current situation, what relative weight should be given to the traditional concentration on bilateral relations versus transnational global issues and multilateral diplomacy?
– What should be the role and organization of an embassy? Does the current configuration, developed during the Cold War, meet current needs? Is the current policy of near universality of embassies in almost every country in the world still make sense?
– How can the Department best organize to carry out its consular responsibilities? The inevitable reduction of junior foreign service personnel has a disproportionate impact on visa issuance and other consular functions – but the demand continues to increase.
– Can the traditional bureau-based structure of the Department be configured to meet the new challenges? What is the proper information management system for the Department and how can it be financed?

STRATEGIES AND RESPONSES

We now turn to the efforts of the Department to address the issues outlined above and to develop an organizational structure to deal with them. This process began during the final years of the Bush Administration and continues under President Clinton.

Reforming the Overseas Post Structure

Perhaps the most important diplomatic requirement emerging from the end of the Cold War was the need to establish posts in the newly independent countries of the former Soviet Union and in other similar situations. As a result, 20 new embassies were opened during the period 1991–6 (although some involved upgrading consular posts to embassy status). They were:

Alma-Ata, Kazakhstan	Riga, Latvia
Ashkabad, Turkmenistan	Sarajevo, Bosnia Herzegovina
Baku, Azerbaijan	Skopje, Macedonia
Bishke, Kyrgyzstan	Tallinn, Estonia
Bratislava, Slovak Republic	Tashkent, Uzbekistan
Chisinau, Moldova	Tbilisi, Georgia
Dushanbe, Tajikistan	Tirana, Albania
Kiev, Ukraine	Vilnius, Lithuania

Ljubljana, Slovenia   Yerevan, Armenia
Minsk, Belarus   Zagreb, Croatia

The Department received no supplementary funds to establish these embassies. For many of the most remote, the Department used an innovative and cost effective system to get the post up and running. All of the equipment needed for an embassy was packed in one container – furniture, communications equipment, office supplies and so on. This enabled staff to begin effective operations immediately on arrival at the new site.

The new embassies in Europe and Central Asia were only a part of the restructuring of posts that took place. Between 1992 and the end of October 1996, numbers of posts changed as follows:

Year	Embassies	Consular/Other	Missions	Total
1988	142	101	11	254
1992	162	102	11	275
1993	162	88	11	261
1994	163	91	10	264
1995	163	89	10	263
October 96	162	77	10	240

Source: Office of Management Policy, Department of State

Many of the consular posts that were closed were located in Europe as modern communications made it possible to transfer many of their functions to other posts. In addition, the number of State Department personnel has been reduced at most overseas posts.

Department Reorganization

Shortly after taking office in 1993, the Clinton Administration announced several organizational changes in the Department designed to meet new priorities. Assistant secretaries were now placed under the direct authority of under secretaries. (Prior to this time the assistant secretaries had direct reporting responsibilities to the Secretary and the Deputy Secretary). An under secretary position was redesignated to be responsible for global affairs. Several bureaus were reorganized and given new responsibilities, including the former Bureau for International Narcotics Control which was given additional responsibility for international crime; the former Bureau for Refugees which increased its portfolio to include population and migration issues; and the former Bureau of Human Rights Affairs which took on added duties in the promotion of democracy and oversight of international labour issues.

The new emphasis on global issues represented a marked change from the traditional focus on bilateral relations. The backbone of the Department always has been the regional bureau – Europe, Inter-America, Africa, East Asia, Near East and a new Bureau of South Asian Affairs created during the last years of the Bush Administration as required by Congress. Although the 1993 reorganization changed this to some degree, the regional bureaus still constitute the core of the Department's foreign policy activities. In terms of management changes, a new bureau – Resources, Plans and Policy – was created to be the Secretary's arm for resource issues involving the entire budget for the foreign affairs community, the 'Function 150 Account', which includes foreign assistance, State operations, contributions to international organizations, USIA and several other foreign affairs related accounts. Previously, this function had been carried out by a smaller unit in the office of the Deputy Secretary. It now became a more significant player in the Executive Branch.

Personnel Levels, Policies

Under the 'Reinventing Government' rubric, the Department was required to reduce personnel to help meet President Clinton's pledge to cut overall Executive Branch personnel by some 272 000 employees. The following Table 13. 1 illustrates the general trend in personnel levels since 1992.

Table 13.1   Department of State Full-Time Personnel Population

	Foreign Service	Civil Service*	Total
September 1992	8896	5582	14 478
September 1993	8792	5622	14 414
September 1994	8512	5436	13 948
September 1995	8207	5208	13 415
September 1996	7936	5247	13 183

* includes the International Border and Water Commission
Source: Department of State Bureau of Personnel

In addition to the Foreign Service and Civil Service personnel, there is a third important component of Department personnel: Foreign Service Nationals. There are between 6000 and 7000 of these personnel who are engaged and paid locally. Their numbers have been drastically reduced in the last five years, although some of them have been replaced by contract personnel. Thus the total full time employees of the Department has been cut from some 23 000 in the early 1990s to something less than 20 000 at the present. The reduction in the Foreign Service has been about 11 per cent.

The FSO population has been reduced by lower annual intake, which is down from approximately 250 per year to less than 200, and by fewer promotions, especially to the higher ranks, forcing retirements. Generally, the Department is also dealing with the reduction by not replacing civil servants who leave, centralizing some support activities, thinning out staffs in almost all bureaus and by better workforce planning.

In the late 1980s, the Special Embassy Program (SEP) was established. Some 30 smaller embassies were designated as SEP posts. The premise was that the personnel of these embassies would be limited; the Chief of Mission (COM) would have less authority over personnel but embassy requirements – especially administrative and reporting requirements – would be reduced to permit effective operation with smaller staffs. The problem was that many requirements were the same for a tiny post like Koror in Micronesia as they were for Cairo, the largest US embassy in the world. The SEP programme has made some progress, but it has been more effective in reducing personnel than in cutting workload.

In overseas missions generally, the ambassador as COM has traditionally had a good measure of control over personnel from all agencies. The President provides each Ambassador with a letter of authority which specifies that no changes in embassy complement (by any agency) may be made without permission. In the past, COMs have tended to approve staff increases by other agencies and compete for State Department staff increases. Because of cost factors, they now recognize the need to constrain staffs. Actual overseas Department personnel levels have been set in negotiations involving the COM, the regional bureau and the Personnel Bureau. The Department currently is engaged in the most comprehensive effort to date to identify better real personnel needs and establish specific personnel levels for each post. These levels will be based on documented embassy needs (see below under Planning), and to the extent it is successful will be a radical departure from past practice.

Planning

It is often said that 'State Department Planning' is an oxymoron. Many efforts have been made to institute a programme/planning process in the Department dating back to the Kennedy/Johnson period, but none have been successful. The culture of the Department did not accept the concept of planning, and the unpredictable nature of international relations means that crises arise or issues come to the fore than cannot be anticipated – the Rwanda–Burundi ethnic conflict is just one recent example. The Department must be in a position to deploy resources quickly to meet dynamic situations.

Closely related is the need to set priorities as part of the planning process. The factors noted above also made it difficult to set priorities within the

Department, its regions and its overseas missions. The Department began to address this issue in a systematic way in the late 1980s with the inception of a planning process for all levels of activity. Previously, embassies had been required to prepare yearly 'Goals and Objectives' statements, but these were not linked to resources. The new programme required them to prepare Mission Program Plans (MPPs) which evaluate performance in the previous year, set out prioritized goals for the coming year and identify resources needed to carry out the objectives. The MPP is negotiated with the regional bureau, and on completion it represents a commitment by the Department to which objectives should be pursued by the mission and on the resources to be provided and used. In the early days, many MPPs were completed in a cursory manner and were not used as management documents. This is changing, and while not universally accepted, the MPPs now are used in actual management decisions both by posts and the Department.

The next step in the process, Bureau Program Plans (BPPs) has been harder to implement. The concept is to amalgamate all the MPPs for a region, add in domestic requirements and use this as a regional management tool. The process is difficult because many of the bureaus in the Department have relations with or support numerous missions but do not have management responsibility for them. As a result the overall BPP process becomes confused. The BPPs are ultimately to be used to construct a Department Program Plan that sets overall priorities, including those among the various bureau. The Secretary and senior officials could then act as a kind of Board of Directors for Department operations based upon this amalgamated Department Plan.[19]

Referring to these recent changes, one article observes:

> After the end of the Cold War, significant changes continued.... the Bush administration authorized aid to the former Soviet Union. In 1994, the Clinton Administration reorganised the international affairs budget into categories supporting six major objectives: (1) promoting U.S. prosperity through trade, investment, and employment; (2) building democracy; (3) promoting sustainable development; (4) promoting peace; (5) providing humanitarian assistance; and (6) advancing diplomacy....[20]

It is interesting to note that these six budget categories were not widely employed or referred to in later Department speeches and memos, leading one to believe that these categories are not being widely used nor are they acknowledged as definitive or central to any sort of Departmental 'corporate plan'.

Other management innovations

The end of the Cold War, along with the NPR provided the Department with an opportunity to review its entire range of management and administrative activities. A recent undertaking in the Clinton administration was the Strategic Management Initiative (SMI), whose purpose was to find ways to increase the efficiency and effectiveness of foreign policy making within the Department of State. In response to a question posed in *State* magazine, the director of SMI noted:

> ...the fact is that SMI isn't about cutbacks and reductions. It's about streamlining, it's about delayering, it's about prioritizing and reallocating. ...if our budget is sharply reduced by Congress, then the SMI tools that we are fashioning are going to be all the more important.[21]

SMI pushed information resources management modernization heavily as one critical way to bring managerial improvements into the Department (see below). The SMI mandate also seemed to be the focal point in the Department for promoting new public management initiatives (often referred to as 'corporatization'). But in the same interview cited above, the director indicated that progress along these lines was slow. Specifically, he noted that: (a) the decision was made not to order specific reductions in deputy assistant secretaries (a recommendation of several previously cited studies of the State Department) and that (b) the devolution of authority to lesser-ranking officers had some way to go yet.

The then Under Secretary for Management, Richard Moose, gave a mixed evaluation of SMI. He noted its strong support for investing heavily in information systems, which Secretary Christopher had pushed in his Congressional testimony, calling it the Department's highest investment priority. But he also commented that SMI had come up with 'lots of things we should do but with almost nothing that we should stop doing' – a near universal indication of the frustration over the difficulties in setting priorities and dealing with shrinking resources, especially in the absence of a clear mission statement and policy guidance from above.[22] Former Secretary Eagleburger also refers specifically to SMI but finds it insufficient.

> Previous attempts to redress the department's flaws, most recently the 1995 Strategic Management Initiative, have been narrowly conceived and cosmetic in effect. The State Department cannot regain its leading role in American foreign policy by merely reducing its operating expenses or closing overseas posts. It needs an ambitious overhaul.[23]

Improvement in the information resources management system

As SMI efforts indicate, many feel that perhaps the most important area for improvement is the Department's information management system. The Department has long had several different systems for communications, financial management and other information requirements. Even at present

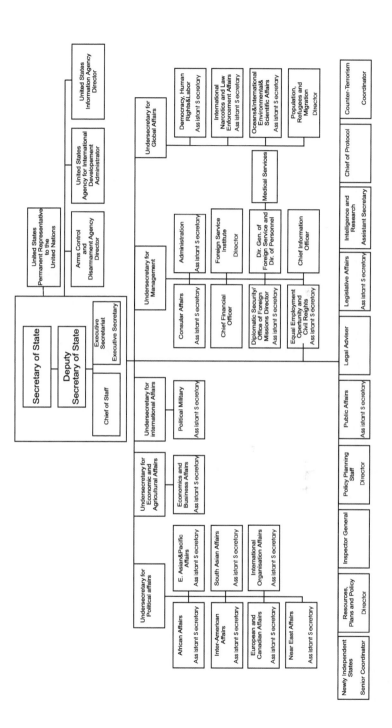

Figure 13.1 The State Department's Organizational Structure

it is necessary for many employees to have two work stations to carry out different types of information activities. The Department is developing one system to meet all needs but it will require extensive financial resources and a major reorientation of current systems.

The development of regional centres for management support
Another area for scrutiny when seeking efficiency and savings is the cost of doing business overseas, which has increased sharply during the past 10–15 years, as has the complexity of US missions. Successive under secretaries of State for management have emphasized the need to find better – and less expensive – ways to maintain overseas presence.

For many years there have been overseas regional financial centres mainly for disbursing and accounting support for missions. In recent years, the Department has expanded the scope of these regional centres and moved some to the US, taking advantage of information and communication technology improvements.

- One example is the Miami regional support centre for Central and South American posts, which provides general administrative services, shipping and other services for all posts in Latin America, thus allowing individual posts to have smaller administrative staffs.
- Another example is a finance centre in Charleston, South Carolina which will centralize many of the financial activities of posts around the world and of the old regional finance centres that were located abroad.
- There is a new centre in New Hampshire for processing immigrant visa applications that is expanding its activities to support programmes other than the Moscow Jewish emigration programme.

Cost recovery for non-state personnel
A major problem for the Department is recovering the costs of the support required for personnel from other agencies stationed abroad. By Presidential directive all US Executive Branch personnel stationed permanently abroad (except for those under a regional military command) are under the authority of the Chief of Mission and are members of the diplomatic mission. For many years, the Department has paid a disproportionate share of the support for these mission personnel, based on the theory that certain administrative activities would be accomplished at posts even if there were only Department personnel assigned.

As this arrangement evolved, the Department had about 40 per cent of the personnel stationed in missions, but provided some 70 per cent of the support for the entire mission. A new system, the International Cooperation Administrative Support Services (ICASS), has been developed to provide more equitable cost recovery. Under ICASS, agencies will move toward a per-capita basis for supporting their employees. This should help the Department meet the cost of maintaining missions overseas.

The Bottom Line – Financial Resources

As always in dealing with management issues, a most important factor is financial resources. Although resources for foreign affairs come from many parts of the budget, the 'Function 150 Account' – funding for the Department of State, AID, USIA, and ACDA, constitutes the major part of this funding and is one indicator of the US priority for all of international relations. The Function 150 expenditures declined in actual dollars from almost $25 billion in 1991 to about $18.6 billion in 1996. The Department's operating budget has been relatively stable, although there have been more significant reductions occurring in the other agencies. The accompanying Table 13.2 demonstrates this; funding for 1997 is likely to be approximately the same as for 1996. The problem is that the Department must accommodate one of its largest and highest priority programmes – the new information management system – out of the proposed budget. There was $16 million in Capital Investment in 1996 for this programme, but the Department states that a 'bare bones' system will cost $90 million, which may have to come from further post closings and personnel reductions.

Table 13.2 Department of State Operation Budget (in $millions)

Activity	1992	1993	1994	1995	1996
Diplomatic/Consular	2031	2164	1745	1724	1719
Salaries/Expenses	–	–	363	383	365
Capital Investment	–	–	3	0	16
Buildings	539	560	400	392	385
Total	2570	2724	2511	2499	2485
In 1996 dollars	2878	2969	2661	2573	2485

Source: *US Foreign Affairs Resources: Budget Cuts and Consequences*, (Institute for the Study of Diplomacy, Georgetown University,: 1996)

Reports have it that the then Secretary Christopher and the then Secretary-designate Albright made a strong plea for maintaining the 1998 International Activities budget at roughly 1997 levels and succeeded in that the Administration will ask for a Function 150 budget request of $20.3 billion as compared with an Office of Management and Budget plan calling for about $1 billion less.

CONCLUSIONS

The challenges facing the Department of State and the US foreign policy-making system are significant but far from unique. As this volume demonstrates, examining how other nations are adapting to these challenges may be of assistance to the US. In this spirit, a few concluding observations are presented, juxtaposing the US situation to that of other countries based on an impressionistic rather than a comprehensive systematic comparison.

There are many forces for change operating on foreign ministries, and not all of these are working in the same direction. Perhaps the best example of this is the widespread existence around the world of strong domestic pressures to reduce the costs of running foreign ministries at the same time that the external pressures of a more complex, less structured, more fragmented post-Cold War world require more rather than less from foreign ministries. The domestic and external forces for change require significant and substantial change in the functioning of foreign ministries. These changes are permanent and require more change on the part of foreign ministries than just a larger budget.

For foreign ministries to adapt effectively to these changes requires more political will and awareness from the top levels of government down. The chief national executive must strongly and publicly support the continuing, changing and changed role of the foreign ministry as critical to the national interest and a key goal of the government itself. This is necessary to provide a degree of balance when the foreign ministry is competing against politically more powerful agencies. It also sends a message to the legislature. The foreign minister must also make it abundantly clear that the institutional and organizational 'health' of the foreign ministry and the foreign service are key personal goals. At the same time, the minister must do and say things that make perfectly clear the critical need for adaptation to (a) new resource realities; (b) new domestic political realities, and (c) new international realities. The foreign minister may well have to be a much stronger political figure in order to bring about this adaptation.

There was a sense at the outset of the second Clinton Administration that Secretary of State Albright would be a stronger and more prominent political figure. Early on she demonstrated an ability not recently seen to articulate foreign policy effectively to the domestic political constituency as well as to other countries. She acknowledged the need to work with the Republican controlled Congress and especially the Senate Foreign Relations Committee chaired by Senator Helms. In her early actions, she also recognized the relationship between the institutional and organizational health of the foreign policy community and the ability to carry out her foreign policy agenda.

In addition, the foreign minister must demonstrate the critical nature of this adaptation by means of the priorities that are set by the foreign ministry.

The ministry should not appear reluctant to change; rather it should project an image of proactive change that deals with these new domestic and international forces. One key is to assure that the adaptation project involves and is headed by foreign service officers with the highest status and rank; these important positions should not be filled by political appointees or by FSOs 'waiting for an embassy'.

Finally, the culture of the foreign ministry is usually very strong and not always supportive of the sorts of change that may be necessary. Positive steps may be needed to assure that high quality *external* inputs and ideas are injected into the adaptation process, especially in the area of management modernization. All of this highlights the necessity of foreign ministries taking control of the change and adaptation process rather than abdicating this role and leaving it to others. Avoiding change is not an option; the US State Department is no exception.

NOTES

1   This section draws heavily on M. East, 'Foreign policy-making in the post-Cold War era: new public management and the case of New Zealand', paper delivered at the 1996 International Studies Association Convention, San Diego CA.
2   One recent example is The RAND Corporation's *Strategic Appraisal 1996*, edited by Zaimay Khalizad for their Project Air Force. It reviews global and regional challenges in light of three scenarios for the US: neo-isolationism, multipolarity, and global leadership.
3   C. Kegley and E. Wittkopf, *American foreign policy: pattern and process, 5th edn* (New York: St. Martin's Press, 1996), p. 343.
4   After the assassination of President Garfield in 1881, Congress, in its law governing succession, placed the Secretary of State second in line, after the Vice President. However, in 1947 the law was changed to place the speaker of the House of Representatives and the President pro temporare of the Senate ahead of the Secretary of State. See 'Brief history of the State Department, 1861–95, *US Department of State Dispatch* 2: 7, 18 February 1991, pp. 119–120.
5   Kegley and Wittkopf, American foreign policy, p. 385.
6   Kegley and Wittkopf, American foreign policy, p. 383–4.
7   It should be noted that one author (East) was involved in two recent major studies looking at US foreign policymaking in the 21st century. *See The Foreign Service in 2001* (Institute for the Study of Diplomacy, Georgetown University, 1992); *State 2000: A New Model for Managing Foreign Affairs* (Report of the US Department of State Management Task Force, December 1992). The other (Dillery) is a recently retired former US ambassador who also recently worked on management issues within the State Department.
8   East, Foreign policy-making, pp. 4–6.
9   *State* (formerly the Department of State Newsletter) 368, July-August 1993, p. 2.

10   Lawrence S. Eagleburger and Robert L. Barry, 'Dollars and sense diplomacy: a better foreign policy for less money', *Foreign Affairs* 75: 4, July/August 1996, p. 3.

11   Ellen C. Collier and Larry Q. Nowels, 'New foreign policy organization and funding priorities', *Mediterranean Quarterly* 7: 2, Spring 1996, p. 95.

12   See note 7 above.

13   This point was made recently by Ambassador L. Craig Johnstone, in his keynote speech to a State Department Town Meeting co-sponsored by the Patterson School of Diplomacy and International Commerce at the University of Kentucky. See *State* 398, August 1996, p. 2.

14   See for example, Michael Mandelbaum, 'Foreign policy as social work', *Foreign Affairs* 75:1, January/February 1996, pp. 16–32.

15   This account relies heavily on Collier and Nowels, 'New foreign policy organization', pp. 98–102.

16   Jim Anderson, 'Singing the blues', *Foreign Service Journal*, September 1995, pp. 44–9.

17   Collier and Nowels, 'New foreign policy organization', p. 97.

18   See I. Destler, L. Gelb, and A. Lake, *Our own worst enemy: the unmaking of American foreign policy* (Simon & Schuster, NY, 1984) for an interesting discussion of this relationship. Kegley and Wittkopf (1996) provide an overview of the Bush and Clinton administrations' relationship between the NSC and the State Department, pp. 359–66.

19   New Zealand is one example of where the momentum for new public management initiatives have been well developed in the foreign ministry. See East, 'Foreign policy-making'.

20   Collier and Nowels, 'New foreign policy organization', p. 97.

21   'Sizing up the Strategic Management Initiative: an interview', *State* 391, August 1995, pp. 2–3.

22   '. . . Moose assesses the impact on State of a US balanced budget', *State* 395, January 1996, pp. 2-5.

23   Eagleburger and Barry, op. cit., p. 3.

14 Foreign Ministries in National and European Context

David Spence

This chapter focuses on two underlying themes of this book: the increasingly contested notion that foreign ministries, embassies and diplomats are the sole or the most apt defenders of national interests abroad and the issue of whether governments and foreign affairs administrations have reacted consciously and strategically to several fundamental changes to the diplomatic agenda.[1] Diplomats are wont to stress the continuity rather than the change in the diplomat's role,[2] yet they are virtually all, nevertheless, engaged in reviews and studies which underline the fact that change is the order of the day. In the Member States of the EU, there is a distinct additional context to this change. A series of unparalleled new tasks and challenges for European foreign ministries have arisen as a result of two specific foreign ministry responsibilities: the coordination of domestic ministries' affairs for EU business and participation in the European Common Foreign and Security Policy. This chapter describes and analyzes the developments involved.

The first section covers developments specific to intra-EU relations: the implications for foreign ministries of the rise of domestic ministries as major bilateral actors in European interstate relations.

The second important feature of specific relevance to EU foreign ministries falls outside the sphere of the European Community (first) pillar of the European Union. In the specific area of European foreign policymaking, there are not only ever closer contacts and collaboration between the foreign ministries of the partner states. In addition, there are new relations abroad both between Member States' Permanent Representations in Brussels and between their embassies in countries outside the EU. Of equal importance are relations with the evolving External Service of the European Commission, either in Brussels in the form of the five quasi-ministerial Directorates-General involved in foreign policy formulation (DGs I, IA, IB, VIII and the European Community Humanitarian Aid Office) or abroad through the 127 Commission delegations and offices outside the EU.

FOREIGN MINISTRIES AS COORDINATORS OF DOMESTIC POLICY WITHIN THE EU

The Europeanization of the Policy Process in the EU Context

The EU policymaking process involves nominally sovereign states in a process of international bargaining, of which the outcomes are binding in domestic law. But, policy implementation is often managed, and always supervized, by a supranational institution: the European Commission. Further, Member States of the European Union are subject to challenge by the Commission before a supranational European Court of Justice if they fail to implement policy. Throughout the process of expanding EU competence the ministries of foreign affairs of the Member States have been confronted with the central issues of their status and raison d'être in the new, supranational system. They have largely concluded that it is prudent to attempt to strengthen the traditional foreign ministry role of 'gatekeeper' in relation to the international policies of domestic ministries and thus monitor issues traditionally outside the purview of diplomacy. In the attempt to avoid other national actors bypassing their authority in the field of foreign affairs, they have constructed a far closer relationship and more integrated task management structures with domestic ministries than have foreign ministries outside the EU framework.[3]

Negotiations in the EU framework are ultimately about how governments defend the 'national' interest in the search for an acceptable European compromise to which they are then, by treaty, committed. Coordinating a national position to be defended in the Council of Ministers is thus vital to effective overall management of Member States' European policy. Governments must arrive at a 'line to take' in Brussels that will be consistently supported by all officials and ministers and thus be an effective contribution to the EU policy process. Since officials and ministers may be outvoted in Brussels, the process of influence and persuasion in which ministries and interest groups are both obliged to participate, cannot be restricted to the national level. Indeed, an integral part of the policy process is the influence of individual ministries, firms and pressure groups on Commission policy and other Member State governments both directly and through the Permanent Representations in Brussels. Sometimes lobbyists and national officials work together. Sometimes their views of the national interest conflict. And just as there are conflicts between private interest groups, there may also be conflicts of interpretation between government departments, between a department and its 'clients' in the private sector and between the 'Brussels team' and the home team. The ability of public administration to coordinate effectively between the potentially conflicting views of ministers and their officials, the various levels of government involved and the private sector is all the more crucial in that 'in escaping from the shackles of capture at the national level, the EU process also escapes from country-based democratic scrutiny and accountability'.[4]

It is certainly the case that the focus of interest groups has already shifted from the purely national level, as has the working environment of many national officials.[5] 'Their' government may not end up defending 'their' line on a given issue, whereas the European Commission, or a majority of other governments, may. As the focus of legitimacy moves from the national to the supranational level, the ground is created for a shift in allegiance from the national to the European forum, and, almost as a by-product, a potential relegation of both domestic and foreign ministries to the status of mere cogs in the European wheel. One current UK Labour minister once ruefully argued that 'European politics are now domestic politics with a vengeance'.[6]

The reach of EU policy now covers every domestic ministry and all levels of government, be they local, regional or national. This omnipresence of the European context coupled with the specific nature of interest diversity in the lobbying process and the means adopted by the European institutions to cope efficiently with the results[7] underlines the indispensability of efficient arrangements for national policymaking and coordination. Significantly, the Europeanization of domestic policy in EU Member States has tended, in all Member States, to require more rather than less of foreign ministries, given the supranationality of the EU process, the consequent blurring of the distinction between foreign and domestic policy and the continuance of the foreign ministry's gatekeeper role on the margin of the domestic–foreign policy divide.

As the gatekeepers, unlike in pre-EU days, foreign ministries are now subjected to influence from all levels of national government and the private sector and their staff must adjudicate between the resultant pressures in an endeavour to adjust strictly national priorities into European interests which remain palatable at national level. To do this they are required to lobby not only other Member States in the Council, but also domestic constituencies. They need to strike and gain support for bargains in Council and to ensure implementation of the subsequent legislation. They do this within a correspondingly enhanced relationship between local, regional and national interest groups and 'their' foreign ministries, (albeit with no formal attempt at redefining these relations). As the following analysis makes clear, what is involved is work of a new kind and perhaps correspondingly less work of the kind associated with traditional diplomacy.

Foreign and Domestic Ministries and the Conduct of European Union Affairs

There are three integral parts of the machinery of national policymaking in EU affairs, common to all EU governments: the 'lead ministries', foreign ministries with a monitoring and coordination role and the Permanent Representations to the EU. In some Member States there have always been additional coordination mechanisms outside the ministerial framework. This is the case, for example, of the European Secretariat of the British Cabinet Office and the French Secrétariat Général pour la Coordination Interministerielle des Affaires Economiques Européennes (SGCI). Significantly, nowhere do foreign ministries today have the sole right to the gatekeeper function in EU affairs, and everywhere there is evidence of a shift in the important role of coordinator/arbitrator from foreign ministries to such central authorities, either through formal, constitutional structures, as in the French or British cases, or through the more political instances of the offices of heads of government, as is the case with the German Federal Chancellor's office.

Lead Departments and the Foreign Ministry's Role as Coordinator

A system common to all Member States now operates where lead ministries enjoy a high margin of manoeuvre in their Community dealings without undue interference of a centralized kind. Coordination in terms of information flows to other ministries is usually routine. Domestic ministries responsible in Member States for policy areas of exclusive Community competence have a symbiotic relationship with the Commission's directorates-general and have developed close, co-operative (rather than rival) links with their counterparts in other Member States.[8]

European policymaking in domestic ministries was originally managed by international divisions, responsible not only for Community affairs but all international aspects of the policies within the responsibility of the ministry concerned. Subsequently, as workloads and Community competence increased, international divisions spawned European coordinating divisions. These were not involved in the day to day arrangements for specific technical negotiations or the implementation of Community legislation. Their function was to coordinate the principles of policy as opposed to the detail and to manage, horizontally, the various European aspects of concern to their ministries. The coordination divisions of domestic ministries now work in close liaison with foreign ministries in preparing specialized meetings of the Council of Ministers and ensuring that the national input into negotiations is prepared coherently, in particular taking due account of other ministries' priorities and the views of the foreign ministries themselves.

Guidance or coordination is of course required in cases of disagreement between ministries or where the implications are complex. Foreign ministries often have specific expertise, such as the diplomatic skills required for international negotiations, knowledge of how the EU system works and the ability to put national perspectives on policy into European context. The latter frequently involves trade-offs between policy sectors, where the pro-prietorial feelings of a particular ministry may have to be bruised. That foreign ministries possess such capabilities and that they are clearly the most appropriate coordinators of daily business is generally accepted. Diverse systems of national policymaking for EU business thus share the recognition of a continuing necessity for foreign ministries to monitor domestic policymaking. Problems arise when foreign ministries appear to be defending their own interests at the cost of a specific domestic ministry. Where national systems differ is in the strength or weakness of the reporting and coordination mechanisms which ensure that information flows ade-quately and also that agreed policy lines are respected by officials from all ministries. Furthermore, they differ according to the strength of the percep-tion of an increasing need for a central arbitrator in cases of differences of opinion.[9]

How Foreign Ministries Coordinate

Foreign ministries provide the institutional framework of day-to-day coordi-nation. They monitor the activities of government departments and coordi-nate between national capitals and Brussels through, usually, two EU departments, one dealing with policies having domestic implications, such as internal market, environment, energy, and so on, and the other focusing on external issues, such as trade, development and the Common Foreign and Security Policy (CFSP). This arrangement mirrors the two versions of the Committee of Permanent Representatives in Brussels, meeting as CORE-PER I (domestic – Deputy Permanent Representatives) or COREPER II (external affairs – the Permanent Representatives themselves). Departments in foreign ministries dealing with bilateral relations between Member States are involved only to a limited extent. They do not take the lead in European affairs, and their future role is currently the subject of much reflection in capitals.

The EU Departments

European Union departments in foreign ministries fulfil four functions. The first is the routine coordination function of daily business, the 'postbox' function of receiving and distributing all material from Brussels, including Commission reports and proposals, European Parliament Committee reports and motions, telegrams concerning the day's meetings, and so on. Foreign Ministries also transmit material from domestic ministries in national capit-als to Permanent Representations for further handling, though the wide-spread use of facsimile machines and the increased proficiency of domestic ministries to coordinate in their own policy areas frequently means foreign ministries are bypassed. The volume of Community business probably justifies this, though it does represent a weakening of the chain of command and challenges the gatekeeper role of the foreign ministry.

Second, foreign ministries provide the key link in the coordination process by encouraging feedback and consultation between domestic ministries on policy issues. Where the system functions badly, as in some Member States without a tradition of domestic policy coordination between ministries, or where coalition governments produce interministerial rivalry, the deleterious effects on policymaking are easily perceived.

The third major function of the EU departments in foreign ministries is the preparation of briefing for Council Meetings. While lead ministries themselves prepare meetings in which their own Minister takes part, each Council is part of a complex pattern of ministerial meetings where trade-offs in negotiations can draw diverse policy areas into package deals. Given their overall responsibility for coordination of such ministerial meetings, foreign ministries become a partner in domestic ministries' decisionmaking processes.

Finally, tasks of a horizontal coordination nature, such as preparation and participation in Intergovernmental Conferences or the management of crises, such as the EU–Canada fishing dispute of spring 1995, usually lie with foreign ministries. These are issues where the necessary coordination of domestic ministries raises the potential for substantial disagreement about the policy responsibilities involved. Where the susceptibilities and proprietary feelings of those coordinated are at stake, Member States with coordination mechanisms outside the foreign ministry benefit from an added focus of independent authoritative coordination and decisionmaking.

Bilateral Departments

EU departments in foreign ministries do not manage bilateral relations with European countries whether EU members or non-members. Western, Eastern or Southern European Departments handle bilateral affairs. Since lead ministries manage their own bilateral relations with their opposite numbers (and with pressure groups) in other Member States, good coordination would normally require bilateral embassies and bilateral departments in ministries of foreign affairs to be kept informed of direct approaches. Yet, it is clearly impossible, if only for reasons of staffing, for foreign ministries or bilateral embassies to conduct or even monitor closely such bilateral relations across the gamut of domestic policy areas now part of the EU purview. Unless their role is redefined to encompass this specific task, there are legitimate grounds for doubting their overall utility in the new European context.

The role of bilateralism within the EU and the foreign minstries' continuing concern with it is arguably in need of redefinition. Traditional forms of bilateralism have clearly declined as domestic ministries take on increasing responsibility for European affairs and European policy ceases to be regarded as 'foreign policy'. An enhanced role for bilateral embassies, for example as pre-negotiators within the EU, could be imagined. But, the recognition of such potential importance of bilateralism in the EU framework has hitherto not been wide and is certainly not matched by an evolution in the role of bilateral desks in foreign ministries or embassies within the EU. The crucial challenge for foreign ministries is that the growth of complex bilateral relations between Member States has taken place with scant regard for the gatekeeper function of bilateral departments in foreign ministries and has thus led to a decline in their role.

The Permanent Representations to the EU

Permanent Representations are usually seen as Brussels extensions of foreign ministries, since the Permanent Representative is customarily a senior diplomat and the Permanent Representation itself exercises traditional diplomatic functions. Yet all Permanent Representations are at least equally staffed by officials from domestic ministries. First secretaries with responsibility for technical affairs such as the internal market, transport or customs and excise are usually secondees from the domestic ministries concerned. Indeed, over time, the balance has switched from foreign ministry staffing of such posts to the lead ministries, itself arguably a trend underlining the foreign ministry's failure in the historic endeavour to retain a gatekeeper role. It is thus misleading to view the Permanent Representations as the extended arm of foreign ministries, as distinct from the extended arm of national capitals. Yet, the fact that the Permanent Representatives themselves continue to be diplomats, that the embassy structure prevails and that foreign ministries provide an operational role model in Brussels underlines the mind-set of European policymaking.

The daily coordination function not only provides a significant new role for European foreign ministries, but also for the Permanent Representations. The Permanent Representations mirror, on the spot, the coordinating role of the EU departments in national ministries of foreign affairs, while providing the main actors in the negotiating and lobbying framework, whether with the Commission, the Parliament or the other Member States in the Council framework. Of course, where meetings are highly technical or scheduled to take place simultaneously with others falling under the portfolio of the Permanent Representation's officer concerned, they are attended by the appropriate desk officer from lead ministries in national capitals. Often, meetings are attended, at least part of the time, by officials both from the lead ministry and from the Permanent Representation. The Permanent Representative himself attends COREPER, the prime coordinator between

Member States of the General Affairs (foreign affairs) Council and the European Council. The *Financial Times* once described COREPER as 'an exclusive male club with an accent on classical diplomacy and intimate deal-making, usually over lunch adding, with some exaggeration, that 'One of the best-kept secrets in Brussels is that 90 per cent of EU decisions are resolved informally in COREPER before they even reach ministers.'[10]

Efficient bargaining in Brussels requires officials in Permanent Representations to maintain close contacts with their opposite numbers in the Commission. They act as a kind of permanent national lobby influencing the Commission's forward thinking, obtaining early warning of proposals and providing the partners for most pre-negotiation. To be effective Permanent Representations must act long before formal notice of new proposals, when they are mere gleams in the Commission's eye. After consultation with national ministries, Permanent Representations encourage those proposals which suit national priorities and attempt to divert the Commission from those ideas which do not. They do this by making lead ministries' views known to the Commission or setting out implications Commission officials may not have thought through. The salient point, however, is that while their staff have diplomatic status, they are not career diplomats and are not part of the line management of foreign ministries. They are viewed by their colleagues in capitals with respect tinted with circumspection. One Permanent Representative has even informed journalists, with perhaps tongue in cheek, that he is known at home as the 'traitor' to rather than the representative of the national cause.[11]

Foreign Ministries: Neither Coordinators and Arbitrators Nor Gatekeepers

It seems obvious that lead ministries cannot settle differences with other ministries without some impartial arbitration mechanism. To be effective, the arbitrator may have to be proactive, must be seen as the repository of skills and knowledge in European affairs of use to policymakers and will certainly depend on effective prior coordination on a daily basis before issues reach the stage of outright bureaucratic rivalry. Increasingly, day-to-day coordination is the stuff of foreign ministry responsibility, whereas trouble-shooting and arbitration are drawn into the ambit of prime ministerial offices or other forms of central, non-foreign ministry coordination. The day-to-day coordination provided by foreign ministries and permanent representations is thus but one part of the coordination function. Ensuring information flows between colleagues with interests in other ministries is essential, but conceptually different from coordination as mediation and conciliation between rival ministerial interests.[12]

Member States arbitrate between sectoral ministerial interests in a variety of different ways. The French and British systems can be seen as the centralized end of a continuum of European policy coordination, with the decentralized and, at times, uncoordinated German system at the other end. In the UK[13] and French[14] cases, the Cabinet Office and the SGCI are central coordinators under the direct responsibility of the respective prime ministers. Arbitration is thus kept above the interests and objectives of individual Ministers and their departments and overall European strategy is not determined by a ministry with its own interests to defend. Whether the Foreign Office or the Quai d'Orsay could efficiently play the policy mediation role of the Cabinet office and the SGCI is relevant of course. After all, other Member States do not have such overarching coordination mechanisms.

In Belgium and Germany, responsibility for coordination and arbitration is shared between the foreign and economics ministries, though it is significant that much of the responsibility for authoritative guidance and mediation is now provided in Germany by the Federal Chancellor's office (*Bundeskanzleramt*). Denmark leaves the foreign ministry responsible, while in Greece there is rivalry for power between the Ministry of the National Economy and the Ministry of Foreign Affairs. But discussions with officials having responsibility for EU affairs in other states demonstrates that there is high regard for the UK and French systems.[15] The significant aspect of these various national approaches is that the foreign ministries' monopoly over the gatekeeper role is far from assured.

The Impact of CFSP on the Working Methods of Foreign Ministries

As Member States have moved towards establishing a CFSP, foreign ministry structures and working methods have perforce adapted to the changed focus of policymaking. Diplomats now find themselves obliged, by dint of the CFSP, to share their traditional prerogative of foreign policymaking and to consult and negotiate with their opposite numbers in Member States and the European Commission. The reality is now the need for a European reflex in response to external events.

It is a reality of which some diplomats remain to be convinced. Nuttall argues that specific sections of foreign ministries have become 'committed' to CFSP, while others view CFSP as 'Euro-crap'.[16] Yet, there are some incontrovertible facts of international life to be borne in mind. The combined GDP of the EU states is larger than that of the USA and Japan. The EU's contribution to aid, both of the developmental and humanitarian kind and its total population (and thus market) is greater than any other advanced country or similar regional grouping. The degree of policy integration between Member States is further advanced than in any other attempt at regional integration; the EU contribution to the UN (34 per cent of UN regular funding, 37 per cent of the peacekeeping budget) is higher than the USA or Japan. As a result, EU influence has clearly grown. There is an

expectation abroad that the EU should speak with one voice and an identifiable emergence of a willingness to do so.

The Growth of CFSP and the Dilution of National Diplomacy

The CFSP was established under the Treaty on European Union (TEU)
signed at Maastricht in 1992 and signified a bold new venture linking
Member States' foreign policies into a new web of institutionalized, albeit
still intergovernmental, policymaking based on the institutional framework of
the EC, now the EU.

The TEU's Article B stated boldly that the EU was to 'assert its identity on
the international scene, in particular through the implementation of a common foreign and security policy including the eventual framing of a common
defence policy, which might in time lead to a common defence'. This did not
imply, however, that the individual foreign policies of the Member States
were at an end. Provision was made for exceptions to the rule of common-
ality; but the point was that the exceptions were intended to prove the rule.
'Common' policy was also not 'common' in the sense of the Common
Agricultural Policy. In foreign policy it was to apply only in those areas
where Member States agreed that it should apply; in short where they had
important interests in common. In other areas, they merely agreed to keep
each other informed of their intentions. CFSP was thus less a *policy* than a
set of procedures with which to pursue the objectives of systematic co-
operation, achieving common positions. Yet there was now to be the potential for 'joint actions' to respond to crisis situations.

Foreign Ministries are, in principle, in sole charge of the CFSP. Yet, in the
absence of a specifically European army and defence structure (*pace* the
declaration in the TEU that the Western European Union should be the
defence arm of the EU), the prime tool of European foreign policy remains
the *acquis communautaire*.[17] By implication, to enforce concrete political
measures taken in the second (CFSP) Maastricht pillar, first pillar (EC)
treaty articles and methods are necessary – economic assistance, sanctions
and changes in trade policy. The obvious need, indeed treaty requirement, to
coordinate the two areas of policymaking suggests the necessity for foreign
ministries to play a careful role.[18]

The complication arising from the decision to keep 'a single institutional
structure' for the work of all three Maastricht pillars[19] created a series of
problems with regard to the management of links between the pillars. Not
least of these was the further layer of coordination required to ensure that
deliberations and decisions in the CFSP framework reach the General
Affairs Council having transited through this single institutional structure,
that is through Council working groups and COREPER and not, as was
formerly the case, through separate intergovernmental working groups and

meetings of the political directors of EU foreign ministries. In EC affairs COREPER is the coordinating body and negotiating instance of last resort before foreign ministers and Heads of State or Government meet.

The shift in responsibility for coordinating European foreign policy from the meeting of political directors to COREPER, which now stands hierarchically above the Political Committee and reconciles the aims of CFSP and the means of the first pillar has implied a shift of focus from national capitals to Brussels, indeed arguably the beginning of a shift from intergovernmentalism to the 'Community method'. One former Permanent Representative has commented on the reluctance of diplomats in the political committee to accept these implications:

> You cannot separate external economic and trade relations from external political relations. They are closely linked and since the Union is largely a civil power, its main element of pressure frequently is financial aid, economic concessions and trade concessions. These are political instruments which need to be managed in a coordinated way and sometimes coordination between the Political Committee and COREPER is less than one might wish.[20]

The evolution from purely national policymaking to agreement on procedures to make policy in common had profound implications for the machinery of foreign ministries. 'Going it with others' implied a new series of meetings for foreign ministry officials in Council working groups and the obligation to cover all issues arising.

For the larger Member States, this did not imply an enormous leap in the geographical and functional spread of foreign policy. But for the smaller states, there was a requirement to cover areas where there had been no identifiable national concern and where there was no embassy structure to assist in information gathering and policy formation. As the 1980s brought increasing concern with foreign ministry spending, there was a pressing need to justify involvement in the common foreign policy while maintaining the search for cost-effectiveness.

CFSP Machinery: Shifting the Policy Focus to Brussels

The Maastricht Treaty provided that 'The Union shall define and implement a common foreign and security policy covering all areas of foreign and security policy' (Article J1). It further stipulated (a point confirmed in the Amsterdam Treaty), that the European Council decides the guidelines and principles of particular policies, with the Council of Ministers taking decisions on implementation of the resulting common positions and joint actions, sometimes by qualified majority. Maastricht also created a new right of initiative for the Commission equal to that of Member States. Not a sole right, as in

EC affairs, but with Brussels as the confirmed venue for policymaking, this new right marked a change of emphasis. The Commission had moved from often total exclusion from discussions to a position of full partner with foreign ministries. It now participates at all stages of the CFSP, where it not only enjoys this right of initiative, but is called upon, through its executive responsibility for some tools of foreign policy, such as trade policy and for the EU budget (which *inter alia* covers the CFSP), not only to make and defend policy, but to implement it in the name of the EU.

Developments in the CFSP as presaged in the Amsterdam Treaty do, however, retain the intergovernmentalism which characterize the operation of second pillar matters. But two important innovations are set to swing the locus of decisionmaking further from national capitals to the Brussels forum. Consistent with intergovernmentalism, Member States retain their own right of initiative and moves towards qualified majority voting have been hedged in with the now traditional *caveats* of national veto. However, the proposed 'High Representative of the CFSP' and the establishment of a 'policy-planning and early-warning unit', both based in the Brussels Council Secretariat are harbingers of further change. The decision not to use the existing Commission facilities, by appointing a foreign affairs Commissioner as High Representative and upgrading the Commission's existing foreign policy planning unit, illustrates Member States' reluctance to move from intergovernmentalism to the Community method.

Nevertheless, the salient feature of the new arrangements is the slide from national capitals to Brussels of these two key foreign policy functions. It expresses continuity in the manner in which the current CFSP arrangements have grown. They began from a specifically national base with a small degree of coordination from the national capital of the Presidency and first evolved into a flying secretariat with a rolling presidency based on the *Troika* system. Administratively, this involved foreign ministry secondments between the past, present and future presidencies. Developments have culminated after the changes introduced by the Single European Act in 1986, the TEU in 1993 and the envisaged adjustments in the Amsterdam Treaty, in a Brussels-based system, which is briefly examined below.

Conclusions of European Councils and General Affairs Councils, in which foreign affairs are considered, are now prepared by foreign ministry officials at levels approximating the machinery of EC affairs. Central to the preparation is the network of European Correspondents based in national capitals and the Commission. They form the administrative interface between foreign ministries, the Council Secretariat and the appropriate Directorates General in the Commission. They are responsible for the COREU (soon CORTESY) cipher network, which currently exchanges in excess of 20 000 communications per year. Of political importance, however, are the CFSP Counsellors in the Permanent Representations in Brussels and the Commission. Still higher up the hierarchy is the Political Committee (POCO) composed of political directors (ambassadorial level) from foreign ministries and the Commission.

REPRESENTATION OUTSIDE THE UNION AND THE ROLE OF THE COMMISSION

To the sceptical, the existence of Commission delegations abroad is unnecessary. 'EU missions are being set up in some of the remotest places . . . and have been turned into fully-fledged diplomatic missions' stated the *Sunday Express* in a damning, but misguided article.[21] The Commission's obligation to collaborate with the Presidency in ensuring coherence in foreign policy, its management role in foreign trade policy, development aid and technical assistance coupled with the fact that other international actors increasingly see the Commission as the prime focus of the European input into international affairs all increase the visibility of the Commission and contribute to its evolving role.

Representation of second pillar issues, that is the specifically *foreign* policy of the EU, remains the responsibility of the Presidency of the Council, within the framework of the *Troika*. A political *démarche* by the EU abroad would normally be led by the ambassador of the Presidency in office. The problem is that purely trade related issues are the responsibility of the Commission and the Head of the Commission delegation would normally present the EU position if there were trade implications.

Commission Delegations represent the EU in all areas within first pillar competence, notably economic co-operation and external trade, development co-operation, financial and technical co-operation and, on occasion, such issues as the environment. They also ensure, in co-operation with diplomatic missions of the Member States, consistency in all external actions of the EU. They monitor and report to the Commission on the political, economic and social situation in the host country and serve as a permanent link with local governmental authorities, firms and NGOs, informing them in turn of the activities of the EU and of the Commission.

They promote awareness and knowledge of the European dimension and endeavour to improve the perception of leaders and Third World public opinion on the role played by the EU as the world's largest provider of development aid and the most important actor in world trade. They prepare official missions of the Commission and other institutions. They manage food aid, humanitarian aid (656 million ecu spent in 1996, mainly in fomer Yugoslavia and the Great Lakes region, but in a total of 60 countries),[22] human rights, NGOs, AID programmes and the fight against drugs. The Commission's role in representation varies from region to region. In Lomé countries the main task is development aid, in Washington, Tokyo and Geneva trade relations, while in Eastern Europe and the former Soviet Union, the concentration is on technical assistance through the PHARE and TACIS[23] programmes, now accompanied by the pre-accession strategy.

The TEU's Article J10 relates these general first pillar responsibilities to the particular task of international representation in stating that:

> The diplomatic and consular missions of the Member States and the Commission delegations in third countries and in international conferences, and their representatives in international organisations, shall cooperate in ensuring that the common positions and common measures adopted by the Council are complied with and implemented. They shall step up cooperation by exchanging information and carrying out joint assessments.

Commission heads of delegation are thus involved through the *Troika* at ambassadorial level in the advocacy of CFSP policy on the spot and the coordination of diplomatic *démarches* in the host country. Its status as a permanent part of the *Troika*, particularly in its enhanced version outlined in the Treaty of Amsterdam, makes the Commission the only permanent element in the changing constellations of external representation through the Presidency of the Council of the EU. A counterpart to the Commission's permanent status is the fact that the ambassadors of the Member States are in principle involved for a potential maximum of 18 months (during their *Troika* period) in seven and a half years. But, this is of course only if the Member State concerned has an embassy in a given country. For the larger Member States, the 18 month period is, of course, a minimum period, since they represent the EU where the presidency is held by a Member State with no embassy. In reality, for most Member States in most countries of the world, their participation in the *Troika* is rare. That confusion abounds in the minds of public and foreign governments alike is not surprising.

The salient point is the departure from purely national foreign ministry control that these complex arrangements signify. There have clearly been significant changes in relations between the Commission and foreign ministries and Commission delegations and Member State embassies outside the EU. The Commission's status as the only permanent member of the six-monthly fluctuating *Troika* of Council presidencies is but one structuring factor in these changes. There are Commission delegations or offices in 127 countries or international organizations outside the EU (more than most Member States). This network of representation employs some 700 officials and 1600 local staff (see Table 14.1). Lest the picture be created of an exceedingly powerful, indispensable Commission, it should be stressed however that Member States' diplomatic staff have been somewhat reluctant to treat the Commission as a full partner, and the roles and competences of

Table 14.1 Commission and Member State Diplomatic Representation

	Commission	France	UK	Greece	Belgium	Netherlands	Luxemburg	Germany	Spain	Portugal	Italy	Denmark	Sweden	Finland	Austria	Ireland
Total staff at home	2645	3000	3400	660	673	1795	118	2819	2450	778	2923	993	916	1150	745	528
Total home based staff abroad	623	6000	2400	936	543	984	72	3619	1550	376	2816	633	550	650	850	210
Total staff abroad	2467	11000	10000	1526	1811	1943	227	5968	6550	2071	6416	1573	2250	1400	1457	446

foreign ministries and the Commission are still jealously monitored and guarded.

The Impact on Foreign Ministries – Towards a European Foreign Service?

The principle of collective action, while hitherto slow to be accepted on the ground, appears to be increasingly part of the horizon of the national foreign ministry official. Despite the enormous growth in Commission responsibility, it might be argued that there is no zero-sum game between European and national priorities and interests, and that the burgeoning of activity does not alter the integrity of traditional diplomacy. On the other hand, there is a clear sense in which more diplomacy centres on the new CFSP arrangements, rather than enhancing national competence and activity. Underlying CFSP in terms of the work of foreign ministries is that all geographical and functional desks are caught up in a process of constant information exchange and negotiation with their counterparts elsewhere.

Discontinuities and incoherence may abound, not least because of the inherent instability in a system based on a six-monthly rotating presidency, generally run by states with no policy tradition and no formal representation in most countries of the world. However, a glance at the typical agenda of the CFSP Administrative Affairs Council working group underlines increasing perceptions of synergy and willingness to collaborate in policy formation. Issues now cover joint training for foreign ministry officials (organized by the Commission), secondments between foreign ministries, both to head offices and to delegations (and including the Commission's Brussels directorates-general and its delegations throughout the world), shared embassy facilities, comparisons of staff conditions, comparisons of the changing profile of diplomats, comparative use of performance indicators of staff and a whole range of similar discussions undertaken with the tacit assumption that where there is co-operation there is synergy, mutual learning and, potentially, gains in efficiency.

It may be that CFSP still represents 'procedures without policy, activity without output, while American arms and diplomacy still determine the course of western interests',[24] yet the fact of daily collaboration is doubtless creating a European reflex, which clearly provides a context for national foreign ministry action and an incentive to seek administrative and policy-making synergies and cost- effectiveness. This has important implications for the overall theme of this book, since the EU's enlarged scope in diplomacy might be interpreted as the basis for an evolution towards a European Foreign Service, despite the absence of any clearly expressed intention to move in this direction.

The consciousness of the strategy and, indeed, the final outcome of the process may be far from clear, yet the growth of CFSP underlines that Member States wish to enhance EU foreign policy, including strategies for representation outside the Union. Significantly, they are also increasingly willing to entrust the Commission with the management of major aspects of external policy.[25] This is partly a result of the gradual process of Member States being constrained to do more with their EU partners than before. But, it is also due to the clear expectation of the international community that 'Europe' speak with one voice – an objective yet to be achieved.

EU Member States increasingly entrust the Commission with much of the operational side of European foreign policy. The Commission runs the huge technical assistance programmes of PHARE, TACIS and MEDA. It also runs the EU's humanitarian aid effort. It provides financial management and coordination in such cases as the civil administration of Mostar and it provides the focus of non-EU representation to the Union through the accreditation to it of 165 non-EU missions in Brussels. *Volens nolens*, therefore, the Commission is increasingly seen by Member States and their international partners as a privileged actor in world affairs. Whether or not this is the desired effect, the overall impact on European diplomacy is that the Commission is now a powerful actor on the world stage. This potentially diminishes the roles of individual states – a development resulting from the underlying actor capability[26] of the EU itself, and enhanced by the EU's apparent inability to provide an alternative focus, as the 1996 deliberations on the issue of 'Mr CFSP' underline.

This is not to deny the continuing significance of national foreign policies. The attempts of President Mitterrand to intervene in the name of France in Bosnia, while EU Member States grappled unsuccessfully with the challenge of concerted action there underlines the point. Similarly, Greek reticence on Turkey and Cyprus or the UK interest in Gibraltar are cases of minorities of one blocking the emergence of common policy. At an administrative level, the UK refusal to share embassy facilities with its EU partners in the new Nigerian capital of Abuja is a telling example of the entanglements of national political priorities with economic and financial constraints, where the otherwise prevalent desire for cost-saving is not in evidence.

As some of the chapters in this book demonstrate, since the 1980s many EU states have been constrained by financial pressure and management rigour to close embassies and consulates. It is ironic that this cost-consciousness has accompanied the increase in the number of states worldwide. But joint representation through a European Foreign Service as an answer to the problem is not yet on the agenda. Meanwhile, non-resident representation provides a growing alternative to embassies. Faced with the growth in the number of states and the countervailing growth in financial constraints, some states are turning to the conduct of relations with other states from home or from representations in third countries.

While the overall increase in the number of states in the world does not necessarily imply the creation of strictly national interests in every EU Member State, there is an identifiable overall European interest. For the Commission, precisely in the new states being created, there is a legally necessary role in terms of European trade policy and the management of trade associations (Community competence) or aid/technical assistance of the PHARE/TACIS variety (mixed competence) and, in the current period, preparation for EU enlargement. The Schengen arrangements (due to shift into the first pillar) and the increasing currency of the idea of a European visa regime offer interesting prospects for streamlining certain of the services provided by embassies or even provision via non-governmental or at least inter-European agencies at EU level. Likewise, coverage of economic issues (excluding trade promotion, which is clearly national) is largely already duplicated by Member States and the Commission. CFSP provides an increasingly rigid structure for political and economic reporting. The absence of short-term national interests is thus no guide to the existence of an interest for the EU as a whole. The question is how this interest should be represented.

The prime concern for individual EU states is how to maximize effectiveness without permanent missions – an issue frequently discussed in those hard-pressed foreign services with an historic presence throughout the world. The smaller Member States have not had to undergo such soul-searching, not having enjoyed worldwide presence. One national response could be for EU members to reassess their global spread, assess where their prime focus should be and envisage a move to multiple-accredited missions. There could also be the recourse to job-sharing among staff and there is increasing discussion of the need for all staff to cover consular, economic, commercial and political affairs. A different approach would be to review the arguments for an EU response, at least through EU missions, if not by the creation of an EU foreign service. The European Parliament proposed an interim solution to the issue in 1996, recommending that

> the necessary steps should be taken to have a diplomatic representation of the Union established in third countries where fewer than four Member States have diplomatic representation

A much canvassed idea is co-location with other Member States and/or with the Commission or even joint missions. There are already shared UK/French/German embassies in Almaty and Minsk, and Nordic joint embassies in Windhoek (Namibia) and Dar-es-Salaam. Colombia, Mexico and Peru have some joint embassies and a yearly revolving responsibility to provide the Ambassador. This could be a model for the EU. Its current attempt to create co-located missions to the new capital of Nigeria, Abuja, could thus be a harbinger of things to come. Meanwhile, it is important to note the increased sharing of facilities (buildings, health services, education, transport, communications), increased joint reporting and increasing interchange of staff.

CONCLUSION

Two key points emerge from this analysis. The first concerns the foreign ministry role in the now Europeanized domestic policy agenda and the fate of bilateralism. Within the widening EU, the role of bilateral embassies is arguably in structural decline, as their job is either done by others, transformed into a hosting facility for visiting royalty or statespeople or no longer required as the EU deepens and foreign policy effectively becomes 'domesticated'. It may be, as Jorgensen has argued, that it is 'incorrect to argue that the demise of the bilateral embassy in Western Europe demonstrates the withering away of bilateral diplomacy' and that 'we are witnessing changes in form and function, not disappearance'.[28] Indeed, the decline of foreign ministry orchestrated bilateralism within Europe is matched, as we have seen, by an increase in a new area of foreign ministry responsibility, namely the monitoring and coordination of domestic policy. Yet, even here this chapter has identified a counter-trend in the removal of the highest level of domestic coordination of international policies to central coordination structures such as the Cabinet Office or the French SGCI, or to the offices of Heads of Government, such as the *Bundeskanzleramt* in Germany.

The second point underlined in this chapter is the creation through CFSP in national foreign ministries of a European reflex and the consequent strength of the logic of a European foreign service. Notwithstanding the scepticism with which such an idea is received, it seems logical that the forces outlined by Hocking in the introduction will militate in favour of such new thinking. In terms of the external affairs of the European Union there are, in principle, clear lines of separation between economic and political affairs. Economic policy, such as trade or agricultural policy – that is international policies arising from agreements between the Member States on issues of EC competence – is the responsibility of the European Commission. Increasingly, after the implementation of the Amsterdam treaty, this will also be the case for most of the Maastricht pillar III provisions. As to pillar II, the EU's CFSP is legally intergovernmental. Member States formally state that they wish to guard strictly their rights and prerogatives. Yet, this chapter has highlighted the fact that the principle of separation of competence between Member States and the EU and its institutions is increasingly hard to maintain in day-to-day practice.

To sum up, foreign ministries in Western Europe have been obliged to adapt to changed circumstances. They may have adjusted the scope and methods of their international activity, in particular by assuming a new, or at least enhanced, role in terms of the coordination for EU business of domestic policy issues. Yet, outside the EU, foreign ministries now have to justify the existence of embassies increasingly in terms of export promotion rather than in terms of what many would define as the traditional functions of diplomacy. And, as other chapters point out, there is growing recognition of the need to find alternatives to the simplistic view that representation of such interests must be through embassies.

Increasingly, this implies the search for synergy on the operational side of foreign policymaking with other Member States and the Commission, a search without a definition of the end goal. There is certainly no formal move towards a European foreign service, yet the incrementalism identified in this chapter is forming a context which would make fundamental change potentially smooth. EU states already have a single trade policy and a single agricultural policy. They have neared completion of a single market and a single currency. They no longer speak of 'political co-operation' but of a *common* foreign policy. They have decided that 'all declarations, démarches etc. under CFSP are no longer made on behalf of the "the EU and its Member States" but on behalf of the EU only.' The pressures for foreign ministries to adapt (not least for financial reasons) to this changed policy environment are likely to increase and, as Hill argued in 1983, 'there is little point in EPC reviving the fortunes of Europe's diplomats if an excess of enthusiasm is going to blind policy-makers to the perennial need to keep ends and means in balance.'[29] In this perspective a European Foreign Service rising to the challenges of the changed policy environment, though not on the Member States' agenda may well be on the cards.

NOTES

1   See D. Newsom, 'The new diplomatic agenda: are governments ready?', *International Affairs* 65:1, Winter 1988/9.
2   For an academic defence of this thesis, see G. R. Berridge, *Diplomacy: Theory and Practice* (London: Prentice Hall/Harvester Wheatsheaf, 1995).
3   I use the term 'gatekeeper' in a more precise sense of more relevance to the bureaucratic issues of concern in this book than David Easton in his seminal *A Systems Analysis of Political Life* (New York: Wiley, 1964) pp. 86–8.
4   H. Wallace, 'Towards the European regulatory state', *Journal of European Public Policy* 3:4, 1996, p. 575.
5   See S. Mazey and J. Richardson 'A European policy style? in S. Mazey and J. Richardson eds, *Lobbying in the European Community* (Oxford: Oxford University Press, 1993), pp. 246–57.

6   G. Robertson, 'Britain in the New Europe', *International Affairs* 66:4, 1990, p. 699.
7   For an analysis of some of the implications, see A. Héritier, 'Policy-making by subterfuge: interest accommodation, innovation and substitute democratic legitimation in Europe – perspectives from distinct policy areas', *Journal of European Public Policy* 4:2, 1997.
8   W. Wallace, *Britain's Bilateral Links Within Western Europe*, (London: Royal Institute of International Affairs/Routledge, 1984).
9   See D. Spence, 'The coordination of EU policy by Member States' in M. Westlake ed., *The Council of Ministers* (London: Cartermill 1996).
10   See L. Barber, 'The Men Who Run Europe', *Financial Times* 11/12 March 1995.
11   Ibid. The German Permanent Representative was using a play on words in the German, describing himself as the 'Verräter' (traitor) rather than 'Vertreter' (representative).
12   See Spence, 'The co-ordination of EU policy'.
13   See Spence, 'The Role of the National Civil Service in European lobbying: the British case' in Mazey and Richardson, *Lobbying*.
14   See, in particular, C. Lequesne, *Paris-Bruxelles: Comment se fait la Politique Européenne de la France* (Paris: Fondation Nationale des Sciences Politiques, 1993).
15   See L. Metcalfe, 'Comparing Policy Co-ordination Systems: Do the Differences Matter?' unpublished paper to the Fifth Erenstein Colloquium 30–31 October 1987 and L. Metcalfe and E. Zapico Goni, *Action or reacation? The role of national administration in European policy-making* (London: Sage, 1991).
16   S. Nuttall, *European Political Cooperation* (Oxford: Clarendon Press, 1992).
17   The French *acquis communautaire* is the commonly accepted term for the accumulated legislation and political practice of the EU member states.
18   The Treaty on EU mentions in various places the obligation to coordinate policy. For example, Article J 2 obliges Member States to ensure their national policies conform to the EU's common positions and to coordinate their action in international organisations. Article J 6 covers co-operation between diplomatic and consular missions. Article C requires consistency in external relations, security, economic and development policies.
19   The third is Justice and Home Affairs, with the terrorism and immigration sections of the third pillar replete with implications for the work of foreign ministries.
20   P. de Schoutheete, interviewed in *European Voice*, 4–10 December 1997.
21   'Scandal of EU Missions in paradise', *Sunday Express*, 14 January 1996.
22   European Commission, 1996 *Annual Report from the Commission to the Council and the European Parliament on Humanitarian Aid.* (COM(97) 437 final.
23   PHARE stands for Assistance for Restructuring in the Countries of Central and Eastern Europe. TACIS stands for Technical Assistance for the Commonwealth of Independent States.
24   Forster and Wallace, 'Common Foreign and Security Policy', p. 420.
25   On the painful evolution of foreign policymaking in the EU framework with particular emphasis on the Commission's gradual involvement in the process, see S. Nuttall, The Commission and Foreign Policy-making in G. Edwards and D. Spence *The European Commission*, (2nd edn) (London: Cartermill, 1997). For a more recent view see F. Cameron, 'Where the Commission comes in: from the Single European Act to Maastricht', in E. Regelsberger, P. de Schoutheete, W. Wessells, *Foreign Policy of the European Union*, (London: Rienner, 1997).

26   The concept of actor capability is discussed in G. Sjoestadt, *The External Role of the European Community* (London: Saxon House, 1977).
27   European Parliament, *Opinion of Parliament on the Convening of the IGC* PE 197.390, 1996.
28   K. Jorgensen, *PoCo: The Diplomatic Republic of Europe* unpublished manuscript.
29   C. Hill *National Foreign Policies and European Political Cooperation* op. cit. p. 190.

Index